TICKING
All The
BOXES

To Grace,

May you never need internet
dating!!

by
Kelly Carter

Much love

Kath x

aka
Kelly Carter!

authorHOUSE®

AuthorHouse™ UK Ltd.
500 Avebury Boulevard
Central Milton Keynes, MK9 2BE
www.authorhouse.co.uk
Phone: 08001974150

First published by AuthorHouse 11/3/2008

ISBN: 978-1-4389-0977-6 (sc)

Printed in the United States of America
Bloomington, Indiana

This book is printed on acid-free paper.

To Tony, the best of brothers

'Sometimes love doesn't come to us. We have to go out hunting. It's like pigs looking for truffles. It's called dating.'

PATTY LUPONE

Chapter 1

IT NEVER RAINS BUT IT POURS

Finding the right man. Got to be easy hasn't it? I mean, they're everywhere aren't they? But is that really true? Parties? Sick of them. Clubbing? My legs are past it. Sport? Get real. Evening classes? Spare me. Church groups? I'm beyond salvation. Men at work? Danger!

This is what I was thinking as my exasperating friend Karen stared into the Pronuptia window with all the concentration of a Dickens urchin front of a sweet shop. It was absolutely pouring down – 'teeming' as we say here in Manchester – but that didn't stop her. She was utterly transfixed by the sight of so much flowing chiffon, silk and lace, and probably spinning a fantasy of herself stepping out of a carriage and four wearing one of those frothy concoctions. The ultimate hopeless romantic, she was in and out of love more often than Amy Winehouse in rehab.

'For God's sake Karen, come on or we'll end up catching pneumonia. Get a move on!'

I held the sou'wester fashioned from a discarded newspaper above my head, and water ran down my arm. Damp patches made my trousers look like combat fatigues, and my prize suede slingbacks were coming apart. By now I really was at the end of my tether...

'Right, we're off,' I snapped, frogmarching her to the fuggy shelter of a Costa Coffee, where we gratefully sank onto the nearest sofa.

Karen held the cup of cappuccino in both hands, clearly glad of its warmth. As she greedily scooped off the froth, she left herself with a comic moustache, white speckled with amber. In her excitement though she was not aware of it, nor of my amused expression.

'I'm telling you Sally that dress with the ivory corset thingy's the one for me – that one with the tiny red roses round the–'

'Hang on a minute,' I held up my hands to quell her enthusiasm. 'You're not even engaged – you're not even seeing anyone unless there's something you're not telling me? Well, have you–'

'No, I haven't got a bloke in tow. Not yet anyway but I've joined one of those Internet dating sites – not something you'd need to do; you've probably got scores of blokes after you – and I absolutely know it's going to work! He'll probably be in the Forces, bloody dishy as well, just like Prince William – I love men in uniform and …'

As she merrily prattled on about 'our future home' – an old ivy-covered vicarage to convert [in *Manchester* for God's sake], I took stock of my own situation like hers in so many ways, but without the *Brides* magazine overlay. It was more than a year now since I'd ventured, with a little apprehension and a lot of hope, into the vast expanse of computer dating

A blast from the past

I don't feel like dancin', dancin' …If I hear that damn song one more time, I'll chuck a pint pot at the jukebox!

' Two pints of Boddies please Sal.'

'OK Smithy, just a sec. Steve, the pump's on the blink again – can you see to it?'

Saturday night, the mad hubbub of music, raised voices and raucous laughter with me in the thick of it all busily dispensing pints, and trying to maintain some semblance of order. My friend, Marie, owned The Fox. Marie, with her BMW convertible, villa in Spain and diamond Omega, all courtesy of a short-lived but *extremely* lucrative marriage to an overweight, balding stockbroker.

I really liked that part-time work, so different to my 'day job' in the uninspiring world of financial training. It was fun meeting people, even if I was slaving away, and everyone else was enjoying themselves. It was a welcome change to the stuffiness of the bank – and more importantly, there was just a chance I might meet someone.

'Hi Sally, how are you? It's been ages.'

The *voice* was familiar. Spinning round from the optics, I saw Anne, on old school-friend. She looked great; she'd lost a lot of weight, the highlights made her look younger, and the navy trouser suit was really flattering.

'Oh, Anne, great to see you – when was the last time? Wasn't it at Janey's thirtieth?'

'Dead right – took me a week to get over that hangover!'

'But what are you doing here? Not out with the usual crowd?'

'No, I'm not ... not tonight' she added coyly.

Hmm, I remember thinking ... am I imagining this? Anne's so relaxed tonight; confident too. I followed her beaming smile to the man sitting patiently below the 'Don't do drugs and drive' poster. Wow! This was one of those 'Jane Austen' moments you read about – weak knees, missed heartbeat, irresistible urge to drop a handkerchief. 6'1"/6'2", slim but with broad shoulders, casually dressed, thick hair, well-defined eyebrows, long dark eyelashes, heavy eyelids and the most startling blue eyes … and, whoops! Yes, he caught me giving him the once-over … mmm, that gorgeous, gorgeous smile to die for … Anne's words curtailed my growing fantasy … 'Ah yes, Stuart. He *is* rather gorgeous, isn't he,' she giggled, in a proprietorial tone, rather like the proud owner of the winning Burmese at a regional cat show. 'Where, where, where …?' I asked her, my eyes still locked onto this positive god with the unerring accuracy of a heat-seeking missile.

'Where did I find him, do you mean? [She was positively oozing self-satisfaction].You'll never guess, but when me and Malcolm split up, I did bugger all for months except eat and drink too much and generally feel sorry for myself. Then I read about Dateandsee.com in *uFlirtu* magazine. You know Dateandsee don't you – one of those Internet dating sites?'

What?! I couldn't believe this … Anne, plain, dowdy Anne [as was] and Internet dating sites? 'Dating sites?' I spluttered. 'Tell me more!'

I tossed and turned in bed. I had this image of Anne, happy, flushed with success. A complete transformation. Was it really possible to find love, marriage even, on the Internet? Most people sneered at the very idea of Internet dating, with disparaging remarks like 'only fit for losers', 'bound to end in disaster'. I must confess that had always been my feeling too; I'd always been pretty conventional in my thinking; I suppose I'd just ignored the evidence. The rocketing divorce rate suggested that traditional methods of meeting a partner were no guarantee of success. I remembered when I got married ... At first, life with Paul was absolutely brilliant. We valued the same things, sharing a great sense of fun and a strong desire for children. Both of us had promising careers, a wide circle of friends and the love of close families. A marriage made in heaven ... Yes, if only.

The problem had been children – or rather, the lack of them. The fateful meeting with the consultant gynaecologist was the last straw. We drove to the clinic in an uncomfortable silence. Paul simply stared ahead, gripping the steering wheel so tightly that his knuckles whitened. He strode ahead of me, crunching the gravel, pausing only to scowl when I asked for the car keys as I'd forgotten my handbag. The waiting room resembled the lobby of an exclusive hotel. Deep sofas, fresh flowers, an atmosphere of unhurried efficiency; the NHS was a million miles away. The consultant's dour expression told me all I needed to know: sadly I was 100% right – I'd never carry a baby full-term. That was it. End of story.

I'd come late in my parents' marriage though, if anything, I was all the more loved for it; I was an only child as well and I'd often wondered whether Mum had suffered from the same complaint as me. Difficult though – people of Mum's generation just didn't discuss matters like this.

From that point on, my marriage was in total freefall, and we were divorced within the year. Some months later, I heard that Paul had remarried; he'd also been promoted and moved to Reading. In a way I was luckier than other women – my job, family and friends helped me to rebuild my life, but a deep, raw wound remained.

But dwelling on a sorry past wouldn't deliver a happier future so it was time to pull myself up sharp; the Internet itself might not heal the wound but could perhaps help me find someone with a plaster.

Meeting men – easier said than done

I mulled over the possibilities of the workplace. The men were pleasant enough but none really caught my fancy – Derek, who attended séances, and Brian, Twitcher-in-Chief, the bank's answer to Bill Oddie.

Then there was Roy in data services, a regular worshipper at Old Trafford – never without his Man U baseball cap leaving no one in any doubt as to his prime loyalty. This wasn't exactly a major turn-on as far as the girls were concerned, and I was no exception.

There was the girls' nights out – these normally ended up with a splitting hangover and the notable absence of any knight in shining armour. Then, there had been the evening classes featuring portly Julio [*Spanish for Beginners*], camp Desmond [*Interior Design Made Easy*], geeky Scott [*Microsoft Office Part 1*] and the truly unforgettable Michael – known to the students as 'Metal Mickey' [*Car Maintenance for Girlies*]. Sport ... hmm, yes, there had been the tennis club and the unwanted attention of the coach William, 'please call me Willie', who substituted perspiration for inspiration. No, my exposure to sport convinced me that the unwelcome cocktail of streaming sweat and Lancôme 'Attraction' could turn a man's head but, sadly, in the opposite direction.

Amateur Dramatics had been another possibility but my view of 'luvvies' was indelibly coloured by painful memories of my stunning childhood debut in pantomime. The church hall was packed to the rafters. Proud mums and dads, clasping cameras, eagerly awaited the entrance of their beloved offspring. The spotlight found me, collapsed on a milestone [aka dusty piano stool] mopping my brow with a huge red-spotted handkerchief and hollering 'Ten more miles to London and still no sign of Dick.' The resulting guffaws reverberated around the hall. No, not even the RSC could tempt me back to the boards.

So, Internet dating, a whole new world; perhaps a second opinion would be advisable. Time to call Caroline, friend, confidante, fashion guru and life coach. Also, a bottomless well of tact, trust, prudence and patience.

'Yes, hello,' muttered a weary voice.

'It's me – I just thought–'

'Do you know what bloody time it is?' snapped this erstwhile Mother Teresa. 'Sorry Cazi – God is it that early? It's just that I've got something on my mind right now, and–'

'Yes OK but I've had a crap few days too: Louise's teacher complaining about her global warming project, Richard my 'why-am-I-the-only-loser-in-Year 9-without-an-iPod' son, and now you ringing up in the middle of the night – oh, and yes, I've got lover boy next to me, snoring like some hibernating mammal and occasionally roaring 'Nice one, Rooney boy, nice one! And another thing–'

'Hang on, I'm not phoning to whinge. Listen, will you? You know those computer dating sites, don't you – Love letters, CherishU, yeah, that's it. Well, I'm going to have a go. What do you think?'

Silence.

'Cazi, are you still there? Right, remember Anne Jackson from school? What do you mean the 'Sumo Wrestler'? That's a bit unkind – a size eighteen is average for a fifteen-year-old these days. You'd barely recognise her now though – no, I don't think it's been a nip'tuck job but she's definitely been reading Paul McKenna. Well, anyway, she was in The Fox last night looking fantastic! Not surprising really since her eye candy was Mr Drop Dead Gorgeous. Think Daniel Craig. And ... wait for it ... all through this Internet thing. What do you think?'

Deafening silence.

Typical. This was Caroline at her negative worst. First time in months I'd a decent idea, and she gave it the sort of welcome Posh Spice would get at Slimming World.

'Do you *really* know what you're getting into? You're seeing Daniel Craig; I'm seeing Hannibal Lecter. You won't know these weirdos from Adam and you'll probably end up in the sack with them.'

'All right *Caroline*,' I retorted. 'Tell you what, if I do end up with Mr Axe Murderer, I'll give him *your* email address as well. ALLBLOODYRIGHT?'

'OK, sorry – but you'll have to be very careful and if it does go tits up, can I have your silver earrings?'

'Absolutely not. Look, I *am* going to have go, so full details of my first conquest later. OK?'

'I suppose so but don't make a move without running it past me first, agreed?'

'Agreed, sorted, whatever. Bye, love.'

Sunday afternoon and I was ready for romance cyber-style. I took a deep breath, uttered a quick prayer to St Jude, patron saint of lost causes, and googled 'Internet Dating'.

Heartsdesire.com – this had to be Doris Day territory, I could almost hear her trilling 'Que será, será'.

And next?

Udate.com – certainly more attractive.

Hump.com – outrageous but I don't think so.

And then:

DatingDirect.com – hmm … clever title, easy layout and not costing a fortune either – one for my Favourites.

And, by way of contrast:

Gayescorts.co.uk – not my kind of cocktail.

The list stretched on …

Dateandsee.com – Anne's site – umm, a veritable banquet of manhood! Bon appétit. And what about that *'Dave – Electrician'* there? Yes, *very* sexy, and local too! I went back to the list of sites …

Thrills&swoon.com – full marks for invention.

And finally …

Ladiesandgenitalsmen.com …rapid exit!

Decision time. I'd always been a great believer in consumer feedback so, based on Anne's testimony, it simply had to be Dateandsee.com [and Dave's obvious promise sealed it!].

Getting it right

I needed a photo and my best one at that. One of those taken in the Algarve perhaps but not from the start of the week – lobster red wasn't my colour. More pressing was the need to draft my profile – vitally important for success. The site suggested I put in a bit about myself and about what I was 'looking for in a man'. Mmm … easy enough; 'sex god', 'virile' or 'indefatigable', but then, common sense prevailed. I was looking for something much more than just a lover; I needed to write something witty enough for Catherine Tate and certain to attract interest.

I discarded the first draft – too much *Mary Poppins*. And the second – *Baywatch* babe. My third attempt nailed it – a short but perfectly formed description. It was amusing, original and intelligent – or so I hoped.

I selected the photo [not happy with the hair but it would have to do], uploaded it and then entered the profile.

THE PROFILE:
Name: Sally
Age: 39
Location: Manchester
Status: Divorced
Children: None
Job: Financial Services
Height: 5'6"
Build: Slim
Appearance: Attractive
Eye Colour: Blue
Hair: Blonde
Religion: Christian [non-practising]
Star sign: Virgo
Smoker: No
Drinker: Moderate

INTERESTS: Cooking [Italian], travel, the arts, cinema, restaurants, literature, and theatre.

> ABOUT ME: *Brace yourself boys, here goes. I'm quite a lively character but never before eleven on a Sunday morning. I'm confident and sociable. My drug of choice is humour. I'm interested in new ideas and different approaches to life. Before an impending nuclear attack, I'd stock up with Bolly, Belgian chocolates and Brad Pitt. I'm looking for a fellow, preferably of noble lineage and 'old money'. Otherwise, I'll settle for someone intelligent, articulate, solvent and with a real sense of adventure. My printable paranoias are garden centres and anything remotely connected to sport. Are you totally turned off by now? If not...*

I lay in bed imagining a thousand eager fingers composing urgent replies, protesting undying love ... then I remembered that I was, after all, just one of ...what? 250,000 similar hopefuls? Suddenly, I sat bolt upright. What if someone had *already* contacted me?! I leapt out of bed and trotted into the living room. Click. The laptop purred into action, its bright screen amid the gloom even more mesmeric than usual

... EUREKA! There *was* a message. OK only one but at least it was something. Who could it be? A Daniel? A Brad? ... no, it was a Derek, a Derek from Dudley.

> *THE MESSAGE: Hi Sally. Loved your bit about 'brace yourselves boys', reminded me of that fabbo bra poster. No, honest, sex isn't my obsession. Read my profile and you'll see why. Derek.*

THE PROFILE:
Name: Derek
Age: 42
Location: West Midlands
Status: Separated
Children: Two
Job: Auto Engineer
Height: 5'9"
Build: Medium
Appearance: Attractive
Eye Colour: Blue
Hair: Dark Blonde
Religion: Christian [non-practising]
Star Sign: Scorpio
Smoker: Yes
Drinker: Moderate

> *INTERESTS: Sports, skiing, rallying, Grand Prix, restaurants, modern jazz, Internet, photography, travel, pubs/clubs, movies.*

> *ABOUT ME: I like to drive in the fast lane of life. I'm a very dynamic person, it's the drive I've got in me. More cylinders than a Maserati in fact. Romance is very important to me; I think it's the petrol of life. Yes, my sporting interests are great. They'd be even greater with the right 'sportswoman' by my side — whether it's whizzing down the slopes of Klosters or reattaching my ears after Le Mans! Why not join me in the pit lane and you could be my oily rag.*

Oh dear … forty-two years of age, with a gold chain around his neck and *so much* hair gel … surely a presentation reserved for boy-bands and footballers.

> *MY PREFERRED REPLY: Dear Lewis Hamilton, hi, it's your favourite model here. I'm wearing nothing but my 17" 15 spoke alloys and a full beam. Check out my rear spoiler, run your hands over my luxury upholstery and finger my climate control button. Make sure your cylinder is fully turbo charged; I'll blow your exhaust then you can fill my tank to the brim.*

I read it back with a growing sense of shame. It was far too cutting and unnecessarily rude. Thank God I hadn't pressed 'Send'. Instead, I settled for a flat, stock reply – this would fit the bill.

> *MY ACTUAL REPLY: Thanks for your message but I don't think we are well suited.*

I leant back, drumming my fingers on the table, wondering if I could do better. Was my profile a bit too clever by half? Was the photo good enough? Yes, I'd have to revisit both and probably get a photo tailor-made for the job ... otherwise I could end up serving a life sentence at The Fox or cruising the bars or even [God forbid] reviewing my workmates in a fresh and hopeful light!

Chapter 2

PHOTO SHOOT

I have to be honest; this wasn't one of my best days at work. Firstly, it was Monday – enough said; secondly I had much more important matters on my mind – how to improve my *obviously* limited appeal on the website. So, to a certain extent I simply went through the motions – replying to emails, responding to phone calls but never taking the initiative – reactive rather than proactive, to use the jargon. I kept thinking about the photo I needed, convinced that the holiday effort I rushed into had been a mistake. Perhaps I could use the one taken by Mum during a day out at the Trafford Centre, but I didn't think the backdrop, the 'Finger Lickin' Good' sign, was exactly suitable for dating purposes. Then, I thought about omitting a photo altogether and referring to myself as an 'enigmatic' woman who preferred to 'surprise' possible suitors but figured this was far too subtle for most blokes [photo essential for a considered appraisal of the product].

No, I'd just have to get one done. I could ask Chief Twitcher Brian to do the honours. He was basically a really kind bloke but, oh dear, he did tend to go on a bit, boring everyone rigid with numerous photos of blue tits, grey tits and robin redbreasts. And, in contrast to the great majority of his workmates, he really couldn't see any pervy undertones in all of this. So no, forget Brian. I couldn't think of a reasonable excuse for asking him and anyway, he might think I was interested in being Miss February [cold tits?] in next year's Twitchers' Annual.

Caroline, yes Caroline would have to do it, despite her initial lack of enthusiasm for the project. At least I'd have artistic control e.g. subtle lighting [careful though, a halo effect might attract the god squad] telling her to stand some distance away [say next door] so I didn't look overweight. Right, I decided to phone her there and then before she turned on the TV to catch *Jeremy Kyle* – she was addicted to the cringe-inducing stories and public humiliation of the ever-willing participants

'Cazi, yes it's me – yes, I know it's on soon. That's why I'm ringing now – I'll be quick, honest. Thing is, need you to take my photo asap and naturally I expect to look like SJP on it.'

'What the hell is that? Sounds like something you might pick up from a holiday fling.'

'Bloody hell what planet are you on? Did you get a lobotomy as well as five kettles when you got married? SJP – Sarah Jessica Parker, one of those gorgeous, sexy, very 'now' women with fabulous figures, A-list credentials and wealthy husbands.'

'Who do you think I am – Mario Testino? Anyway, it'll have to be later on tonight, because me and Bob have to go off to a parents' evening and talk nice with Mrs bloody Walker – you know, the Myra Hindley lookalike. I'm determined to get our Louise out of that St Thug's Upper School but Ken Livingstone here won't hear of it. "A comprehensive education was good enough for me and it'll be good enough for my kids as well." Sometimes I think he's a raving communist.'

I sighed; I wasn't going to pursue this any further.

'All right then, yes, about half-nine's fine and can I borrow your frilly blouse that looks so much better on me than it does on you? I want to wear it for the photo. It gives me a waist – no, don't titter! – and if I wear my push-up, the cleavage will be just enough to excite the punters without attracting the *Readers' Wives* lot.'

'OK, OK. Now, is that IT?'

'Yes, and when you come round you can read through my profile, you lucky thing you. Took me ages. Pretty good though if I do say so myself!'

'OK, fine – if we get the photo done, I'll be able to view the entire Sally package on display to every pervert, rapist, and gold-digger in Manchester, if not the entire European Union.'

'You know, there *are* times when I wonder why I love you. See you later and don't forget that blouse. Be nice to Myra!'

'That's a laugh – bye honey.'

Rarin' to go

3.25 pm ... My God, doesn't that damn clock ever move? I was seething. I was DESPERATE to get home and read the avalanche of emails certain to have followed the tantalising profile I'd posted ... surely Derek from Dudley wouldn't be my only catch?

I worked in the very heart of Manchester, close to the Bridgewater Hall, a concert venue of some distinction but more importantly even closer to Deansgate, Manchester's very own Oxford Street, boasting a number of the country's top stores including Selfridges and Harvey Nichols. The bank had one of those imposing late-Victorian neo-Gothic edifices; in contrast the interior was state-of-the-art modernity with the ground floor dedicated to the normal high-street banking activities.

A group of us were on the first floor, sharing a vast open-plan area. We had placed signs of ownership at our desks, photos of family, friends and favourite celebrities and all sorts of bright animal miniatures, receptacles for staples and pencils. The office needed these as the overall colour scheme was hardly inspiring: dull grey computers everywhere, pale walls relieved only by the inevitable work flow charts. My desk had a photo of me and Caroline in Ibiza circa 1990 and a mug inscribed 'Never go jogging – it makes the ice in your glass jump'.

There was a restroom at the back of our floor where a thoughtful management provided coffee and magazines. The facility provided sanctuary from difficult customers and doubled as a drop-in centre for discussing the week's current 'affairs'.

3.40 pm …and I was still there, fretting at my desk.

Who needs Barbados?

3.45 pm … Short of doing an impromptu pole dance around the central column, what could I do to hurry time along? And then … from the corner of my eye I became uncomfortably aware of a looming presence. Yes, it was Brian. He sidled towards me. Spare me. [Not another conversation about the lesser-spotted wagtail known only to the migrant tribesmen of outer Uzbekistan – and Brian.] Then I felt guilty – only a few hours earlier I was considering him as my photo saviour; I had to be civil.

He perched on the side of my desk, looking down at me with an expectant smile. 'Hello Sally. Just wondered if you had a minute?'

'Brian, nice to see but sorry – deadline,' I replied, pointing at my screen. 'If I am not finishing zis, mein Führer Villiams vill remove my biscuit privileges und tranzfer me to ze filing room, a fate vurst zan death ja?'

He looked at me wearing his Rolf Harris 'this-puppy-will-be-destroyed-if-you-don't-ring-this-number' expression. 'That's OK. I know you're always busy. I don't want to bother you; I just wanted to tell you about this trip Twitchers' Weekly are planning to view exotic birds.'

'Really? Where to? The Isle of Man?'

'No, Barbados actually.'

'Barbados?' I echoed, unable to believe my ears. 'BARBADOS!' I instantly dismissed the urgency of the Departmental Expenses Q2 Report and swivelled round, looking at him with new interest.

'Brian, are you actually going to Barbados or simply reading the advert before booking a week in Rhyl?'

'Well, I'd really like to go. These birds are very rare you know – you can see them on those David Attenborough programmes or in Chester Zoo, but it's not the same as seeing them in their natural habitat.'

'So, what's stopping you then? No passport?'

'Oh no, I've got a passport. I had to get one when I took Mother to Lourdes to cure her cystitis. And it's not the money either. After all, you don't spend much sitting in a hide every weekend. I'd willingly pay it and for a companion too if only I had one ...' Rolf's endangered puppy expression had morphed into that shot of Bambi when he realises mummy's never coming home.

Shameful thoughts flashed through my brain. Could I possibly consider this? On the one hand, Barbados with the blazing sun, golden beaches, rum punches, warm seas, star-spangled nights. Sensational! But with Brian...?

No, no, and thrice no, I decided.

'Look, there must be plenty of other enthusiasts who would love to go. Why don't you place an ad in the magazine expressing your interest and ask if anyone else fancies it? But DON'T say you'll pay or every scrounger in the land will be writing to you.' [Unlike 'moi', I thought, smug about my own obvious lack of mercenary qualities.]

'I suppose you're right. Maybe I will, but I don't really want to share a straw hut with a complete stranger.'

I struggled to mask my incredulity. Straw hut? 'Hmm, well you'd certainly have to mention the straw hut bit. I mean, you wouldn't want to lure someone to Barbados under false pretences would you now? Anyway, I'd really suggest that you give some thought to the ad but I simply have to get back to this report now, or we can kiss goodbye to this month's expenses – sorry.'

'OK, well thanks for the advice Sally. I knew I could rely on you. Bye for now.'

And, with a final lingering glance, he trundled off.

3.52 pm ... if I eat another biscuit I'll be fat girl with no fella rather than sad girl with no fella, I mused. I'd definitely decided to leave at four, telling Herr Villiams I had a dental appointment. In fact I *would* rather have root canal treatment than sit in the office for another hour

'Hiya gorgeous,' murmured a male voice. I rolled my eyes to heaven. What was going on here? First, the Birdman of Alcatraz and now Roy of the Rovers.

'Hello Roy,' through gritted teeth.

'Watcha been up to sexy?' leered Roy, pupils dilating as he surveyed the entire millimetre of my exposed cleavage.

'Oh, nothing much. Colin Farrell gave me a good seeing to last Friday when we were in Venice. How about you?' STUPID GIRL. WHY DID I ASK THAT? WHY INVITE THE INEVITABLE?

'... And then in the 16th minute, Rooney slipped one past that dago goalkeeper only for the ...' I knew exactly what was coming and silently recited with him – 'four-eyed, clueless, mentally retarded bastard referee to disallow it.'

'Oh dear, how awful for you Roy. It must be nearly as bad as finding out your girlfriend's contracted Chlamydia or something. Sorry, but I've really got to go.'

Roy shot me a particularly venomous look, muttering 'Miserable cow' as he sloped off.

With that, I grabbed my bag, and practically ran to the car, barging past Ryan, the pimply work experience boy. I shouted a quick 'Sor-ee Ryan'. I couldn't wait to get home.

Formula 1

'And now, heeerz Susie with the Travel news,' boomed manic Micky Moon, Piccadilly Radio's most popular DJ.

'Thanks mate,' said Susie, all breathless and giggly. 'There's certainly a problem out there this afternoon.'

'I could give you a problem every afternoon,' guffawed Micky.

'Ee, though, you're such a cheeky bugger you Micky Moon,' she giggled. 'Anyway, here's the Travel news – unfortunately, for all you unlucky drivers out there, the main route into Sale is completely closed due to a–'

A lone policeman was waving his arms like an excited bookie at Ascot. What the bloody hell was he on about? I could see his eyes bulging with a mixture of fear and fury. 'Left, left, go to the left' he boomed above the roaring traffic. I screeched to a halt.

'Eh up love, what's your hurry?' gasped the officer, his troubled breathing aggravated by the acrid smell of burning tyres.

'Yes, I'm so, so sorry – my Jessica's having her puppies you see,' rolling my eyes in an outrageously theatrical butter-wouldn't-melt-in-my-mouth manner.

'Puppies?' the officer looked blankly at me.

'Yes, you know, puppies, woof, woof, big brown eyes, button noses and paintbrush paws. It's an emergency. She's been in labour for over three days now and there's eleven of them and if I don't get home asap, some of them will die horribly, horribly,' I choked, reaching for the packet of Kleenex in the glove compartment.

'Look love, this road is completely closed. There's no way through so you can save the Gwyneth Paltrow routine for the Oscars.'

'Plonker,' I muttered.

'What was that?' he said with increasing exasperation, adopting a Judge Dread expression.

'Err nothing ... Sergeant,' I simpered, switching to flirting. 'Where do I have to go please?' eyelashes all a-flutter.

'Turn left here then second right then first right and you'll rejoin Washway Road further up past the spillage.'

'What was spilt exactly?' I asked, affecting a concerned interest.

'A Boddington's delivery wagon shed its load. We've had as much trouble stopping the lowlife pinching the bitter as we've had clearing away the bloody vehicle.'

'Well, if I'm offered a cheap pint with my pickled egg tonight I'll know where it's come from won't I? Bye for now Officer!'

He responded with a withering look as I executed a perfect left turn into the previously unknown and tree-lined Acacia Avenue.

Say 'cheese'

Charging into the kitchen, I snatched a sandwich and was just about to log on when Caroline called.

'Hi Sally, you OK? Look, bit of a problem. Bob's going to be late so I've had to move all the teachers' appointments back an hour which means I can come over now to do the photo rather than after parents' evening. Is that OK with you? It'll make life much easier for me.' Bloody typical. I've broken the land speed record to get home and now reading my emails (if there are any) will have to wait.

'Sure, no problem. Come round soon as you're ready.'

'OK, hon, see you in 'bout ten minutes.'

'OK, bye.'

I had to tidy up my living room for the photo – some of it could appear in the background – I didn't want my hunk to think I was living in some festering squat. I cleared away all the newspaper supplements – unread, again – from the dining table and placed two table settings with deep burgundy napkins to complement the cream runner. I added dark wood coasters for the crystal wine glasses, sparkling now after a quick clean, and, in the centre of the runner, the Georgian cruet set – one of the few relics of my marital home that I really treasured, buffing it up to enhance the shine. From the kitchen windowsill I retrieved the pretty yellow tulips, cutting them down so that they stood well in a medium-size glass vase. Next, the sofa – the throws would have to go; they were only there as a 'temporary measure' anyway because Ringo, next door's neglected pussy cat, had become a frequent visitor in recent weeks. Then I plumped up the deep red cushions, the wheat-coloured suite looking really comfortable in the warm light of the table lamps. On the TV set was a cherished photo of Mum and Dad taken a couple of Christmases ago. I tidied up the bookshelves, put the CDs and DVDs into some semblance of order, and ran the Hoover over the carpet. From behind the mirror above the mantelpiece, I removed the postcard with its Mediterranean scene – 'Magaluf is fab – and so are the blokes!'– from Janey, one of my racier friends, and then checked that the small water colours of Venice were correctly spaced. Finally, I rearranged the fruit in the bowl on the coffee table, making sure the brighter oranges were at the front and on top, placing next to it my *Cucina Italiana!* cookery book which I'd barely had time to dip into because of work pressures. I stood back and smiled, pleased with the results of my labours.

Caroline heralded her arrival by singing lustily … 'If a picture paints a thousand words …' into the intercom.

'God, someone's been busy in here – didn't recognise the place it's so tidy. Are you sure you're not auditioning for *The House Doctor* or that other one, that *Location* thing – you know, the one with the toffee-nosed type with the big arse in it and–'

'Yes, Cazi, very funny, ha ha, but you're here for the photo shoot of the millennium, remember?'

'Yes, I know, only joking but look, I'm expecting a bit of bother up at the Gulag that passes for a school, so don't expect me to take a million photos just so you can sit back and pick out your favourite at leisure. You don't look like SJP and you never will right?'

'OK, keep your hairnet on. Where's that blouse?'

She glanced to one side, and paused, almost guiltily, before handing over a crumpled mass of fabric.

'Oh, you could *at least* have put it on a hanger. I've got to–'

'Hey,' she countered, clearly irritated, 'I've got two kids, and an idle bastard who is reputedly my husband. It was in the ironing basket OK!'

'All right, all right. But this'll take longer than fifteen minutes because I've got to iron it – don't forget, first impressions count remember!'

'Just get on with it … QUICKLY!' she snorted in reply.

I ironed the blouse, got dressed, dimmed the lights and pouted at her camera like Victoria Beckham.

'My God, you look like an ad for one of those 0870 lines – ITALKDIRTY4U or something. Just relax and smile naturally.'

I tried but it must have come out more like a grimace.

'Now you look like something from *Bad Girls*.'

'Oh great, thanks. Look, I haven't time to be "natural" – you're hassling me. God, I bet supermodels don't have this problem.'

'Calm down, tell you what – why don't you just walk around? I'll follow you, and while we're chatting I'll take photos.'

My initial movements were probably somewhat laboured, resembling those of a wilful supermarket trolley in dire need of lubrication.

'For heaven's sake, walk properly will you, this isn't a camcorder I've got here... now you're strutting around like Camilla with a riding crop shoved up her arse!'

'OK, sorry – I'm doing my best you know. It's not every day of the week I can play the diva!'

I wasn't wholly convinced of all this pantomime but remained desperate to get it done, not least because the Wonderbra was pinching me something chronic. She followed me, a few paces back, snapping all the time, a blizzard of flashes strobing the living room. It was all a bit false but I genuinely laughed out loud when Caroline told me she intended telling the childless Mrs Walker that her *Ten Steps to Happy Teens* could be put to good use in a Baghdad Public Toilet.

'Sally, wait, look, this is the one. Great smile and sparkling blue eyes. Get that computer switched on.'

I deleted the first photo, uploaded the replacement and then clicked on my profile. My image, as if summoned by a genie, magically appeared and beneath it the text.

'Ah, the famous profile,' cried Caroline. 'Let's have a quick read through. Yes, yes – that's good, love it, full marks for wit and originality. I especially like the reference to Bolly – that'll weed out the Brown Ale Brigade. But you will be very careful won't you?'

'Of course, Mother, and I promise to tell you everything I do, down to the last throbbing detail.'

'Excellent,' she said, picking up her jacket. I could sense that, though she would hate to admit it, by now, she too was visibly warming to the whole exercise. 'My life,' she moaned, hand on forehead, 'my life is totally devoid of adventure but at least I'll get to live this if only second-hand. Night, sweetheart.'

'Night Caz. Thanks for taking the photo and for the blouse. I'll wash AND iron it before I give it back – AND I'll even lend you a hanger!'

Tubas, Tories, and Tuscany (well, nearly)

Right, alone at last. I'll just switch off the phone then close down my profile and check for messages. Three of them! Bless you one and all! There's hope for me yet!

First up there was … Jeff, from Barnsley … the Bali of the North … my heart sank.

> THE MESSAGE: *How do Sally. I like what you put especially about being musical because I play the tuba in the brass band here. I think we would get on. Look at my profile and you shall see what I mean. Jeff.*

Tuba … brass band … my heart sank even deeper. What had I got myself into? Perhaps Caroline was right after all when she'd said originally, 'No love, this is one bad move – Internet dating is for losers: every weirdo from Wigan to Winchester does it! No, forget it. I'd rather see you join a convent.' But, impelled by mounting curiosity as much as by a fierce determination to prove my cynical friend wrong, I scrolled down to take in Jeff's profile … perhaps things would improve? … wouldn't they? …

THE PROFILE:
Name: Jeff
Age: 41
Location: Barnsley, South Yorkshire
Status: Single
Children: None
Job: Technician
Height: 5'11"
Build: Medium
Appearance: Average
Eye Colour: Blue
Hair: Blonde
Religion: Methodist
Star Sign: Virgo
Smoker: No
Drinker: No

INTERESTS: Music, walking, cooking, sports (watching), DIY, gardening.

ABOUT ME: I want to meet someone nice me. It is more fun to do things like putting up shelves or potting on if you have got someone with you. My garden is very big and I have a nice shed where I do my tuba practiss. I also use my shed as an office because I am the secretery of the North West George Formby Fan Club. I like people what are warm and kind. My favourite things to eat are suet puddings. If you can make them it would be great.

Gardening? The tuba? George Formby? Suet puddings? Perhaps all of this could have been overlooked had this first earnest suitor been in any way attractive but, sadly, he was quite ordinary. He looked a good deal older than his stated age and was balding prematurely, with a hint of the Bobby Charlton comb-over. The photo too had left him with a series of unfortunate blotches on his forehead and cheeks. His paisley tie reinforced the picture of a man old before his time. I knew instantly the sort of reply I'd liked to send.

> *MY PREFERRED REPLY: Dear Jeff, thanks for your message. Unfortunately the prospect of glittering social events in Morecambe Palais with other George Formby devotees does nothing for me. Personally, I always thought his true vocation was to entertain the Japs as a deadlier alternative to the atom bomb. Why not try something new? Otherwise I fear the only thing you'll be humping is that oversized trumpet.*

No, this wouldn't do – no point in trying to be so clever; that would get me nowhere. The stock reply proved useful again.

> *MY ACTUAL REPLY: Thanks for your message, but I don't think we are well suited.*

Now, who was next in line? Phil from Chester.

THE MESSAGE: Hello Sally – glad to see I'm not the only one hermetically sealed in my duvet on a chilly Sunday morning! Chocs and champers – yes already ordered for you. Read my profile and with luck we might be sharing them! Phil

THE PROFILE:
Name: Phil
Age: 43
Location: Chester
Status: Single
Children: None
Job: Computer Analyst
Height: 6'1"
Build: Medium
Appearance: Average
Eye Colour: Brown
Hair: Dark Brown
Religion: Christian [non-practising]
Star Sign: Pisces
Smoker: Yes
Drinker: Moderate

INTERESTS: Pop music, movies, theatre, rock climbing, restaurants, travel, the Internet.

ABOUT ME: *Getting started! This is always the hard part, isn't it? Bit like redecorating your house – where on earth do you begin? Anyway, I could launch into some Booker winning prose describing myself as a Renaissance man, Renaissance but contemporary too. You know, fluency in several languages including Latvian, principal violin in the Northern Philharmonic, co-discoverer of DNA, counsellor with the Samaritans, Liberal Democrat, EU positive, Apollo in Armani. But the Booker prize is given for fiction isn't it? And yes, I might win with the above! But back to reality. I speak English fluently until my third bottle of Chablis that is. As for being a musical virtuoso, well, the truth is I'm a dab hand at the paper and comb. The only science I know is from Star Trek [I have all the videos but never made it to the convention]. I'm a raving Tory and I don't like foreigners. I'm dressed by George at Asda. There I've said it – but, in my defence, my friends think I'm a decent sort of bloke. Caring [I never miss birthdays], honest to a fault, hardworking and GSOH big time. If you haven't reported me to the authorities yet, why not get in touch? It might be fun.*

A bit too full of himself for me and the reference to Star Trek is seriously worrying.

MY PREFERRED REPLY: Dear Mr Spock. Everything was fabulous up to and including Apollo in Armani. Wit and articulation are a heady mix for me. Imagine my disappointment to find out …you're 'dressed by George at Asda'. Valets back in fashion are they? Does he also slip in a recheck of your inside leg measurement every now and then? And …you're a Trekkie. What turns you on about that? I bet its Scotty's 'Beam me up' machine. How else did you get so far up Uranus?

MY ACTUAL REPLY: Thanks for your message but I don't think we are well suited.

Well, still no Sean Bean, but I remained hopeful – one more to go, and it was … Mike from Crewe. Aagh! Crewe … trainspotters – please God not a trainspotter!

THE MESSAGE: Hello there Sally or should I say 'choiao siggorina'. Me and Italian cooking, well I love it and the good news is it's much cheaper at home than in the eye-ties. A bottle of vino and its Saluti! all round. Hope my profile interests you as much as yours interested me. Mike

THE PROFILE:

Name: Mike
Age: 40
Location: Crewe
Status: Divorced
Children: One
Job: Financial Services
Height: 6'0"
Build: Slim
Appearance: Attractive
Eye Colour: Green
Hair: Dark Brown
Religion: Christian [non-practising]
Star Sign: Capricorn
Smoker: No
Drinker: Moderate

INTERESTS: Mediterranean cooking, theatre, movies, wine tasting, contemporary music, TV/radio, stock market.

ABOUT ME: My friends tell me I'm a very supportive kind of fellow. Caring, reliable and responsible. I enjoy good comedy on the TV – the witty, ironical, contemporary sort – more The Office than Two Pints of Lager and a Packet of Crisps. I genuinely miss having a lady in my life. Nothing better than seeing a play or a film and talking about it afterwards. I've lived and worked in Crewe

> *all my life but I do feel the need for a change of scene sometimes. You know, bargain breaks – UK or Europe: for me, no frills airlines are the best invention since the jet engine itself. Would much prefer to see Venice, Barcelona, and Amsterdam – wherever – with the right company. What do you think? Why not BMI baby (get it?).*

Even I knew I wasn't a 'siggorina' but I reminded myself that this was about dating not attending an Italian evening class. So what about his looks? Although he was no oil painting, there was something quite attractive about him. The contrast of his green eyes and brown hair was unusual and lent him a certain feline quality. He had a confident look and a smile that invited a response. His range of interests had much in common with mine … this added to his appeal.

> *MY PREFERRED REPLY: Standard reply not required! Mike sounds worth a shot!*

> *MY ACTUAL REPLY: Molto bene Mike – there, that's my Italian exhausted! Thanks for your message. Nice profile. Especially loved the BMI pun – very sharp! You'll notice that I work in Financial Services as well; I'm a trainer for Barclays. So come on Mike, what about you? Chief financial analyst perhaps? – but not for Northern Rock I hope.*

Come on baby light my fire!

What's the time? Nearly ten already … God this is addictive – I've been sat here for hours. Can't be bad though – first trawl and one decent salmon. Must phone Caroline; she'll be fascinated. No, better not do it now – after speaking to the teachers she'll still be roasting the kids on an open spit.

I was really quite pleased. Dateandsee was definitely made for me. No problems with the technology. I'd taken to it like a duck to water and I'd enjoyed a modicum of success, though just a few replies were not exactly the Christmas post. What about having a go myself? Casting my own net over the Cyber Ocean, I remembered that juicy electrician … what was he called again? Dave, that's him. Yes, I'd certainly contact him and have a look for anyone else worthy of my bait.

Umm, Davey boy, what was it about him that I liked apart from his dark, brooding good looks? I pulled up his profile and mentally reviewed it. I chose to ignore the appalling grammar 'We was really stuffed down the Taj Mahal last week', preferring instead to concentrate on the bits I liked namely his high *phwoar* factor!

> THE MESSAGE: Hi Dave. I liked your profile especially the photograph and the bit where you compared yourself to George Best – you know, you've both spent thousands on wine, women and song and merely wasted the rest. Maybe you'll read my profile and decide to spend even more! Sally
> P.S.   Is it true sparkies do it in the dark?

Ummm, that 'P.S.' might be a bit too forward but too late now. Next up it's Andrew, definitely Andrew from Alderley Edge – might as well follow the rough with the smooth. He was certainly personable, to put it mildly. His brown eyes stared resolutely, almost challengingly into the camera. His hair was thick and curly, his jaw square and strong. Nice GSOH too: 'Love cooking – the books that is, oops sorry Chancellor, only joking', 'As they say, travel broadens the mind – sadly it also expands the credit card. The prices in St Tropez these days! I think they named it after trop [Fr. = too much – in case your convent education didn't extend to everyday French]' and the clincher, 'One of my girlfriends said I had more than a passing resemblance to Ben Affleck – mind you, she was blindfolded at the time.'

So, motivated as much by the vision of a magnificent mansion with sweeping lawns as by his obvious wit and fine features, I decided to explore the delights of rural Cheshire.

> THE MESSAGE: *Hello Andrew in Alderley Edge. What's a son of the landed gentry doing ploughing the fertile fields of Cybershire? I went to the country once and got rather wet. Maybe next time you'll be there to dry me off? We might meet up and perhaps you'll swap your brolly for my Bolly? Sally*

There, done – with any luck, this would certainly prompt a positive response.

But now the answerphone was flashing. It was from Caroline. 'Hello, Sally,' grunted the ill-disguised voice. 'Well, you do look sexy. My name is James. I'm 6′ 2″, handsome, loaded and … my friends call me 'Donkey'… give me a call – I'm sure you will.'

I returned the call at once and the instant the receiver was lifted said brightly, 'Hello, donkey dick.'

'Well, hello there Sally,' Bob drawled, 'I see my wife's been sharing one of my finer points with you–'

'Oh, hi Bob. Sorry – little joke between me and Cazi.'

'Oh it's no joke sweetheart – nor is it little. Has my dear wife told you about the surgical truss she …'

I heard Caroline snap, 'Shut up Bob, that's enough. Let me have the phone.'

'Hi Sally. Look, do me a favour – please don't wind him up or I'll have to endure a double helping of his lurve machine.'

'I wasn't winding him up. I thought you'd answer. Anyway what do you want?'

'What do you think I want? A recipe for a chocolate cake? I obviously want to know how many replies you've got to your "Available immediately" advert.' [Her sarcasm seeking to conceal her growing interest.] 'Where on earth have you been? I've phoned four times and the mobile too – everything's switched off.'

'Sorry! I've been shopping for a soul mate you know not for a new pair of tights. Anyway, I didn't want to disturb your date with Corrie.'

'Taped it. Now I'll have to wait an hour to regain control of the TV from Bob. He won't let me watch it until "Cosmetic Surgery Live" is over. Anyway, what's happened?'

'Well, guess what? I've had four replies altogether – not bad eh?'

'Four? You've not had that many men after you since your top fell down in the school disco. Come on then, what are they like?'

'Three no-hopers and one contender.'

'What do you mean "no-hopers"? I hope you haven't been too quick to judge?'

'Quick to judge? Listen, the first is president of a George Formby fan club, plays the tuba in his shed and is looking for someone to help him with potting on duties. The second is further to the right than Attila the Hun AND a Trekkie. The third is a grease monkey with a penchant for instant lubrication.'

'There, you see,' she said, with just a trace of 'I told you so'. 'That's what I meant about this Internet lark. It's like Disneyworld for tossers.'

'Hang on, I've not told you about Mike from Crewe or the two fellas I've written to.'

I read out loud Mike's profile and message. We agreed that he sounded promising, *provided*, Cazi emphasised, *provided* that his references to saving money – home cooking and no frills airlines – were not a thin disguise for a Grade A tight-arse [my antennae twitched briefly.] As for Dave, I was honest enough to say that what he lacked in sophistication he more than made up for in specification.

But it was when I mentioned Andrew that she immediately perked up. 'It's him! It's him! He's "THE ONE"! You can get married in his house – sorry, lodge: bound to be a lodge – surrounded by the downtrodden estate workers, all hurling their flat caps high in the air shouting, "Three cheers for Mistress Sally!" I'm going to look stunning at your wedding. I've been flipping through the *Brides* magazine I bought for you in Sainsbury's by the way. What about a Christmas wedding? That'd be something really different to look forward–'

'Cazee! Enough.'

'No, but just think about it Sally. Snow blanketing the countryside, stars twinkling above, roaring log fires and you could wear a fur-trimmed hood instead of a veil.'

'What ARE you on? You've been reading too much *Woman's Weekly* and not enough *Heat*.'

'Oh she's go-ing to the chapel and she's gon-na getta-ma-a-arried ...'

'Bloody hell, give it a rest will you? -You're beginning to sound like Karen .... you really should be writing Mills and Boon! Look, it's getting a bit late; I'll be in touch towards the end of the week – OK?'

I put my no fat, carb free, low cal sewage for one in the microwave... as the dish slowly rotated, I wondered with a mounting sense of excitement, how long it would be before my own *life* heated up.

Chapter 3

ENTER THE GOODFELLA?

Mike's reply was promising.

> Hi Sally, no, I'm glad to say I don't work for Northern Rock – I work for the Halifax. I've been with them since leaving school, in the not too distant past I should add, and on the whole I enjoy it.
>
> I was wondering whether you'd like to get together for an Italian. I know we live about thirty miles apart and probably should meet somewhere in the middle but the place I've got in mind is 'Pizza da Pietro' – just a couple of streets from the station, Crewe's only claim to fame!. I've been there several times, it's the genuine article and not too expensive. What do you think? Do you mind travelling to Crewe? Anyway, I'll give you my phone numbers [01270 838999 or 07986 635721] and you decide whether you want to go ahead or just mail me back if you prefer. Regards, Mike.
>
> P.S. Thursdays are a good night for me.

I paused to reflect on his message. A 'genuine article' pizza place. Good choice for a first date – relaxed, informal, cosy. Red check tablecloths, candles in Chianti bottles, light opera in the background, the pungent aroma of garlic and olive oil, and if I got really lucky, some good-looking

Italian waiters telling my escort how 'bellissima' I was! Slight worry about its location – stations aren't normally in the more upmarket areas but then again Crewe station IS famous if only with trainspotter anoraks. Travel to Crewe. Well yes, a bit further than I'd like to go but he deserved the benefit of the doubt – after all, he'd put some thought into choosing a place he knew we'd both be comfortable in. Mobile AND home numbers supplied. Good. No worries about him being married. So why did I have an uneasy feeling? Was it the reference [again] to something being'… not too expensive'? Would Caroline's description – 'Grade A tight-arse' prove ominously prophetic? Or was it that twenty-odd years with the Halifax implied a dull, tedious existence perfectly suited to a trainspotter [the Crewe connection was really worrying]? Was I in some danger of getting into a relationship with someone who actually enjoyed pen-pushing, bean counting and folder filing so long as he had enough time to pursue his two great loves – stamp collecting and membership of The Carpenters' fan club? Oh come on, I reprimanded myself, this wasn't a *relationship* – it was just a date, a one-off, something I'd done dozens of times before, and anyway I needed the practice if this whole Dateandsee thing was going to work for me. At least he seemed safe enough, more likely to attack me with a brain-numbing discourse on the penny black than a machete. I felt it wiser not to reply immediately – mustn't appear too eager: [Chapter 2 'Men are from Mars, Women from Venus'].

Enter Ms Bossy Boots

The following day at work started with unusual interest. Our new boss, Lesley [female] was dropping by for a day or so, beginning with an informal 'meet the team' session before commencing duties proper in the month ahead. I knew for certain that I would really miss Eric Williams, my previous boss. Calm, unflappable Eric – he would never achieve a million dollar coup on Wall Street but everyone, colleagues and customers alike, agreed he was rock solid. He'd always taken an interest in me, offering that extra guidance when difficult situations arose. At fifty-eight the bank had made him the archetypal 'offer you can't refuse' and he was now set to stroll contentedly down the nineteenth fairway of life with the 'chaps' at the local golf club.

Lesley made her entrance. What is it people say about buying a house? You know in the first thirty seconds whether you like it or not. Lesley wasn't a house but that didn't stop me making the same snap judgment about this viewing. Her entire demeanour radiated as much heat as a single bar electric fire in a national grid failure. There were no handshakes, fewer smiles. Her mouth seemed permanently fixed in an inverted crescent of dissatisfaction, as if she'd chewed a wasp or something. She was tall and willowy, hair closely cropped like Judi Dench as 'M', flat-chested, no make-up, blank, cold eyes unblinking behind rimless glasses, fingernails unadorned and squared off. Put this together with a long black jacket draped over dark, plain trousers and you've got the bad bitch from *The Matrix* for a boss. Christ, I thought, what's her game? Was this whole look simply to impress/intimidate the troops? Come back Eric!

She immediately took control of the proceedings. An informal 'meet the team' session was effortlessly transformed into a particularly scary episode of *Dragons' Den*. Her feeble attempt to generate a relaxed atmosphere consisted of rearranging the chairs as if at an Alcoholics Anonymous meeting to 'maximise the scope for interaction' [Chapter 108 'Management Matters']. Oh dear, I groaned inwardly. Tasks were assigned to 'help me cope with the steep learning curve'. Or was this in fact some sort of covert vetting, a test to gauge the abilities – and, more importantly, the compliance – of her minions?

Curiously too, she seemed to assign the more difficult tasks to the prettier young women – a further worrying sign. In less than half an hour, all those present, muted by this hound from hell, were left in no doubt at all that...

'Q3 is going to be particularly challenging'

'There are no problems only opportunities'

'Being nice is good, being profitable is better'

And finally my personal favourite:

'I won't ask you to work harder, just smarter.'

Oh dear! ...In fact, she was rather like Sir Alan Sugar but without the good looks and charisma. She persisted in chanting a litany of management mantras, culled no doubt from countless hours of 'Leading the Way' courses. No comfort breaks were allowed, particularly distressing for Peter, Mr Bureau de Change, who'd told me just before the meeting that a 'dodgy burger' he'd scoffed the day before whilst fishing the banks of Lake Eerie [aka Salford Canal] was now "ip 'oppin' in me belly'...he really was a no-hoper. No coffee was ordered, as 'the immediate priority is to strip out all unnecessary running expenses.' Predictably, therefore, as soon as the meeting reached its longed-for conclusion, the attendees stormed off, heading like a herd of thirsty wildebeest for the nearest watering hole or trampling each other underfoot for the sanctuary of the toilets. Clearly this new regime was going to be very, very different.

Later in the day, I noticed that my young colleague, Lucy, was unusually quiet. Lucy was, quite simply, a sweet little thing. She had a small frame and a neat, trim figure. She generally wore her black hair in a bob, which – with her really pretty features – made her look closer to fifteen than twenty. Occasionally she wore glasses and this completed the look of a wispy junior clerk at the local council. She had joined the bank in the previous year when her A-level grades failed to reach the target necessary for university; she had a pleasing, winsome personality, and was undoubtedly clever. If she had one fault it was a marked lack of self-confidence that I was determined to boost, seeing in her a young girl capable of so much given the right guidance. I moved over to her desk.

'What's up Lucy? You don't seem yourself today.'

She didn't answer immediately but just stared at her screen; her hands, palms down, were splayed out over the keyboard like two stranded starfish. Her eyes were noticeably moist.

'Come on, Lucy, what is it?' I asked softly.

'Well,' she replied, almost choking on her words, 'you know that meeting this morning? Well the new boss wants a summary of all our South American transactions, country by country, from the last three years; it's Thursday afternoon now and she wants it by tomorrow afternoon so she can study it over the weekend. I just don't know where to begin. I'm hopeless, and she'll sack me.'

I could immediately see the way to set about the job, but I didn't say so. I recognised too that Lesley had set an impossible deadline but kept this to myself as well, not wanting to add to the girl's distress.

'Now, sweetheart, don't get into a state. Look, tell you what, let's get in early tomorrow and I'm sure we can polish it off together by teatime, OK?'

Relief spread over her young features. 'Oh, that's so good of you; I was beginning to get really anxious about it.'

Truth was, I could have done without this additional pressure. To give Bitch of Britain what she wanted would mean staying late tonight to do some preparatory work, and Lucy was in no fit state to assist. Of course I was dying to get back home to check the website but decided that the dating site would have to wait; I couldn't let the poor kid down.

Mr Posh and Mr Pablo

It was close to eight by the time I got home. I'd forgotten it was opening night for *The Sound of Music* at the Opera House and 250 [mostly gay] Marias marching down Oxford Street singing 'Doh, a Deer' added over half an hour to my journey. What a day! First of all, the fearsome Lesley, then lunchtime with sandwiches eaten on the run, streams of emails, scores of phone calls made and received, lukewarm coffee unceremoniously swigged down, Lucy's *cri de coeur*, and then finally the bloody Von Trapp lovers.

Now then, at last – click! To my wide-eyed delight, the site opened with a message from Andrew. He was the Company Accountant from Alderley Edge, already identified as Caroline's Bridegroom of the Year to my Lady Bountiful.

> *Hi Sally, many thanks for the reply. You know, it doesn't rain in Cheshire all the time but I must admit the green wellies and the Barbour do come in useful more often than not. I'd love to swap my brolly for your Bolly, can't get enough of the stuff, comes from being in the trade I suppose.*

Wow, I'd missed that bit about 'in the trade' – this was getting better by the minute! These opening sentences, warm, friendly and personal, made me press on eagerly only for the next sentence to cause me some alarm.

> *Now for the hitch I'm afraid. Things are really happening business-wise at the moment and I've got to fly out to Cape Town at the weekend. I'll be away for about a month. So, I won't be able to share your Bolly just yet, but I will contact you as soon as I'm back, promise, so will you keep it on ice until then please? In fact, why don't I give you my email address and we can 'chat' a bit whilst I'm away? It's* andrew@finewines.com *– look forward to hearing from you. Andrew x*

So, business pressures were the problem, thank God for that – he wasn't married, bankrupt or a recovering junkie. Well what about that, I thought, somewhat deflated. This was just my luck. Was his humour there to cloak a rejection? Was I being binned off? No, I didn't think so – there was too much detail and the email address AND the 'X' at the end. No, I sensed his interest and so what if I had to wait a month or so? Enough time to lose half my body weight and squeeze into that little black dress – perfect for what was sure to be a classy first date. There was no way Andrew would suggest a pizza parlour just off platform 2 – he seemed to be far more lobster than Lambrusco. Playing it cool didn't enter my head. I replied immediately.

> *Hi Andrew, thanks for your message. I'll be teetotal until your return, promise. Thanks for the email address, I'll drop you a line to ask how the Stellenbosch Impala 2001 is doing. Don't get too close to any lions! Take care. Sally*

No kiss – let him come on to me. He was bound to be impressed by my comprehensive knowledge of South African wines (OK, so I knew one) a fellow connoisseur without doubt.

Filled with fresh optimism, I scrolled down – ah, another hit. Mmm … dishee! Andrew was unconsciously filed away for future reference as I took in the Internet's answer to Antonio Banderas. I quickly scanned the bio. Mmm … a European dimension, that's new. Pablo Gonzales, chef in Harrogate. This was really quite interesting …

> *Hola! I have 23 years. I do Tango to you and speak you about footballs and the fighting of the bulls here in Barselonas. I have no wives now since I am celibacy. Pleese to type me and I will promise to you many Sangria and much Tappas.*
> *Adioss. Juan Pablo*

Ah! A character at last! Gonzale*s*? Barselona*s*? Tappa*s*? Adios*s*. Signor Gonzales was about as Spanish as Sir Jimmy Savile.

> *MY PREFERRED REPLY: Hola Don Quixote! Or should it be hiya luv. You see, amigo, despite your swarthy looks I suspect you're closer to Dean Martin than Ricky Martin. I bet your total exposure to Spain is limited to watching Real Madrid on TV, ploughing through a piled plate of Birdseye Paella, feet resting on a crate of San Miguel! Drama student perhaps? Hasta la vista baby!*

> *MY ACTUAL REPLY: Thanks for your message but I don't think we are well suited.*

Hmm, disappointingly, there was no reply from Stockport Dave. Had he actually read my message? Yes, there it was 'Message read yesterday at 11.47 pm.' Probably just back from six pints of Tiger and a vindaloo; he'll definitely reply, as he won't be able to resist my comparing him to George Best.

It occurred to me that you meet all sorts in Cyberland. I'd only been at this a few days and already I had Mr Posh, Mr Sexy and Mr Al Pacino on the go and there were those who didn't quite come up to scratch. Caroline would appreciate an update but first, it was high time I phoned Mum and Dad.

Family Affairs

My parents were now living on the Lancashire coast. This move further north had really made me anxious, as, inevitably, it meant they were leaving behind a well-established circle of family and friends. They were that bit more vulnerable being sixty rather than just six miles away. When I raised my concerns, Dad dismissed them with a laugh, claiming that the bracing sea air would 'knock years off us'; I remained unconvinced.

His eighty-fourth birthday was not too far off now and the family needed to look at dates to arrange a get-together. 'Please leave your message,' intoned the invisible guardian of 24 Sea Parade, Lytham. They'd probably be at their line dancing class. In their early eighties and still bopping, I thought, but oh, how I wished they'd drop the cowboy boots; they went neither with Dad's polyester 'Permacrease' trousers nor with Mum's drawstring-waist pseudo-denim wide-leg 'jeans'. 'You don't understand dear,' Mum had patiently explained. 'The boots are an essential tool for Line Dancing. You can't perfect the Lone Star Linkup or the Wyoming WigWalk without them – it's all a matter of heel–toe co-ordination, you see. You'll understand when you take it up.' I'd chosen to ignore this last remark. I didn't want to hurt her feelings with the obvious comparison between line dancing and the agility trials at Crufts. Besides, I was actually quite proud of them and their enthusiasm for trying new things and getting out and about. I left a brief, jokey message asking how the Texas Toe Tap had gone, promising to try again over the weekend.

It's a date

Right, Caroline next. No, hold on a minute, back to the screen – what about Mike, the Prince of Pizza? Next week was pretty clear and I had to dip my toe into the Internet dating waters sometime – after all, this was what it was all about, wasn't it? Even if the date turned out to be less than memorable, it wouldn't be totally without value and anyway, the telly was total crap on Thursdays. Should I email, phone or text? I wasn't too bothered about speaking to him beforehand and so opted for a text, which would be more immediate than an email and would give him my mobile number as well; I would save my home number until I was sure he wasn't a heavy breather.

Hi mike. pizza da pietro gd 4 nxt thurs. Will b in gd mood – it's payday (lol). C u inside bout 8? Sally

I wondered what the protocol was for paying the bill on an Internet date. I was an old-fashioned girl but there was something different about this kind of date. For example, if I met a man and he asked me out, I didn't expect to split the bill, firmly believing that the type of men I dated would never expect me to pay, or at least not the first time.

But an Internet date was different. Mike had not 'met' me. He didn't know if he fancied me enough to ask me out. We were meeting more as friends rather than potential lovers, and so I resolved to offer to pay my share and see what happened. My musings were interrupted by a text message – it had to be from Mike. *Grt! c u then. Look 4ward to it. I'll put rough guide 2 venice on table so u no its me! Any probs we have mobile numbers now. Choiao! Mike.*

Caroline's word of warning

Then, the phone rang; Caroline. 'OK Jlo. Give it to me. I want the lot, everything, toto! Who, when, where, how many times and I promise not to interrupt.'

'All right. Here we go then, in batting order. First off, Pablo Gonzales, he's – '

'What? A bleedin' dago! I don't think so. They're only interested in one – '

'Cazi, what was that about no interruptions? No, my dear amigo Gonzales wasn't quite the finished article, more Bradford than Barcelona in fact. So it was a case of adios! Now wait for it, you'll love this, get a grip of yourself. I only got a message from the Squire of Alderley Edge, didn't I? Yes, Andrew and more news; he's an accountant BUT for a fine wine importers!'

Sharp intake of breath, and then. 'FANTASTIC! Told you, told you, he's the one – so when you seeing him then?'

'No, hold your horses – mega disappointment. His business is whisking him off to South Africa for a month, just my luck – but he's sworn over his dead mother's soul that he'll be in touch soon as he's back AND he's given me his email address to stay in touch with him AND he signed off with a kiss. So, what do you think of that?'

'Well, his trip's a total bummer! I'll postpone the hat but you know, this could be an advantage – you could lose 10 lbs in a month and look even more fabulous than you already do.'

'Great minds, Cazi, great minds. I've got to squeeze myself into that half price Ghost number sometime.'

'Oh yes, you'd look really fab in that. Anyway, go on; what else – who's next?'

I hesitated. It was no good; I'd have to come clean with her about Mike sometime. 'Well, you remember Mike – Financial Services from Crewe and easyJet fanatic? Well, he's in the frame, for next Thursday in fact. We're meeting at an Italian restaurant.' I avoided being more specific about the actual venue, fearing Caroline would reiterate her tight-arse theory. Silence.

'Are you still there, Cazi?'

'Yes,' voice dropping several octaves to take on something of a more authoritarian tone. 'Look, I still don't think this is a good idea; I've had the heebie-jeebies about this lark from the beginning and I'm telling you – '

'Well, we'll just have to wait and see won't we?' I snapped defensively. Yes, I was somewhat riled, not least because one small corner of my hyperactive brain shared her misgivings.

'It's only a date, you know, a one-off, not a bloody honeymoon, and I'll tell you exactly where I'm going in case I never, ever, ever, return!' I recited dramatically. 'Don't say that, Sal, not even for a joke and yes, make sure you tell me exactly where you're going AND give me all the details.'

To deflect further criticism, open or implied, I changed tack. 'But what about you and the rest of the Osbournes?'

Caroline's toned changed. She was suddenly more serious.

'Actually, Sally, Bob's not too good. He's been having these pains in his chest. Doctor's given him the usual spiel – have a couple of days off work, better diet, quit smoking, cut down on the booze, try some exercise etc.etc. But to be honest, it's come as a bit of a shock and we're all a bit worried. What? Louise? She's driving me round the bend; only thinking of doing some arty-farty subjects for A-level isn't she – English, Art and what was it? Yes, Sociology or something equally useless. I keep on about doing Maths and Economics and getting on the Accountancy gravy train like her cousin David – making a bomb he is – but she won't listen.'

My A-levels had been English Literature and Art, and I gently pointed this out, adding that I wasn't exactly a failure. 'She'll do best at what she's interested in, believe me Cazi – it's her life and she's a sensible girl.'

'I know, I know,' countered Caroline. 'It's just that I don't want her messing up like I did.'

'Caroline, that's all behind you now and it's not going to happen to Louise. She's far more savvy than you were at her age. No, come on, you know that's true. She'll be fine. She's got a great future ahead of her. Now, I'll have to leave it there – early start tomorrow; bit of a problem at work! God, work, yes, forgot to tell you, the new boss came in today – think Margaret Thatcher – and that's when she's being nice. She was probably Dr Harold Shipman's receptionist in her last job. Watch this space. Bye for now and give Bobby a big sloppy kiss from me, poor thing.'

'Will do – but, remember, watch it with Mr Fish's Arsehole or whatever his name was.'

Work before play

I left home well before the rush hour and reached the office in record time. I was amazed to see little Lucy Locket hunched over her desk, hollow-eyed through lack of sleep and nervous exhaustion. On her mouse mat, I spotted a Twix wrapper and a murky, oil-filmed mug of coffee – the sorry remains of an insubstantial breakfast.

'Good morning Lucy,' I trilled, attempting to lighten the mood. 'Right, let's get stuck in, we'll have this lot well sorted by lunchtime, you'll see,' immediately activating my out of office assistant and voicemail.

Like an obedient puppy, she followed my every instruction to a T. Even Roy backed off at the mere sight of my flaring nostrils [speak to me this morning and I'll staple your tongue to your tie!]. We had the report completed by early afternoon when the click-clack-click of her shiny, black boots heralded Lesley's fearsome approach. Now, when were they last in *Vogue*, I wondered – ah yes, the 1936 edition, shot in Berlin.

She made a beeline for Lucy's desk. 'Well?'

'Ah, Lesley,' Lucy said in a low voice, scarcely daring to look her in the eye, 'yes, here's that South American report you wanted. I hope it's OK,' she volunteered anxiously. From my own desk I noted Lesley's cold stare. There was no trace of emotion – her entire face seemed botoxed, flat, smooth, expressionless – a death mask of indifference. She snatched at the report, cursorily flicked through a few pages, face suddenly darkening, eyes flashing with anger –

not at the contents of the report but at the knowledge that, on this occasion, her attempt to humiliate and intimidate Lucy had been thwarted. She continued to look sternly at the proffered pages before fixing her stony gaze on her anxious victim.

'Well yes, but next time make sure it's double spaced,' she said scornfully. 'That way it'll be easier for me to correct your mistakes, won't it?'

With that, she turned on her heels and was gone. I smiled over to the Lucy who was still shaking at Lesley's caustic remark.

'Don't worry, sweetheart, the first hurdle is always the highest and you cleared it easily! Now, she gives you any more Mission Impossibles, discuss it with me BEFORE getting into a state. OK?'

The week raced by, punctuated by several calls from Mum and Dad and their attempts to find that elusive weekend to suit everyone – God, they're busier these days than ever before, I thought – and an incessant but predictable series of demanding emails from Her Lesleyness ['I'm sure we can effect a little more leverage in the start-up business sector'].

Today's post

More encouragingly though, there was a steady stream of messages from hopeful suitors including the gorgeous Dave from Stockport – hurrah! He was off to a stag weekend somewhere [… I somehow doubted it would be in the Cotswolds …] but would email when he got back on Tuesday. Of the others only one caught my attention. And how! Graham from Solihull was not just good-looking, he was irresistible. He was a manager in retail – womenswear; this was getting better and better. His interests included IT and design.

> *I produce all my own birthday cards and Christmas cards. And oh yes, by the way, I'm bi but, at the moment, I'm in one of my seasonal male phases. I feel sure there must be lots of equally adventurous potential friends out there.*

I looked at the screen in disbelief and read the paragraph once again. No, there was no mistake 'I'm bi'; he was actually putting his sexuality out there for all the world to see.

> *And what about you, Sally? I have the feeling you're not the sort of girl hidebound by the traditional but destructive pigeonholing of personalities and sexualities. Are you tempted to, shall we say, think a bit laterally?*

Bi? How could people be so pedestrian about things like this? He spoke as if bisexual was as mundane as 'short-sighted'. I didn't really care what he was – that was up to him – but I was horrified to think that he could even imagine I might be interested in him. He was so good-looking …

and yes, there was even a hint of guy-liner on his photo but hey, even a modern girl has her limits. No, Graham from Solihull was fated to be chained – he would probably enjoy that as well – to his Mac, churning out Christmas cards featuring a transsexual Santa, ecstatic elves and a visibly aroused Rudolph. After this wholly unexpected message from the dark side, straightforward, conventional Mike from Crewe seemed a positively welcome prospect.

Pizza4U

Thursday evening. Now what to wear? What kind of impression did I want to make? Professional business woman? No, too cold, too standoff-ish and I had enough of that from Monday to Friday. Active, casual, hip look? Walking into JJB Sports brought me out in hives but I did the Reiss casual look quite well but no, not sexy enough. Full-on glamour? For a pizza joint in downtown Crewe? No way.

Smart casual? Ah yes, smart casual, that old standby, never lets you down – that secure no man's land between cheerless formality and gay abandon [sorry Graham, no pun intended]. It would be the black trousers with a black and white top with just enough cleavage to test his distraction level but not enough to make him think I was easier than Jordan.

Shower, hair wash, new blade in the Venus, liberal dose of body lotion AND perfume – might as well give him the full blast – clothes on, ritual ten minutes in front of mirror rearranging already perfect hair, examining stomach from every possible angle, and then I was ready. I blew myself a kiss in the mirror and left for my date with destiny. It was a fair distance to Crewe, and I had thought about taking the train but decided against it because a) I wanted the comfort of being able to leave at high speed if necessary and b) the 11.10 pm from Crewe to Altrincham was probably either a ghost train with just the one dickhead to bother me or, a 'football special' complete with its marauding fans.

Finding Crewe station was easy, but I did have to ask a taxi driver for directions to Pizza da Pietro. As he looked me up and down, his smirk offered me little reassurance – ninety seconds later, I realised why. The establishment was sandwiched – appropriately enough – between a Chinese takeaway and a Dial-a-Kebab. This was the smart area; as for the rest, well it would certainly qualify for a twinning scheme with Baghdad. Apart from the usual features of urban blight, it was liberally scattered with fast food confetti – waste paper, scrunched up takeaway boxes and hunks of decaying pizza. Reeling from this initial shock, like a soldier edging his way through a minefield, I picked my way forward, stopping for a moment to remove a particularly stubborn, reddish wedge of Napolitana from my heel – thank God I'd decided against my party shoes.

The musty, doughy smell – heavily impregnated with garlic – hit me immediately. 'Pizza da Pietro' – the sign was framed in the white, green and red of la bella Italia. The grimy windows were plastered with out-of-date menus, their curling borders picked out with the belching fires of Mount Vesuvius. In the centre was a flotilla of gondolas, manned by miserable gondoliers, straining at their oars; this evocative scene was intensified by the beaming faces of muscular peasants, merrily toiling in the sun-blessed vineyards of Tuscany. The layer of mist on the front window suggested an internal fug that made me start with apprehension. Talk about having second thoughts ... but, too late, as, between verses, I caught my name ringing out from inside...

Stiffening my resolve, I stepped warily inside. My eyes swept across the room. Through the gloom, I could make out a dozen or so tables, some boasting a red check tablecloth, others not. Mine host had, however, done his best to impress the clientele. Each table had a bulbous Venetian-style vase with multi-coloured tulips, some days old now and way past their best, twisted through the heat into all sorts of contorted shapes; additionally, there was salt and pepper and the positive jewel of a bottle of ketchup proudly occupying the central spot. Gordon Ramsay, eat your heart out. The handful of diners stared at me in disbelief; I could only assume that rarely did an attractive young woman, apparently on her own, grace their humble hostelry.

'Hello Sally, over here!'

I took it all in an instant. The creased brown suit, the brown and beige striped jumper, the cream and brown check shirt – yes, check ... WITH stripes! – and that most heinous of fashion crimes – black shoes with beige socks. Think Alan Partridge. Instinctively, for this was definitely not a case of love at first sight, I stretched out my hand, the tried and trusted social device for avoiding an unsolicited kiss or embrace. His limp handshake had me fearing the worst. He *was* tall, but this was the only discernible positive so far. Then I noticed two biros in his breast pocket, one black, the other red. Did he intend to take notes? To grade me perhaps? We sat down. I suspected he was undertaking a similar appraisal of me.

To my consternation he began fiddling about under the table, before brandishing an Asda bag. From it, ever so slowly, he withdrew a bottle wrapped in light, green cellophane. Then with a triumphant flourish, worthy of a stage magician reconnecting the head of his startled assistant, he produced a bottle of … Lambrusco. God, do I always have to be right about things? Just once couldn't you surprise me with a better deal than I anticipate? He then summoned over the proprietor, a rather grumpy-looking character whose round face was segmented by a huge, drooping moustache.

Mike turned to greet him. 'Bony Sierra siggnor, three of your sparkling wine glasses if you please! Grazio!'

Even as early as this, his voice troubled me; it had a certain anaesthetic quality, capable of comatosing the frenzied studio audience for *The X Factor*. 'Oh, I do like it here,' continued the reedy inflection, 'and I'm sure you will too. It's so … so … Italian.'

Three's company

It was only then that I took in the full significance of his words. Three – three wine glasses? Why on earth three? Then, looking down, I noted three table settings, three sets of cutlery guarding a place mat of the Pope. At that moment, a rather gangly youth emerged from the Gents and made his way, a little haltingly, to our table; it was clearly the last place on earth he wanted to be. I noted how much he resembled Mike, a similarity emphasised by the boy's rather sad attire.

'Ah, here's Gerald, my son,' said Mike brightly. 'They do three meals for the price of two here on Thursdays and it seemed silly not to take advantage of it. I'm sure you don't mind. Gerald, this is Sally, my latest friend.'

'Latest'? Was he some sort of serial dater, like the Yorkshire Ripper without the gore? And what number was I in his table of totties? The boy looked thoroughly miserable and I was feeling really sorry for him; I was determined to bring him into the conversation as much as I could – it might make him feel a bit more at ease and would, anyway, dilute the stream of anaesthetic being injected from my left. I sensed my eyes glazing over as Mike recounted the number and variety of 'truly wonderful meals' they'd enjoyed here, all quite 'bellissimum' apparently. Uncharacteristically, he paused and I seized my opportunity.

'Well Gerald, it's nice to meet you.'

'Yes.'

'So, you're one for Italian food as well are you, just like your dad?'

'Yes.'

'Are you a Pizza or a Spaghetti man?'

'Don't mind.'

'Have you ever been to Italy?'

'No.'

'Would you like to go there sometime, you know, Rome or Venice?

'Don't know.'

'On holiday, do you prefer hotels or seaside places – they have fabulous beaches in Rimini?'

'Don't mind.'

As I desperately trawled the deepest recesses of my brain for another question, Gerald looked down, and then dived into the unplumbed depths of his Nike bag to retrieve a small bottle of Coca-Cola that he carefully uncapped.

'And how old are you now, Gerald?'

'Fourteen.'

'He's tall for his age, isn't he?' remarked Mike, adding, with a touch of pride, 'He takes after me.'

Lacking professional training either as a psychotherapist or a post-traumatic stress disorder counsellor, I was finding it really difficult to make any kind of headway here. Luckily, the proprietor shuffled forward, his world-weary expression oozing boredom as he plonked the tumblers on the table.

'Now, Sally, do try some of my liquid velvet.'

He filled the glasses with unexpected largesse, roaring 'Saluti!' with all the rousing force of Mussolini.

'Err, oh yes, Salute!' responded I. One sip at a time, my dear, one sip at a time, always sound advice.

Unfortunately, reaching across for the 'Priceless Pizza' menu, Mike knocked over my glass, drenching the front of my very best designer trousers.

'Oh, I'm so sorry,' he said swiftly. 'Here, let me help.' He lurched forward, only to fell a desiccated mini palm tree that was intended to add to the atmosphere, spilling the earth all over the place. 'Oh sorry, very sorry.'

'Don't worry,' I breezed, affecting unconcern. 'Look, why don't you and Gerald study the menu while I just pop off to the Ladies. It'll be OK, I'm sure.'

Baling out

The Ladies, or rather 'Signore', was located through a dimly lit alcove on the far side of the room; a once glossy 1960s photo of a particularly buxom Sophia Loren pointed the way. The Ladies did provide some form of refuge but I wouldn't be hanging around. There was an overpowering aroma of cheap air freshener which made me feel nauseous. To my horror, there was no soap and a single grimy towel from a rusty nail, driven askew into the crumbling plaster. Pink paint was peeling from the walls. I didn't dare enter the cubicle so I stared forlornly into the mirror. The tap, initially obstinate, suddenly spurted into life, and with a tissue from my handbag I did my best to clean away the worst of the wine stain.

When was the earliest I could leave this alternative universe, this Lower Earth? Half an hour to gobble down a pizza then invent some reason for leaving? But what reason? My brain had seized up, incapable of processing anything more than the horror of dinner with the Addams family. Caroline, yes, Caroline! I'll text and tell her to call me in half an hour or so. I'll have thought of something by then.

Am in middle of salvador dali landscape. Ring my mobile in 30 mins. Can't xplain just do it. S x

I lingered for a moment to apply a little more make-up, not to intensify my appeal but rather to waste just a bit more time.

As I rejoined la famiglia Addams, Lurch was waving the menu excitedly. 'Ah Sally, we've gone for the Gokki to start with, followed by a Margaret, what about you?'

Gokki? Margaret? God, Dateandsee, please don't let this be typical of your offerings – even watching back-to-back Panorama specials would be preferable to this.

'Oh, I'll just have a small Quattro Stagioni. I'm trying to watch my figure,' I said lightly, reanimated now by the prospect of imminent release. This reference to my figure caused Gerald to look down at the table in embarrassment but served only to quicken Mike's interest. He leaned forward.

'Oh, I think you're just fine as you are,' affecting an amorous smile, his yellow teeth gleaming in their setting of bright pink gums.

He had a small blue notebook open, each page bearing neat columns and the headings such as Date/Item/Cost.

'Don't mind me,' he said cheerfully. 'This is my Daybook where I record each day's expenditure. It's really great when you find you've spent less in a week than in the previous one. Gerald, how much was the Gokki again?' All of this without the slightest trace of irony, let alone embarrassment. For once, I was lost for words. Caroline was going to love being right: he was obviously as tight as the proverbial camel's arse in a sandstorm.

By sheer good fortune the gnocchi and pizzas arrived just as he was about to prove that Asda's 'No frills' toilet paper was not always better value than Tesco's 'Basics' variety. I nibbled at my pizza like a weight-conscious dormouse. Gerald, poor thing, eyes fixed on his plate, strove manfully to work his way through the 'Margaret', every so often sipping away at his favourite tipple. In startling contrast, Mike attacked his with lip-smacking gusto, knocking back the remnants of the wine with no thought of sharing. 8.45. Come on Caroline for God's sake – where the bloody hell are you? If you let me down I swear I'll tell Bob you snogged his best man at your wedding reception. My mobile rang – there is a god after all!

'Hello.'

'It's me. Where's Salvador Dali? I thought you were in Crewe?'

'Oh, hi Mum. How are you?'

'Mum? What do you mean? Have you been sniffing those felt-tips again?'

'Oh no, oh Mum, I'm so sorry. No, don't upset yourself – it's not your fault. I'll come straight up. I can be there in a couple of hours.'

'I get it. You're with Fish's Arsehole, right? This is your excuse to get away.'

'Yes, that's right. Get yourself into bed and I'll be there before you know it. Is there anything I can bring you?'

'Oh just the usual – some fine champagne and caviar please.'

'Ovaltine and digestives, OK. Bye mum; now stop crying. I'll be there soon as I can. Bye!'

'Mike, I am sooooo sorry,' my eyes downcast in affected distress. 'That was my Mum. She's been out to the line-dancing club and twisted her ankle. Tex had to bring her home. She's in a bit of a state and I'll have to drive up to Blackpool to see her straightaway.'

'Oh no! Just as we were all getting to know each other. I was hoping to share a zabali … zalblagli … zabalgi … that Italian pudding with you.'

'Well, can't be helped I'm afraid,' I replied, pulling out my purse. 'Here's £15; I'm sure that'll cover my half.'

Mike, utterly bewildered, looked at me in dismay as we shook hands formally. I smiled pleasantly, adding 'Best of luck with easyJet, Mike. Arrivederci! And Gerald, don't forget Rimini!' before racing for the door.

I collapsed over the steering wheel. Thank God for Caroline. I loved her even though I would have to sit through squillions of *I told you sos*. Despite the night's disaster, I recovered my composure on the drive home, deciding that I wasn't going to let it deter me … now, what would that sexy sparky Dave be doing next week …?

Chapter 4

RECHARGING THE BATTERY

Hiya Sally. Sorry I couldn't get back to you earlier. Me and the lads went to Hamburg for Tommo's stag night. What a laugh! Tommo's lucky to escape with only one tattoo, too bad we spelt his bird's name wrong – it's 'Gail' but we thought it was 'Gayle'. Anyway, she's still marrying him so no harm done. I was quite surprised to get a message from you. You're dead good-looking and I bet you're a bit posh! What you doing on Dateandsee? You must have fellas queuing up at your door. But I'm glad you did get in touch and it would be great to meet up soon. Where exactly do you live? Are you near a good curry house or do you want to come here to Spice Island? Either way is good for me. Look forward to hearing from you. Dave x

I reduced this to just one sentence: 'you're dead good looking and I bet you're a bit posh ...' Well done, Davey boy! You might lack polish, you might not know your Bolly from your Beaujolais, you might have bhajis for brains but

you think I'm 'dead good-looking'! Good enough for me!
Let's have another look at his picture. Yes, verrrrry nice.

> Hi Dave. So you survived Hamburg. I bet you
> gave the Reeperbahn the once over. Glad you had
> a good time and Gail was able to overlook your
> little faux pas but just think, it could have been
> a lot worse – after all, the ink might have run
> out after GAY! Thank you for your flattering
> comments. I'm not a bit 'posh' although I do
> like nice things and as for 'fellas queuing' at my
> door, well, the only time that happens is when
> the milkman/binman/paperboy line up for
> their Xmas tip. I live in Sale and yes, there is a
> rather good Indian within walking distance so
> if you don't mind travelling, what about going
> there? I'll leave it to you to suggest a particular
> night. Sally x

Now, have any other would-be heroes written to me?
Spare me, no! The tuba puffer from Barnsley's at it again.

> How do Sally. I am sorry you do not think we
> are well suited but thank you for replying. I knew
> you was a nice lass. I must have sent 10 messages
> and you was only the second one to reply. I think
> that's rude me. I would always reply. Anyroad,
> I hope you find what you are looking for on
> Dateandsee. I am writing to

> *this other lass that replied. She is called Iris from Rochdale and she is in the Gracie Fields fan club so ay up, we might have something in common. Bye bye. Jeff.*

I sighed with relief. No reply required and actually the message had given me a degree of optimism. Obviously there was someone for everyone out there, and I was pleased for Jeff.

Sex and the city

Glancing at my watch, I realised I'd have to abandon the computer for the moment as I was going to the pictures with Caroline and Louise. I'd invited Lucy along. She didn't seem to have much of a social life which was surprising because she was really rather pretty. There was less than two years between the girls, and so it should work out OK. I met up with her in the UCI foyer.

'Hiya Luce. You look nice! You should wear your hair up more often – it shows off your lovely face.'

'Hi Sally. Thanks for inviting me. You look nice too, but then, you always do. I really like your jacket – where's it from?'

'Thanks, sweetie. I got it at one of those posh shops in Chester when me and Visa went out for the day.'

I grabbed the opportunity to suggest updating her wardrobe. 'You know, me and you should hit the shops some time – look for designer rip offs in H&M and New Look. What do you think?'

69

'I'd love to! And I've got my birthday money to spend.'

'That's a date then! Anyway, I haven't seen much of you lately. Everything OK?'

'Well I suppose so. Lesley's been away all week on a course about how to discipline staff or something. At least, that's what she said but I saw the invitation and it's actually called "Putting the Human back into Resources". Anyway, I'm glad she's not around. Thanks for showing me what to do with the expenses spreadsheets. Lesley was really pleased. She said she can tell at a glance now who's claimed more than they're supposed to for parking.'

'Blimey, she's a sad case, isn't she? Ah, here's Caroline and Louise.'

Caroline smiled broadly but Louise just glowered. I introduced Lucy, and then turned to Louise.

'Why so glum, love? We're here to enjoy ourselves, right?'

'Nothing.'

'Nothing? Doesn't look like nothing to me. What's the matter – Daniel Radcliffe not called?'

'Oh, ignore her,' Caroline said. 'She's got her period.'

'MUUUMMM,' whined Louise, 'do you have to tell EVERYONE? Why not just buy me an outsize white T-shirt with 'Cursed – sponsored by Tampax on it?'

'Oh do be quiet, Louise. I don't know why I ever treat you to anything. You're the most ungrateful girl at times, you really are! Sally, tell her. We all know what periods are like don't we? Something you just have to live with for thirty-five years or so before osteoporosis takes over. So, don't get the hump – get it?'

Lucy and I laughed with Caroline; Louise wasn't amused.

'I have really, really bad period pains,' Lucy chipped in. 'My mum says having a baby will put a stop to it.'

'Now listen you two, don't you even dare think about that as an option,' said Caroline wagging her finger like some strict school matron. 'Believe me, if the gin's run out, Ibuprofen and a hot water bottle's all the remedy you need and, besides, I'm far too young and beautiful to be a grandmother.'

'And I'm too fabulous to be a grand-godmother!' I chimed in linking arms with the youngsters. 'Look here's something to cheer you up Louise. We're thinking of doing a day's retail. Do you want to come with us?'

'Oooh yes please', she enthused, visibly brightening. 'Mum said we can't afford Miss Sixty but I've seen almost the same things in H&M. So cool!'

'Course you can come. Let's all go – make a day of it. See if your Mum and I can squeeze into skinny jeans and cropped tops.'

'You must be joking Sally – Mum says me and Rich robbed her of a flat stomach and a 22 inch waist.'

'22 inches? That's a laugh! I've known your mum for years and the only thing about her that was ever 22 inches was the length of her miniskirt.'

'Oi you, I had a very trim figure in my youth thank you very much.'

'Well if you say so Caroline,' I said, punching her good-naturedly. 'Come on, let's go and have some safe sex!'

Even Louise smiled. They were going to see the screen version of *Sex and the City*. This was the biggest grossing chick flick since *Bridget Jones*. Reviews were excellent and the gang of four were always good for a laugh. I was pretty sure I'd have to explain the more outrageous scenes, seasoned sex siren that I was. We squandered a quick £20 at the sweet counter avoiding the giant Diet Cokes strategically placed next to mega-sized hot dogs with the lascivious slogan, 'Big enough for Carrie'.

'I don't know why I'm looking for a fella on the Internet,' I said through a mouthful of chocolate. 'Life doesn't get much better than this!'

'The Internet? I didn't know you were doing that?' Lucy said incredulously, her image of me as Super Ms Cool momentarily tarnished. 'Why do you have to do that? You're lovely and all the fellas at work think so.'

'Ah yes, that would be Roy, Peter and Brian right?'

'And Ryan and Martyn and Derrick and Jonathan in Investments and I bet there's loads of others as well. I know you wouldn't be interested in Ryan 'cos he's too young but the others are all your age.'

'Yes, Lucy, they are my age and they're all nice enough but they don't really appeal to me … except for Jonathan that is … it is Jonathan, isn't it, that tall, blond one with the designer stubble and the nice bum?'

Louise sniggered against her will.

'Yes,' replied Lucy excitedly, 'and he drives a fabulous Mercedes. I saw it when he offered to take Bev from Mortgages home – Lesley had reduced her to tears, telling her she'd be in a mortician's not Mortgages if she "screwed up the effing forecast again."'

I knew Beverley – tall, leggy blonde. All 'teeth and tits' according to the blokes. She was the standard office pin-up.

'Erm ... now Lucy, how do you know Jonathan likes me?' I casually enquired.

'Because I overheard him tell Roy not to bother 'cos you were well out of his league and if anyone was going to [she hesitated] ... "do it with you" it would be him.'

I positively preened!

'Lucy, Lesson 1 in office matters of the heart. Never, ever keep this type of information from me again. Drop whatever you are doing and tell me immediately and by the way, what is Jonathan's second name? I just might have to email him tomorrow, about a very important investment training seminar I'm planning.'

'Wilson, I think.'

'Good girl – keep your ear to the ground and the information flowing.'

Caroline led the way into the cinema. 'Right, you two girls sit next to each other so me and Sally can have a chat.'

'Chat? You're supposed to watch the film!' the girls chorused.

'Oh we will, we will, but there won't be anything in it that's new *us*. We are women of the world you know. In fact we're a bit surprised that Warner Bros. didn't take us on as consultants.'

That self-satisfied notion was dispelled within ten minutes when the outrageous Samantha held Carrie, Miranda and Charlotte spellbound with her tale of a 'rodeo ride' with a startlingly well-hung cowboy involving a lasso, saddle and reins.

'Might try that with Dave,' I whispered.

'Dave who?' Caroline whispered back.

'You know, he's that sparky from Stockport. He's back from Hamburg and raring to go. He thinks I'm "dead attractive and a bit posh" would you believe.'

'Ah, special needs case is he?' she sniggered, 'When are you seeing him then?'

'Next week probably. I've left it up to him to choose the day. He's coming over to Sale for a curry.'

'So you can burn the posh label, but, never mind, the "dead attractive" bit will be easy.'

We all agreed the film was a winner and Caroline, with remarkable composure, neatly sidestepped Louise's questions about the more outrageous techniques of oral sex.

I dropped Lucy off at home. I didn't want her catching the train alone even though it was only 10.30 by the time we'd had a cappuccino. Her mother popped out to say hello.

'Oh Sally, it's so nice to meet you. Thanks for taking our Lucy under your wing. She's told me how much you've helped her. I'm really grateful. She seems to be enjoying her job so much more lately.'

'Oh that's OK Mrs Locket – sorry Mrs Hill! I call her Lucy Locket! She's got a lot of promise and she's nice to have around. She keeps me up to date with the latest pop music and showbiz news – believe me, I need it. I'm becoming a bit too much Radio 2 and *Coronation Street* these days. It'll be *The Archers* next.'

'I know the feeling. And call me Liz. Anyway, thanks again. Safe journey home.'

'Thanks Liz. Bye.' I drove off thinking what a likeable woman Liz seemed, and so lucky to have a good kid like Lucy.

An unhappy past – a happy future (?)

A loving mother – yes that could have been me. Had things gone well, my own child would have been a teenager by now. I sometimes wondered if it was a boy or a girl but an early miscarriage meant no chance of ever knowing. Perhaps it was better that way. The miscarriage itself was bad enough but the years of trying to have a baby plus Paul's attitude to adoption had compounded the unhappiness of it all. I really hated dwelling on that sorry episode in my life. I usually only thought about it after a gallon of vodka or when I'd been well and truly disappointed by a man. No, it really was hard but I'd trained myself to bury the pain and disappointment. Only Caroline knew how I truly felt and even she never dared bring up the subject, simply responding with sympathy and tissues whenever I raised it. Lucy had set me off, and I wasn't about to blame the poor girl for that. I let myself in, suddenly feeling rather miserable. The answerphone light was steady, no messages. The flat was quiet, no family. The bed was cold, no partner. I cried myself to sleep.

D is for Darcy, D is for Dave

Hmm … Jonathan Wilson. Just look him up on Outlook. Yes, there he is ext. 46761. I'd write a flirty email to *John Wilson* who appeared just above Jonathan in Outlook then pretend to send it to Jonathan by mistake. He'd never twig … John Wilson was based in Kent and Jonathan wouldn't know him but would assume I'd met him on my travels.

Good day John. Or should I perhaps say Mr Darcy? My, you did look strikingly handsome last week – so much so indeed that a maiden might swoon at the merest glimpse of you. I may just allow you to escort me to a social gathering on the next occasion that I am up in town. It transpires that I am between romantic heroes at the moment and thus somewhat tired of having an empty dance card. Would you, I wonder sir, be gracious enough to consider this possibility? Are you ready to extend some old-fashioned hospitality to a young lady? Miss Elizabeth Bennet.

Send. Ooops, silly me, wrong Wilson! Still in Miss Bennet mode, I wriggled on my chair to effect a more demure position, as if seeking to persuade my stays to be somewhat less constricting. That email called for a celebratory Mars bar from the machine.

Well, well, well, would you Adam and Eve it? There's me with two tickets to the Barclays Investment Bankers' Annual Ball and there's Miss Bennet looking for a new Mr Darcy. I'll forgive you calling me John – we don't know each other very well [yet] but that's soon remedied. It's two weeks on Saturday. So how about it? Think you can find a fine ball gown by then? J x

Blimey. This was really, really excellent! ESSENTIAL to get this reply right.

Jonathan, hi! How are you? Sorry, I'm a bit embarrassed because you see I meant to send that email to John Wilson in the Kent office! He's just above you in Outlook but hey, I'm glad I had a 'blonde moment' and sent it to you instead. Miss Bennet would love to go to the ball and no problem with the gown, got a wardrobe full of them – my life is a constant social whirl. Sally x

Cinderella, you shall definitely go to the ball on August the 27th. I'm going into a meeting now and I'm off tomorrow on a charity golf do but why don't we meet for lunch on Thursday and I'll tell you all about it then? J x

J, I save my kisses for very good boys but as you are taking me to the ball, I guess you qualify. Thursday's good for me so long as it's around one – Miss Whiplash wants to smack my bottom with the quarterly expenses report in the morning. S x

Oooh, now that would be a sight for sore eyes, my glasses are steaming up at the very thought of it. I'll see you Thursday at one. Let's meet up in the lounge at PJ's.

J x

P.S. I'm a very, very, good boy, just ask all those lovely young ladies in FX. Trust me!

My memory reaching back to those distant years in the school choir, I threw my head back, bellowing, 'Drink to meee only with thine eyes and I shaaalll drink to thine …'

'Hey you! Pack it in – you sound like Charlotte Church after a bad night on E.'

Oh dear, Roy had materialised from nowhere like some mischievous sprite.

'Oh yeah, and you can do better can you Roy? I've heard that your turn on the karaoke empties the place quicker than a couple of eager sniffer dogs looking for drugs.'

I turned back round to my PC, determined that nothing was going to spoil my buoyant mood! Roy scowled and, severely rattled, retreated to his cave – the server room. Right, what was that date; yes, August 27th – better check it straight away. I flicked through my pocket diary … August 13th… August 20th … oh, *please* don't let the family do be the following Saturday – and then I felt ashamed at the thought of preferring the ball to the family get-together. But, salvation! The twenty-seventh was clear as Dad's birthday celebration was entered for September.

And the day just got better and better. No one bothered me, not even Miss Whiplash, and the words for the Barclays Training Strategy document simply streamed into place. And there was more; when I got home, there was a message from Dave.

> *Hi! I don't know what a faux pas is but I can promise you, we didn't get up to any funny business on the Reeperbahn, too legless to even think of it. Anyway, wouldn't touch them Kraut birds with a bargepole!*

God he was adorable, so ... so ... thick? No! .... Unworldly, yes, that was the word, unworldly.

> *Anyway, I'm happy to come to Sale but will I need my passport? How about Friday night? I'll come on the train, we can both have a few drinks before the ruby, I won't have to worry about driving and there's no work the next day. If that suits you I'll need some directions so here's my mobile number 07796 354213, or you can email them. Dave x*

So today was Tuesday, Jonathan on Thursday, Dave on Friday, working in the pub on Saturday. This was certainly turning into a top week. I'd contact Dave tomorrow night – I was still keen to meet him but, as I had Jonathan to think about as well, that slightly took the edge off my eagerness. My changing luck prompted me to carry on.

But – what's this? An email from the Count of Cannelloni in Crewe. What on earth can he want – not a return fixture for heaven's sake?!

Hello Sally, just a quick note to ask if you would help settle the accounts of our recent meal. On studying my Daybook I realised that my outgoings last week were £5.78p in excess of the previous week and so I would be most grateful if you would send a cheque to me for £3.06 as soon as possible in the SAE enclosed. This amount is 31p higher than your balance but is required to cover the cost of the first class stamp. I am looking forward to receiving the cheque from you as soon as possible.
Mike
PS: I know you couldn't stay for dessert but I ordered it when you had to go to the Ladies [Gerald really enjoyed it so it wasn't wasted!].

I read it twice and words still failed me.

The screw tightens

Thursday morning. 7 am. 'I believe in miracles… where you from … you sexy thing – you sexy thing you … I believe in …' I hummed along with the radio. Favourite suit, plain white silky sweater, high heels and Chanel Allure. This was to be a special day, which called for a special perfume. Mrs Sally Wilson. Mr and Mrs Wilson. Jonathan and Sally Wilson. Jonathan Wilson and his delightful wife Sally. These all had a lovely ring to them.

11.30 am. 'Ah Sally, hello, yes, about the training expenses report.'

'Good morning, Lesley! And how are we feeling today? Isn't it just a fabulous Thursday? Are you looking forward to the weekend? Got lots of fun things lined up?'

'I don't do "fun". That's why I'm head of this branch and you're not.' Lesley's eyes shot a death ray of disapproval.

I wanted to say 'No Lesley, that's why you're an alien from Planet PissOff with all the appeal of Anne Robinson' but settled instead for 'Well, one makes one's own choices in life Lesley, and I do try to get my home/work balance right.'

'Too bad you don't apply the same principle to the training budget, isn't it?'

I was mystified. 'Training budget?'

'Yes, what's all this crap about providing a buffet lunch for twenty new entrants who ought to be grateful that such a prestigious institution as ours has taken on their sorry arses? Most of 'em won't last the six months' probationary period anyway so I don't think we should spend £4.25 a head letting them think the bank is a playground with pizza and Coke thrown in.'

'But Lesley, look, most of them are kids, straight from school – probably the first time they'll have been away from home, and some will have travelled at least a couple of hours to get here. It'll be good for them to meet each other over lunch – creates the right kind of informality for an induction course. We want them to enjoy the experience, don't we? We want them to know the bank is a caring employer with a happy workforce. Everyone knows a happy worker is a productive worker, right?'

'Oh do we now? Well, thank you Einstein for that amazing revelation. No, here's how it's gonna be in future. Give 'em coffee on arrival and a couple of custard creams then send them to the canteen where they can buy their own lunch – this isn't Jamie Oliver's school dinners you know.'

I sighed heavily. Bloody bitch, she wouldn't know how to create happiness in Barnardo's on a Christmas Eve. I was 'henceforth' instructed to:

- Suspend the practice of giving every new entrant an 'I'm a Barclays bright spark!' mug
- Withdraw payment of inner city parking fees; they could just do Park and Ride
- Cancel the usual order for 500 Comic Relief T-shirts for counter staff; they could just wear something of their own in red. But no, repeat, no football shirts!'… And, worst of all in my eyes …
- Suspend the £100 Marks and Spencer's voucher paid to staff, who came up with a new working practice to reduce running costs

This 'ideas' award had been my brainwave, and, in the past year, over sixty staff had received the £100 voucher. The bean counters reckoned Barclays had saved around

£150K but this was meaningless to Lesley. My department laid out the £6200, but didn't see any of the savings, which were usually picked up via branch expenditure.

'I'll think a bit more about whether I should cancel the annual HR/Learning Sports Day,' she added airily. 'I know it's for charity but that begins at home; the bank has just written off £300 million of Third World debt – how much more do they want? OK, that's it. You can go and tell that bloody moron Roger or whatever his bloody name is to get in here. I don't like his football screensaver – it's bloody unprofessional.'

'Right,' I said, leaving her lair, drained of the power to argue with the Iron Lady for even a moment longer.

I signalled a thumbs down to Roy, who was chatting up one of the girls in the office. 'Royboy, you're on, and don't bother with the Charmometer – she's even more immune to it than me.'

Roy winked at the girl in thoughtless bravado; he then straightened his tie [red and white – what else?], patted down his latest Beckham hairstyle and took a deep breath before knocking softly on Lesley's office door and cautiously venturing inside …

Entertaining Mr Darcy

It was now lunchtime. Thank God for gas powered straighteners, I thought, standing in front of the Ladies mirror and turning my flowing hair into a jet of golden glass. Quick sweep of mascara – think Bambi, touch of lip plumping gloss – think bee sting, extra dose of kohl pencil – think lap dancer, plus generous spray of Allure.

Some ten minutes later, I sashayed over to Jonathan who was lounging on a Conran leather sofa reading *GQ*. This man was seriously, seriously dishy, with his fair hair, blue eyes, and an inviting mouth above a strong jaw. He could easily have passed for one of those public school types who raise the nation's flagging morale by winning rowing golds at the Olympics. Hmm, yummy, he definitely passes my snog test. This test was Caroline's invention, a tried and trusted method of deciding a man's potential. If you couldn't form a mental picture of yourself snogging the man in question then you certainly couldn't imagine doing anything more intimate with him. Jonathan certainly passed this initial test – I had no problem imagining myself flinging his *GQ* to one side, and then diving on top of him like a *Fat Club* absconder swooping down on a chocolate mousse.

He stood up to greet me, a twinkle of approval in his eyes. He was tall and well built. He was wearing a beautifully tailored dark suit that contrasted elegantly with a coral-pink shirt and stylish tie, blue diagonal stripes against a claret background. I leant forward to receive the customary light kiss of greeting.

'Anything interesting in that lad-mag?' I drawled, my right hip thrust forward, Liz Hurley style, before accepting his invitation to sit by him on the sofa.

'Always something new in *GQ* – everything from the latest in designer boxers to the Victoria's Secret email address.'

'Oooh, Victoria's Secret, I love her stuff. I bought a few bits and pieces when I went Christmas shopping in New York.'

'And I can easily imagine your beauty, Miss Bennet, attired in such becoming apparel but I am [and here he ever so gently patted my knee] – as I feel sure you recognise by now – too much of a gentleman to press you for further details. Now, let us peruse the menu.'

'Splendid idea, dear sir,' I trilled, playing along with him before turning to the pretty waitress – I'll have the Chicken Caesar salad and a small dry white wine please.'

'Seafood salad and a still mineral water for me please,' he added with a ready smile.

The waitress smiled back and turned away but not before I saw him check out her pert 25-year-old derrière – his approval was all too obvious … mmm, he clearly likes his ladies …

'So, Sally, I have you all to myself at last. Every time I see you, you're surrounded by admirers – Brian, Peter et al. not forgetting Lesley of course!'

'So you've noticed as well have you?' I laughed.

'Noticed? She makes kd laing look feminine. I don't think it's an "independent woman" thing either. She's the genuine article – probably got more testosterone than Van Diesel.'

'Well she's an oddball, isn't she? You know her latest idea? Cancelling the annual Sports Day would you believe.'

'Oh, now that would be a crying shame. I so enjoyed watching you hopping home last in the sack race. You know …' he leaned in towards me. 'You manage to look fetching even in a sack.'

I flushed with pleasure and, fanned myself with the menu. 'Oh Mr Darcy, my word, that is so awfully flattering of you but I think not, as a sack subtracts from, rather than adds to, my altogether modest store of femininity.'

Lunch progressed in the same light-hearted, flirtatious manner. The ball would be at the rather swanky Midland Hotel, and he would pick me up at seven on the dot. 'Most guests,' he added, are staying over ... and the organisers have negotiated a special rate so I've already booked a room. What do you want to do? Stay over or get a taxi home?' He looked at me expectantly with just a hint of an invitation ... or was it a challenge?

'Well, I usually like to enjoy these things to the full. So, yes, could you book me a room and I'll reimburse you?' I wasn't about to make myself that available and besides if I wanted to sleep with him, sod the room charge!

If he was at all disappointed he hid it well, 'OK, that's good. We can round off the evening with some generous brandy snifters in the clubroom.'

He insisted on picking up the bill. 'My treat, can't let a lady pay. But, you know, there's no such thing as a free lunch,' he said as lightly kissed me on the cheek.

Bloody hell, roll on the twenty-seventh, I thought.

'Thanks, Jon, I really have enjoyed it today and thanks again for inviting me to the ball. I'm really looking forward to it!'

'Can't think of anyone I'd rather be there with' [Stick that up your hot totty arse Bev!] 'And I'd love to take you out for dinner next week but I can't. I'm going away on Saturday to Marbella for a week. Six of us, golfing holiday, you know the type of thing ... early start on the course each day to avoid the worst of the sun, a round of golf, light lunch, pool and papers, pre-dinner drinks, dinner and drinks, post-dinner drinks ... God, it's hell but someone's got to do it. I'll ring you the Monday after I get back and perhaps we can have dinner or lunch again in the week leading up to the ball?'

'Great, yes, that's great. You know my work extension but I'll give you my mobile number – don't know about you, but at work, I try to keep my private life private, and I can feel the draught from Roy's ears flapping whenever I get a private call.'

'Good idea, what is it? I'll put in my mobile now.'

'07869 342167.'

'OK, got that.'

We strolled back to the office and parted when I got out at the first floor well below Jonathan's fourth floor glass ceiling territory. 'Bye, Jon, thanks again. See you again soon and have a great time in Spain.'

'Muchas gracias. Adios!'

Preparing to switch on the lights

I floated to my desk as if transported by a fluffy, white cloud. I settled back easily into my chair, smiling to all around like the winner of a beauty pageant. Such heavenly bliss was, however, destined to be short lived. Up came Roy, destroyer of dreams.

'Hello sexy, you've got a nice smile on your face today for a change – bet you've been out for a lunchtime quickie,' he said, positively drooling at the thought.

'Roy, you have as much class as Matalan and the imagination of a termite. For your information and even though it's absolutely none of your business, I've had lunch with a gentleman – I'll explain the meaning of that mysterious word to you when you've got a spare hour to take it in.'

'Gentleman, my arse.' He grunted under his breath. I chose to ignore him; I would spend the afternoon mentally reviewing potential ball get-ups and thinking about nightcaps *à deux* in the rosy half-light of The Midland Club Room.

Arriving home after this really satisfying day, I desperately wanted to share my adventures with Caroline, but first I had to contact Dave with directions to the Indian, my next little adventure.

> *Hi Dave, hope you're having a good week. The Indian Restaurant is called Rajah's and it's on Washway Rd about 10 minutes walk from the station, and only about 5 minutes from me. If you come out of the station and turn right, you're on Washway Road, there's a pub just before Rajah's called 'The Red Lion'. How about meeting me there about 7.30? I'm sure I'll recognise you – won't be too many other hunks in there! My mobile number is 07869 342167. Sally x*

Right, now I can phone Cazi.

'Cazi? It's me. What's that awful noise?'

'That racket is my son, the would-be Phil Collins, torturing the drum kit his witless father has just bought him.'

'I've not missed his birthday have I?'

'No, you haven't. It's not his birthday. It's a bribe – Bob's way of extracting a promise from this creature from the blue lagoon to tidy his room once a week, improve his school marks and stop picking his nose at the dinner table.'

'Ugh!!'

'Yes, that's my baby boy. Now what did Madam want?'

I recounted my lunch with Jonathan, pleased to hear all sorts of encouraging noises from her: 'Good, excellent, yes; this is the sort of thing we want.'

I could almost see her head nodding like that infuriating bulldog in the car insurance advert. 'And I'm out with Dave tomorrow. 7.30 in the Red Lion followed by Rajah's.'

'Ah, quick word of advice Sally dear – don't take him home with you unless, a) he's brought a note from his parish priest testifying to his good character and, b) he can produce an "Aids Free" certificate from his local GP.'

The conversation was interrupted by the shrill sound of a text coming through on my mobile.

Sally cu at 7.30. Look 4ward to it! Dave x

I smiled 'It's from Dave – he must have been hunched over his PC waiting for me to reply, and I've only just sent the email.'

'What's he saying?'

'Just confirming tomorrow and that he's looking forward to it.'

'Well, it would be a shame to disappoint a visitor to our fair town wouldn't it? I'm sure you'll enjoy it, and I read your horoscope in *Hello!* and it's a good week for Virgos.'

'You betcha! See you, honey, and tell "Phil" to pack it in or you'll brain him with his bloody cymbals.'

'OK, ring me Saturday with a full report!'

'Will do – bye Cazi.'

A very hot Indian

The Red Lion and Rajah's? Easy ... black jeans, ankle boots and a black V-neck cardigan with small diamanté buttons to add just a touch of glamour. I strolled into the pub just after 7.30, a forgivable few minutes late. Most of the clientele looked like extras from *Shameless*, and this made him even more conspicuous. I really couldn't miss him; he was standing at the bar halfway through a pint of Stella. Yes please! He was even better in the flesh. Tall, dark, and clean-shaven with Pierce Brosnan hair and the blue eyes to match. I lightly touched his arm.

'Hi Dave.'

He spun round, and his eyes widened as he took me all in. 'Hiya Sally. How you doing? You look great. Nice to meet you!'

'Hi! Ditto! You found it all right then?'

'Oh no problem. I can usually find my way to a good watering hole. What's your poison?'

'Red wine please.' First mistake.

I loved red wine but the trouble was I never knew when enough was enough.

'Large or small?'

'Oh, large I think. I've got that Friday night feeling.' Second mistake.

He carried the drinks over to a table.

'By the way Dave, I forgot to mention, Rajah's doesn't have a licence but you can take your own drink in. There's an off-licence opposite so we can call in on the way.'

'No problem – I prefer that actually. Not keen on that Indian beer; makes you fart all night that does – I'm strictly a Stella man!'

I chose to ignore this somewhat graphic analysis of the chemical properties of Cobra.

'Can you get Stella in Hamburg then?'

'Oh yeah, they serve it in two-litre jugs but even so we nearly drank the place dry.'

'Sounds like a good weekend.'

'The best. Tommo can't remember much of it but that's the idea in't it?'

The conversation continued. I found out that Gail would be Tommo's second wife – the first having 'shacked up' with his [ex] mate 'Doyley' who was an over-sexed scouser now living in Stockport. Dave had never married but lived with 'Shirley' for five years before they separated owing to the fact that Shirley wanted a baby but Dave wasn't ready to settle down 'for all that family crap'.

Well, it was pretty clear to me by now that his interests were not of the 'Happy Families' variety; as I had suspected from the start – this was about fun and the possibility, no the certainty, of a lengthy session of back-arching, body-straddling, buttocks-gripping lust making!

'More of that red stuff?' His words interrupted my non-too-wishful thinking.

'Yes, please.'

8.15. Forty minutes and two thirds of a bottle of Tempranillo later he had imperceptibly shuffled closer.

His thigh was warm against mine. 'What about one more before Rajah's?'

'Great idea!' I replied, losing any hope of controlling my rapidly rising heart rate.

When he got back, I thought – hoped – he had something rapidly rising as well. He slid his arm across the back of the plush, red banquette. 'I knew you was posh. Red wine. That's a posh drink that is. I'm more used to buying half a lager and black but it's nice to have a change. You're dead sexy you and I love your big blue eyes.'

'Why, thank you, Mr Dave,' I leaned into him until our faces were only a couple of inches apart. 'You're not so bad yourself. You know, when I meet a man for the first time, I apply my "snog test". If I can form a mental picture of myself snogging him, I know I'm going to enjoy myself!'

'Well, stop thinking about it and find out,' Dave said, and kissed me full on the lips, lingering for just a few seconds.

Mmm ... lovely ... nice soft lips, firm but not too insistent and no tonsil-tonguing. I hated that. Who wanted a wet tongue thrust down their throat?

We pulled apart. 'Blimey, I need a drink,' I said, gulping down the wine.

'Me too!' said Dave, settling comfortably alongside me, gently stroking my forearm.

'So, tell me something about yourself.'

I obliged with an edited version of my life, glossing over the real reason for the marriage break-up. I was careful to omit all references to past misdemeanours of the male variety; I made myself out to be a cross between a hot babe and a social worker – sexy but with a heart of gold. He was captivated. The third wine had brought the entertainer out in me. I was increasingly flirty and, as he hung on my every word, I literally shone. We left just before nine. He put his arm round my waist and gently pushed me up against the pub wall for a full on snog. I NEVER, EVER, went in for this kind of public display but the bottle of wine had transformed me into the kind of slapper that Cazi and I regularly scoffed at.

'Forget the curry, I'll just eat you instead,' he murmured into my neck.

'Whoa there, boy. Slow down, if I don't eat something to soak up the wine, I'll be unconscious and you wouldn't like that would you fella?' I lightly prodded his chest for emphasis.

He laughed, and took me by the hand as we crossed the road to Threshers. The meal went completely over the top of my head. I couldn't remember what I'd eaten, what he'd ordered, what he'd said about his gym workouts; I couldn't even remember the bill arriving or being paid. I simply had a fuzzy memory of a steady flow of red wine, punctuated by him kissing me whilst touching my thigh under the table and telling me that protein shakes were a natural form of 'Vie-aggro'!

10.40. The fresh air hit us, and we gulped it in like surfacing divers.

'So Mr Universe, do you want to come back to my penthouse for a drink?'

'You bet I do,' said Dave licking his lips and looking at me unblinkingly, the way a cat looks at a dish of tuna. 'Lead the way.'

It took me several minutes to rummage through my cavernous bag for the keys. I produced them triumphantly shouting 'Bingo!' which brought 'Mr Nosey' at number 9 to his front door. He took it all in, and I instantly imagined him writing the report for the next Residents' Association meeting.

'Ah, good evening Mr Cock – whoops sorry, Mr Cook.' I giggled. How are you this evening?' I slurred. 'Anything good on telly? This is my friend the Incredible Hunk by the way. We're going in now for a couple of hours' fornication just in case you were wondering.' I waved my aghast neighbour away and dragged Dave inside.

'Come here, sparky. Light my fire, light me up, switch on the power or whatever it is you sparkies do.' I lurched towards him – he was never going to put up much resistance after eight pints. I felt as randy as a tomcat.

Coming round!

8.20 am Saturday. Why was the left side of my head pounding? What was that gurgling noise next to me? And what was that smell? I cautiously opened one eye and quickly closed it again. Pain shot through my eyeballs like a red-hot poker. What the bloody hell was all this about? Slowly, I opened both eyes, and was rewarded with a wave of nausea sweeping up from my stomach to my throat. 'I'm going to be sick. I'm going to be sick,' I thought, quickly shutting my eyes again.

'God, me mouth feels like Bin Laden's flip-flop,' a plaintive voice said.

My eyes shot open now, the searing pain and nausea momentarily forgotten. I turned ever so gently and beheld, sprawled amid the sheets, Dave in all his post-eight -pints glory – Pete Doherty after a week long bender. Oh no! I mean ... I couldn't have ...could I? Yes, so help me, I must

93

have done – no Scrabble board in sight! I've sorted the Sparky from Stockport! Now what? Got to get out of bed. Got to get to the bathroom. Got to get on a plane to Peru!

'Erm … give me a minute and I'll get you some water,' I croaked.

'Thanks, babe,' he said rubbing his eyes with his right hand and rubbing my leg with his left.

Help! Where's my nightie? Please, please God let it be under the pillow where Mummy always told me to put it. It wasn't there. Or more precisely, the Janet Reager wasn't there but my 'Catholic girls do it for fun' nightshirt was. Why oh why did I have to have a sense of humour? I wriggled into it and raced across the bedroom to the sanctuary of my bathroom. Not easy because the floor was strewn with all the evidence of unbridled lust. Knickers mixed up with my jeans, bra hook caught in Dave's boxers, three condom wrappers – three? I'd think about it later – and an ancient copy of *Playboy* I kept as a 'prop'.

Locking the bathroom door I leaned my throbbing forehead against the cool of the tiles and placed a hand on the bath to steady myself. Another prayer, 'Please, please god, I'll never have sex again if you just make him get up and go the minute I give him a drink.' I would have loved to jump in the shower, but this would have taken too long. I splashed my face with cold water, changed into my dressing gown hanging behind the door, and filled my 'Smashers have Nice Gnashers' toothbrush mug with water. Finally, mustering the sorry remnants of my dignity, I walked groggily back into the bedroom.

'There you go.' I held out the water. He gulped it down greedily.

'Thanks babe, I needed that! Did we tie one on last night or what?'

'Yes, looks that way – would you like a coffee?'

'Yes please. That'd be great. Me 'edz explodin'. OK if I have a quick shower?'

'Erm ... yes, help yourself, there are clean towels in there,' and with that I sought the relative security of the kitchen.

I did mind him having a shower actually as it would mean another ten minutes in my house. I just wanted him to leave me to die slowly. Then again, at least he hadn't suggested a 'good morning workout'. That would have been far, far worse requiring me to make myself noisily sick to avoid it. I made the coffee with plenty of milk, not too hot so he'd be able to drink it quickly. He emerged from the bathroom looking quite – well, restored actually. Bloody men – all they had to do was shower and use the draught from the door to dry their hair.

'Thanks, babe. Umm, nice coffee. Good night, eh? Don't get too many of them in a year me.'

I did my best to summon up some humour. 'Good job. I'm too old for gymnastics.'

He laughed heartily, adding breezily 'Umm right, well, better be off now,' as he swigged down his coffee. 'I'll leave you to get on with your Saturday. Thanks love, I had a great night and if you want to do it again sometime, then, I'm up for it, as you know!'

I smiled weakly. 'Yes, thanks Dave. It was a good night. I'll be in touch.'

I kissed him on the cheek, letting him out before slumping into the hall chair. What was that I'd read in *Cosmo*? 'Computer-dating: it's terrific if you're a computer.'

Very true; but you're a human being, then computer dating clearly inclines you to lose your head over the first good-looking guy amidst the list of no-hopers. I buried my head in my hands, swearing to stick to my Black Lace story collection and never, *ever* to drink again!

Chapter 5

THE ANTIQUES ROAD SHOW

By early evening I felt a little better. Not exactly 100% but well enough to work for Marie as I'd promised. I'd texted Caroline earlier.

Hi. I've sinned again! Hot night with D – don't think i'll b c'ing him again tho. Xplain when we spk. S xx

She replied in typical style: *U r naughty – carry on & u'll b walking like john wayne by Xmas! Don't spare me the details. C x*

The pub was mercifully quiet and I had time to re-live the date with Dave. In keeping with his professional training, his had truly been an electrifying performance. He was obviously not short of power – had enough of it to turn on all the totty from Tyneside to Twickenham, but sadly that's all there was. He generated heat, no question of that, but I needed light as well. Further dates with him would be simply marking time; I wouldn't be moving forward. I'd email him, saying something suitably flattering but making it clear I didn't think we should meet again.

> *Hi Dave. Thanks for a great evening. You must know I enjoyed it, well, what I can remember of it anyway. But I'm not sure we should do it again. It really was fun but we're very different people and I don't think we'll ever be soulmates. Hope you agree. Sally x*
> *P.S. You're a great kisser!*

The reply was swift.

> *Hi Sally. Yes, it was great and so are you. If you change your mind, I'd definitely be up for a repeat performance. So how about this, if you ever want any work doing I'll bring my toolbox round – I've just bought a new drill and it's really powerful! Dave x*

Tuesday night. All quiet. I reflected on yet another awkward encounter with Lesley. When I'd necessarily enquired about the previous month's expenses, noticeably absent from my pay cheque, she'd frowned darkly and pursed her lips, clearly piqued that I should be bothering her with such a trifling matter.

'Yes, I'll look into it sometime.'

'Please do,' I said firmly. 'I'd be very grateful if you would. It's really quite important to me.'

The previous month had been hectic; I'd clocked up hundreds of miles on the road, delivering training courses throughout the north-west. I'd had to replace my printer as well – why is it that printers always pack up when you're in the middle of a crucial document such as the Clinique offer voucher? Without rapid reimbursement, I'd have to dig out my 'A thousand ways with Mince and Eggs' cookbook or, worse still, face a month of enforced vegetarianism. At best, carrots, celery, parsnips, cucumber, lettuce – even the dreaded broccoli – were merely colourful accompaniments to real food. Scavenging in neighbours' dustbins would be preferable to submitting to this hamster food diet.

The unforgiving ring of my mobile [at a glance I saw it was Caroline] distracted me from pursuing the expenses issue further for then, but I was determined not to let it drop. Lesley seemed glad of the interruption, realising that she was actually in a tight corner on this one, for the truth was, as I'd correctly guessed, that she hadn't bothered to sign off the necessary paperwork. Her deadly eye narrowed at the sight of easier prey – Roy, he of Data Services fame, idling by the water dispenser. She stormed up to him, upbraiding him volubly for having failed to restore her network connection.

'It's been down two hours now! How on earth can I be expected to carry out my responsibilities without the right tools? I want it done right now, this minute!'

Roy, as instructed, sloped off to her lair, feeling rather sheepish – after all, he prided himself on his ability to impress any female [me excepted].

I missed Caroline's call, so I texted to say that I was tied up in meetings for the rest of the day but would phone from home later – who knows, I would probably have some juicy titbits to throw her way.

5.30 pm. Home now, kettle's on, quick cup of coffee, must cut down on the booze – well, early evenings anyway. Fire up the computer – ooh, this does look promising! God, please God – let them be this side of the Ice Age and at the very least capable of walking upright. It wasn't that Dave had bruised knuckles but he did have something of the Neanderthal about him, dear love.

Ping! Who's this? Richard from Widnes. The name's got a nice ring to it – could be a good omen, I thought, blotting from my mind the chemical haze, which enveloped the Widnes area most of the time. There was nothing spectacular in his profile – industrial engineer by profession. That fits. Hobbies? Hmm ... DIY *and* gardening; this could be hard work. Still he was quite good-looking and if his details were true, there was no excess baggage. I read on.

> *Hello there. I'm a pretty casual sort of guy, laid back, relaxed. I used to be called 'Dick' but I'm encouraging 'Richard' these days. Friendship is fine but it's really a relationship that I'm after – meals out, walks in the woods, bargain breaks, the sort of thing you can enjoy anyway but even more so with someone you're close to.*

Fair enough, fair enough, thought I – all pretty sound so far.

> *And I trust you won't find the fact that I'm impotent [too close an encounter with the hedge trimmer I fear] will prove detrimental to developing a real relationship.*

This had to be a wind-up but I blanched all the same. What is it with these men? They can't seem to wait to share the most intimate detail in a first message. First it was Mr Bi now it's Mr Bye-Bye courtesy of a hedge trimmer. My standard reply would come into play again.

> *MY ACTUAL REPLY: Thanks for your message but I don't think we are well suited.*

Now, who's next in line to fulfil my fantasies? Yes, perhaps I am deluding myself? As yet, the site has delivered a patchwork quilt of possibles rather than probables. This was typical of my approach I'm afraid. I so easily wavered between vaulting hopes and sorry disappointments – I just couldn't find a halfway house.

But then, quite suddenly, a shaft of sunlight pierced through the gloom. Ping! Another hit – and he was fit – a fit hit! I eagerly read on. He was strikingly handsome. Lovely soft brown eyes, gazing straight at you, into you. Pity about the bow tie – it tended to age him. Hugh, yes, like it ... antiques dealer, yes, like it more ... Knutsford, now that *is* a classy area ... yes, really like it. Divorced – I bet his ex screwed him down to his last piece of Chippendale in the settlement. His interests were loftier than those to which I'd been recently exposed ... fine art, the theatre, concerts [I somehow doubted he meant Oasis]. He was quite businesslike, almost perfunctory in his approach.

> *You know Sally, I really am inclined to believe that you have something special, nay unique about you. Frankly, I'm attracted by your lively sense of humour as much as by your stunning looks ...*

'Stunning looks'! Gulp! Go on, go on Hugh, I'm listening; in fact I'm positively agog!'

> *… and to put it bluntly and not to beat about the bush, I really would like to meet you very soon – next week perhaps? You may know the Barclays branch in the centre of Knutsford opposite the church. Well, just 100 yards down on the left from there is a really good wine bar called En Primeur. If by any chance you're free next Monday, we could meet there about eight o'clock for a couple of drinks. What do you think? – please say yes. Here's my mobile 07837 865987. Kind regards, Hugh.*

I was sorely tempted. He definitely had a certain style about him and a pleasing confidence, and this did fit the Knutsford setting – so why not? Throwing my customary caution to the wind I phoned him immediately. This wasn't perhaps the wisest opening gambit but, who knows, he could, probably *did*, have an entire harem of beauties lining up for him. But fortune favours the brave so I went for it.

'Is that Hugh? Yes hello, I'm Sally, you contacted me? Thanks for emailing me and yes, I'd love to meet you at that wine bar next Monday. I could make it by eight easily. I'm looking forward to it already.' Oh dear, I reprimanded myself inwardly, have I blurted that lot out in one go? Probably sound like a groupie.

'Sally, well now, how *are* you?' Wow, even his voice was special too. It had a deep resonance that made me positively tingle. Queen's English too, but not plummy. He continued. 'I'm absolutely delighted that you can spare the time from what I'm sure is a packed social life and thank you so much for contacting me so quickly; it really is *so* thoughtful of you ...'

Go on, go on. I'm entranced!

'... And I'll make every effort not to bore you to death with the finer points of Sèvres versus Dresden.'

'Oh, I'm sure you won't do that – leave the tedious bit to me with my dull existence at the bank; can't possibly be as stimulating as your line of work.'

'On the contrary my dear, I detect such an original sense of humour from your dating profile, and I can't wait to be thoroughly entertained with stories from the heady world of international finance.'

'Mmm, well you might just have something there but the atmosphere at the bank only normally gets heady when the air-conditioning breaks down.'

He chuckled. 'You see? I'm laughing already. Now I know my bow tie is a truly awful example of self-indulgence but at least you'll have no trouble recognising me.'

'Er, yes, OK, fine – I'll see you then.'

You certainly will! Au revoir, fair lady.'

I giggled girlishly 'Bye Hugh – see you Monday.'

Now, a more cynical soul might have found him a little unctuous, his manner slightly patronising perhaps, the way he talked rather formal – even a little old-fashioned ... but as for me, well he certainly ticked lots of boxes!

How do you Hugh?

Thanks to its new orbital motorway, travelling round Manchester was so much easier these days and I got back to my flat well before six, satisfied with my day's training in Rochdale. This added to my high spirits as I showered and got ready to meet him. As I applied my make-up, a pitiful cry from the kitchen announced the presence of a hungry Ringo deserted yet again by the neighbours. Just time to feed him.

Now, a cool wine bar in Knutsford – so, what to wear? First thought, smart jeans but maybe not given Hugh's penchant for bow ties. Safest bet is to rely on old faithfuls – smart navy trousers, a simple white silk shirt and some nice understated silver jewellery.

I entered En Primeur just after eight. There was low lighting and comfortable seating; in the background a Jamie Cullum CD added to the air of relaxation.

'Sally, delighted to meet you – how could I fail to recognise you from your lovely photograph – here, do let me take your coat.'

'Hello Hugh. Nice to meet you and thanks for asking me. I haven't been here before but it all looks really nice.'

He was taller than I'd imagined and probably in his late forties, even early fifties. Although he had a slightly prominent nose, he had unusually fine features; additionally, his thick dark mane, and brown eyes (those eyes!) would stir any maiden's heart! He was attractive, courteous and suave but with no edge to him.

'Now, what would you like? The wine list is quite extensive.'

'Oh, a small glass of the Vouvray would be fine, thank you.'

I could safely handle two small glasses, having had quite a full meal at lunchtime and a sandwich before coming out.

'Excellent choice, my dear – I'll join you.'

A waiter took our order and soon reappeared with the wine and some mixed olives. Yes, it was all very comfortable.

'So Hugh, you're in antiques; that's different – must be an interesting way of earning a living rather than me with my boring old computers and financial training.'

'Well, interesting is exactly the right word because we deal in some absolutely beautiful pieces of furniture and fine art – at times, I think how lucky I am to be working with one of my hobbies. But, to be honest, it's also uncertain, precarious even, so much depends on the economy you see. If things are good, people are ready to buy, but you know better than me the swings and roundabouts of people's finances. But as for computers, that's one of my company's real weaknesses – we need to be dragged into the twenty-first century. Spreadsheets, inventories, all that sort of thing.' He took a sip of his wine, its coolness clouding the glass slightly. 'In fact,' he added, warming to his theme, 'perhaps you could give me some IT advice, at consultant's rates of course!'

We chatted away in this easy manner, until I realised the time and thought of my heavy day ahead. 'Well, it's been so good to meet you Hugh, I've really enjoyed it but I think I need to be making a move.'

'My pleasure. Now, please don't think this is too forward, but I wondered if you might be free this coming

Wednesday. Short notice I know but by sheer good fortune – or rather, because I know the curator – I've got two tickets for the preview of the Turner/Whistler/Monet exhibition at the Lowry Centre. This is the exhibition that's transferred from Tate Britain. You've probably read of it in the Sunday papers – you may even have seen it?'

'Well I haven't seen it but I remember those artists from my art course at school.' I eagerly swallowed the bait and, before you could say Pablo Picasso, had accepted the invitation. 'Yes, thank you, I'd love to see it.'

'Excellent! It's from six until eight – then we could go on to a Moroccan restaurant I use from time to time. You'll love the exhibition, and I'm sure you'll enjoy the meal. Don't worry about getting in – simply tell the attendants that you're with Hugh Faulkner. That'll be fine.'

Everything about him suggested style; there was an understated confidence and ease of manner. *'I know the curator', 'You may even have seen it', 'I use from time to time.'*

'I know where the Lowry Centre is, it's not too far from our head office in Manchester where I work, and yes, that sounds a really interesting evening – I'll make sure I'm there in good time.'

'Splendid, splendid – I look forward to seeing you then.'

Tell them I'm with Hugh Faulkner? I thought as I drove home to the unwonted strains of Vivaldi on Classic FM – I'll broadcast it from the bloody rooftops thank you very much!

Problems of the heart

After training in Leeds, I spent Tuesday night at home, reflecting on the previous night's success and looking forward to an equally interesting time at the exhibition on the following evening. The meal at the Moroccan restaurant was sure to be a little more appetising than tonight's fare. Already, my shepherd's pie, on its carousel of incineration, was beginning to splutter in its death throes; fortunately, a high-pitched piping from the microwave triggered off the smoke alarm and dragged me back to reality. From the wall I snatched my kitchen gauntlets [a souvenir from a fireman friend but that's another story] and retrieved the ashes of Pompeii, deftly removing the blistered packaging. Oh well, no bother. Just prise away the carbonised crust, smear the exposed top layer with a liberal coating of tomato ketchup, glass or two of Impala and all will be well; nothing, but nothing, was going to deflate my balloon of bliss tonight.

Noting the time and determined to pre-empt *Corrie*, I phoned Caroline. The answerphone clicked into operation. Strange. She very rarely goes out midweek and she loves her soaps. And what about Bob and the kids? Curious. I dialled the mobile and could immediately tell from the echo that she was speaking from outside.

'Hello love. Just phoned you at home. Where is everyone?'

'Oh Sally, I'm so sorry but I did try to get hold of you at work today – it's Bob,' I sensed the tears. 'He collapsed at work this morning and they rushed him off to the infirmary. I knew he wasn't right.'

'Oh my God, how is he and where are you now?'

'I'm in the car park with the kids, just about to come home. Bob's under sedation and he's sleeping now. The specialist's been to see me to say there's no real danger, and to go home, get a good night's rest and come back tomorrow.'

'Right, good thinking. Now, I'm on my way over and I'll stop off at the chippy. Bob will be fine, just fine. He's in safe hands and he'll be his old pestering self before long, just wait and see.'

'Thanks ever so much love, that'll be great and will you cheer me up with all the news of your latest escapades? I need something to take my mind off this – see you soon!'

I switched off the microwave, and sprinted to my car. Mr Woo's chippy – 'No sushi, lots of mushy' – wasn't too busy. I'd phoned in the order on the way over, so I was in and out in a flash. I remembered how often she'd expressed her anxieties about Bob's lifestyle. He was an HGV driver. Regular fry-ups at Greasy Spoons across the country, followed by several rounds at the local, no exercise and the nervous exhaustion from fifty hours a week-plus at the wheel were hardly conducive to good health.

Once there, I'd just boiled the kettle when I heard the key turning in the lock of the front door. I rushed through the hallway to give them all a big welcoming hug. Caroline and Louise certainly needed it; their faces were drawn, their eyes red and puffy: even Richard, in a rare moment of civility, seemed genuinely pleased to see me.

'Lots of chips, Richard love,' I said cheerily. 'Now eat them all up, don't go all slimline on me will you?'

After an hour or so they went off to their rooms to watch TV and catch up on some homework.

Ticking all the boxes

'Well, Cazi. It must have been some day for you. Let's have a drink and you can tell me all about it.'

A bottle or so later [mainly consumed by her], it became pretty clear that despite her catalogue of complaints about Bob, the day's events had made her think about a life without him, and she was pretty shaken up.

'I don't know – I just saw him lying there, and he was so frightened and he looked so ... grey. I thought, what will happen to us if he's not around anymore?'

'Now, come on love, don't think like that. He's going to be just fine. Yes, this is a warning, but if he gives up the fags and starts eating sensibly and doing some exercise, he'll be as fit as a fiddle again. He's not going anywhere just yet, believe me.'

'Oh, I know you're right but the thing is, I feel really guilty. All this business with you and Internet dating, well, it was making me think I'm missing out on something, and that maybe I didn't want to spend the rest of my life with Bob. To be honest, I was a bit jealous of you. Then this happens. I'm so ashamed of myself.'

She began to sob. I put her arms around her, giving her a big sisterly hug.

'Cazi, come on now love, don't you ever, *ever* be envious of me. You're the *only* person who knows that a husband and kids is all I've ever really wanted. I'd swap my Internet adventures for that any day of the week. So come on, cheer up – everything's going to be OK. Want to hear what's been happening to me?'

She snuffled into her damp tissue, relieved at the change of topic.

'Ooh, yes please, especially the sparky story and where are we up to with your future husband, Mr Alderley Edge?'

To set the ball rolling I exaggerated the unsuccessful approaches of Pablo and soon she was laughing merrily. The bi-guy followed, a warm-up act for luckless Richard from Widnes. When I spared no details of my night of perspiring passion with Dansak Dave, she was back to her old self.

'And, oh yes Caroline, I've got a big confession to make – Margherita Mike from Crewe, remember? You were 100% right weren't you! Mr Tedium. *Gardeners' World* would have been more exciting – and talk about tight-fisted! I'm telling you, this bloke's developed stinginess into an art form. Not only does he bring with him his long-suffering son Gerald, poor lad, because there was a 3-for-2 offer on, but he then proudly displays his Daybook, a tiny pocket book in which he records every, but *every*, day's item of expenditure. No, stop laughing. I'm telling you, promise, this is exactly what it was like and that's why I had to use the old Mum's-just-fallen-out-of-a-hot-air-balloon-over-Skegness trick to escape!'

The memory of 'Pizza da Pietro' had both of us doubled up in laughter. More drink. I decided to hold back on Hugh for some future occasion. As I picked up my car keys to leave, she flung her arms around me, saying she couldn't ever thank me enough.

Dateandsee had certainly earned its subscription simply for bringing a smile to Caroline's face.

As I got ready for bed, I was mindful of another frantic day ahead in the office before the evening's treat with Hugh. The office itself was now threatened by Lesley's searching scrutiny. Individual desks were declared 'a relic of commercial lethargy' and thus 'wholly unsuitable for today's non-stop 24/7 activity – hot desking is what I want.' When I patiently explained all of this to a dumbfounded Brian, his jaw dropped, mouth wide-open like one of his beloved fledglings waiting for some tasty morsel. Hot curries? Yes. Hot tubs even? Yes, but hot *desking?*

The finer things in life

During the day Caroline phoned. Bob was much perkier, and would be allowed home before the weekend. After delivering the training courses on successive days in Rochdale and then Leeds, I was glad to be back in the office and relieved to see that Lesley had not, in fact, enacted her 'working space directive'; the familiar sight of my desk with its photos and gizmos was reassuring. To top it all, she had been summoned 'by head office' to attend 'a management summit' for the rest of the week and so there wouldn't be too many interruptions. I'd have lots of time now to produce my reports, catch up on outstanding emails and/ or phone calls before vanishing at 4.30 to prepare for the suave Hugh Faulkner at the Lowry Centre.

OK. Art exhibition. Hugh, with his bow tie. Moroccan restaurant. What type of outfit did this suggest? Something sharp and sophisticated but also feminine. Of course the event would also attract the arty-farty 'I-look-like-a-bag-of-rags-but-I'm-too-lofty-to-worry-about-mere-accessories' community but I had no intention of doing a Tracey Emin impression. I went for wide-leg palazzo pants and a pearl-grey satin top. With my hair up in a neat chignon and wearing Mum's pearl earrings, I topped off the outfit with a vintage fringed shawl, comforting myself with the far-fetched notion that Botticelli would have loved me. I flicked on teletext to check that Manchester United weren't playing at home; they weren't – it was an away game and so the traffic would be no worse than usual. There was a little used car park near the Midland Hotel, and I took a taxi from there to Salford, only a short distance away.

The Lowry Centre was a temple to modernism. Largely funded by EU money, vast tracts of Salford's *Coronation Street* back-to-backs had been bulldozed away. Sir Alfred McAlpine had splendidly succeeded where the Luftwaffe had signally failed. Instead of the dire townscape made familiar by Lowry's paintings, there were galleries, designer outlets, cool bars and smart restaurants, today's urban chic. Even what had once been a noxious, rat-infested waterway was now an attractive marina, 'Salford Quays', a mini Cannes but without the light and the colour. The area had not been totally transformed, however; the locals' wit had survived unscathed, with the C of Canal Street painted out to welcome inquisitive visitors to Manchester's gay village. Following Hugh's advice, I told a liveried attendant that Mr Faulkner was expecting me. I was then ushered in and, feeling like royalty, escorted to the Lowry Bar. I noted the 'VIPs ONLY' sign by the doorway and suddenly felt very grand. Hugh, unmistakeable in his dark blue and red polka dot bow tie, had clearly been on the lookout for me. He was wearing a light blue cotton shirt beneath a dark blue linen suit – the sort of thing Ralph Lauren knocked out at £800 a go.

After slipping a polite 'Please do excuse me for a moment' to his other guests, who parted like the Red Sea before him, he glided over to greet me with a kiss on each cheek in the approved sophisticated manner.

'Sally, it's wonderful to see you again. Let's have a drink together then I'll introduce you to some of my friends. Now, what would be suitable?'

'Hello again Hugh – oh, I think a small dry white wine would be perfect, thank you.'

His world was predictable and actually rather attractive. His friends were well dressed, engaging and polite; their effortless self-assurance shone through – they almost seemed to be a different and distant tribe, many rungs up the infinite ladder of evolution. That said, I was surprised by how much I felt at ease, comfortably sharing tales and anecdotes from the banking world.

'Now, where on earth could Edward have got to?' wondered Hugh aloud, glancing at his watch.

'Perhaps he's ground to a halt in that snarl-up near the viaduct, you know what it's like there in the rush hour,' volunteered one of the group.

'Well yes, you're probably right Jeremy, but look, let's get moving before the gallery fills up.' His friends willingly followed his lead, like trusting schoolchildren, crocodile style, in the wake of a confident and caring teacher.

The exhibition focussed on the work of the three painters and their treatment of nineteenth century London. They were fascinated by the effects of the mists, the fog and the air, heavy with pollution, especially at sunrise and sunset. Hugh and his entourage talked knowledgeably about the works; he proved the perfect host, constantly on hand, solicitous, interested in my opinions but never putting me on the spot. An hour passed and suddenly, above the swell of conversation, I heard 'Hugh, made it at last – damned traffic! I thought we'd be kipping down on the M6 for the night!' A middle-aged man with a florid complexion, and rather too corpulent for his jacket, came bumbling forward, wheezing for breath. The woman in tow did not seem altogether pleased with life. He was blissfully unaware of this and beamed broadly at everyone.

'Hello everyone, I'm Edward. Now, whatever Hugh has told you about me is untrue: the reality is much worse!'

Pealing with laughter, he then turned to his companion, his hand slipping possessively round her ample waist as he guided her forward.

'May I present Arabella, esteemed resident of West Kensington and illustrator at the V & A.' Arabella smiled thinly.

Hugh then introduced some of his friends and me in particular: 'This is Sally, who has done me the honour of joining me tonight.'

As he summoned over a waiter to order some drinks for the late arrivals, I exchanged pleasantries with Edward and Arabella. Some sort of cloud, however, began to darken my sunny disposition. I couldn't quite seem to connect with her, well nobody could – she seemed prepared to pass the entire evening in a kind of regal detachment. Also, she had begun to irritate me somewhat, almost pushing me aside to get a better view of a particular Monet. Miss High and Mighty, or what thought I? I'd sue the hairdresser who let me out on the streets in that state – she looked like the vital ingredient for one of Mr Woo's bird nest's soup. And as for her satin dress, it was the wrong material for a natural size 16 lubricated into an unnatural size 12 – she had more spare tyres than Quickfit.

And as for Edward – talk about a letch! What was he? Chairman of Lounge Lizards plc or something? He'd been mentally undressing me ever since we were introduced, and was quite shamelessly using the thronging crowd as an excuse to stand as close to me as possible, so close that I caught his aftershave; it was rich and there was too much of it. I almost began to feel sorry for Dame Arabella whose hauteur set her apart and made her look rather vulnerable. But my kind thoughts soon proved to be misplaced, for when Edward leant forward to whisper something into my ear, Arabella Scissorhands, decided to attack.

'So sorry, my dear, what's your name again? Ah yes, Sally, how sweet. Now, do tell about your taste in art?' Hugh, I thought, in desperation, where are you? I'm in danger of sinking here. Help! To no avail. A heavily made-up wraith of indeterminate gender seemed to be monopolising his attention at that moment.

'Well, when I was at college, ...' I began bravely.

Quick as a flash Arabella fired out. 'Which college would that be? The Slade? Chelsea? Goldsmiths?' This was said in a piercing falsetto that reverberated around the group. Her questions were taking on more than a hint of the Gestapo.

'No, it was a sixth-form college, near where I was brought up, here in Manchester.'

She adopted a rictus smile; she was one set up already, and the match had scarcely begun.

'I had this really good art teacher, Mrs Whittaker. Everyone liked her – she encouraged me to do a project on Vermeer.' Is that enough to keep you going you stuck- up cow? I thought.

'Ah yes, Vermeer, well now,' she purred patronisingly. 'Have you seen *Girl with a Pearl Earring?*'

'Oh, yes,' I replied enthusiastically, falling into the ready-made trap; 'I'm up for anything with Colin Firth in it.'

'Oh my dear, how very droll. I meant the painting actually, not that utterly tiresome film,' she replied swiftly, viciously enjoying her moment of victory. I could sense myself flushing, knowing that my fair skin would be making my embarrassment all the more obvious.

What a bitch, I thought grimly. Right lady, your card is well and truly marked. Nearly twenty years of business conferences and tough negotiating had not made me resilient for nothing. I was poised to retaliate, a dart of acid wit ready to reduce the preening Arabella to a gibbering wreck, begging for mercy. But to do so would not have been fair on Hugh. This reception was his occasion, with his friends. No, I would have to hold my tongue and hope for some future opportunity to secure revenge. And then, and certainly for the better, Hugh rejoined us having managed to shake off the social limpet. 'So sorry about that – I had to deal with a rather trying interloper.'

'What was he Hugh – one of your competitors?' asked Edward, affecting wide-eyed innocence. There was laughter all round.

'Yes, well thank you for that, Edward; we know we can always rely on you for an entertaining bon mot!' Then, clapping his hands to gain everyone's attention, he continued. 'Well, my friends, time's winged chariot waits for no man, and I need to take my leave of you as I have another particularly important engagement,' his eyes twinkled at me. 'You all must drop by my splendid, enlarged premises – and do remember to bring your MasterCard with you!'

His entourage chuckled; his charm never failed. As his friends too prepared to leave, he turned quietly to me.

'Right my dear, allow me to introduce you to the exotic delights of the Riad Marrakech, my favourite restaurant!'

As we exited the gallery, I caught sight of Edward and his parting ogle; Arabella stood by his side, stiff, sullen and silent.

The Riad Marrakech was within walking distance. Hugh chatted easily, and as we entered the restaurant, he was warmly greeted by a tall, slim and dusky waiter wearing a finely cut scarlet tunic; his beaming smile revealed two gold teeth and, above his name badge 'Younis', shone a crossed pair of miniature silver sabres.

'Ah Misterrr Folker,' he said in heavily accented English. 'I wish you and your lady fine evening. Your usual table waits you. Please to follow me.'

'Lady', 'Usual table'– this was getting better by the minute.

Moroccan cuisine was totally new to me but Hugh was there to offer advice. I enjoyed the grilled lamb and the couscous even more, finding it lighter and spicier than rice – it must have been the herbs. A glass of light red wine and sparkling mineral water proved the prefect accompaniment. The hours flew by and there were no awkward silences. When he ordered some cognac I couldn't believe it was close to midnight.

'No, Hugh, thank you so much but I mustn't. I've got to get to my car and then drive home; remember, I had some wine at the exhibition.'

'Of course, of course, I quite understand,' he replied, gesturing to Younis for the bill, which, it transpired, was to go on his account.

'Please let me ...' I began.

'No, my dear, wouldn't hear of it – it's been a wonderful evening. Thank you so much once again for the pleasure of your company, I hope we can repeat it some time.'

'Well, love to, but, I'm sorry, I couldn't get through to Edward and ... his consort!'

He smiled. 'Oh, don't give it a second thought. Edward's just a soppy old spaniel who needs a bit of love and as for Arabella, well, yes, she can be brittle. On the business circuit she's known as 'The Shark', after one of Damien Hirst's creations, poor thing! Now, here's the taxi to take you safely to your car.'

I was still chuckling when the taxi purred up. He squeezed my arm gently as we exchanged kisses ...

Chapter 6

THE CALM BEFORE THE STORM

It was already Thursday, and things were definitely on the up. From the unsavoury depths of the Crewe D'Azur, and the easy descent into the carnal hell (or was it heaven?) with sparky Dave, I had effortlessly soared heavenwards with Hugh of the easy sophistication and Jonathan of the ready charm. Not only that – a text from Caroline reported Bob's continued improvement and, for good measure, Lesley had been 'detained' at the management summit. For me, 'detained' had connotations of narrow-eyed psychopaths languishing at HM's pleasure on Dartmoor, or determined asylum seekers, grimly hanging on for dear life to the undercarriage of a Eurostar, before being apprehended by vigilant customs officers at Folkestone. Clearly, neither situation was particularly relevant to Lesley's, although she certainly qualified for the former; but the word undoubtedly had a certain menace to it, and I was keen to discover the full implications.

For the moment, however, on Lesley's instructions, I had to design several new courses: 'From Core Activity to Care Activity' i.e. pretend you love your customers and you'll win more business, 'Cheque out those top accounts' well, at least this was honest, 'Advising the Advisors' – whatever that might mean, and 'Induction not Seduction' – Lesley's hard line approach to young recruits. The more I pondered on the courses I was commissioned to write, the more I was convinced that they were increasingly the same – distinctly 'vanilla', to use the popular jargon. Senior managers were quick to reject anything that merely hinted at increased expenditure. They positively foamed at the mouth if the final results were anything other than corporate bland, observing to the nth degree all the current 'isms', the taboos of racial and sexual politics and inevitably 'elf 'n' safety'.

Not ours to reason why, I mused, my thoughts interrupted by loud guffaws from the water dispenser area. This was Roy's very own Speakers' Corner; true enough, there he was, holding court amid an admiring posse of bright-eyed, well-scrubbed clone recruits; they were all male and thus grist to their raconteur's sense of humour, much influenced by Jim Davidson – hence his popularity with the boys. More than once I'd heard Roy gilding the lily of his relatively mundane set of responsibilities to the extent that Bill Gates himself would have difficulty matching his comprehensive knowledge of 'system synergies', 'streamlining servers' and 'web browser interfaces'. The howls of laughter, I discovered later, stemmed from his preoccupation with Lesley. He had apparently entertained the admiring group – revelling in being the centre of attention – by asking 'What's the difference between Lassie and Lesley? Don't know? I'll tell you. One has bad breath and sex on all fours, and the other appeared in several highly successful American films.' Roy, Roy, I thought, shaking my head in what was almost a gesture of pity, behaviour like that will catch you out sometime, your days could be numbered my friend, think P45!

Later that afternoon I texted Caroline: *Call u later. Luv 2 Bob. X.* So smoothly did the rest of the day go that I was able to get back home in good time, and put out an extra dish of 'Absolutely Pawvellous' for Ringo, whose loving owners were away, again. Soon I was ensconced in front of the laptop, oblivious of the noise of the traffic outside and the manic laughter of *The Simpsons* in the flat above. I felt good, confident, and even a little complacent perhaps. Andrew – AA – currently soaking up the sun in South Africa, yes, why not contact him; after all I did have his email address safely stored in my Favourites.

Hillo Endroo. Hope Kipe Tarn is good for yew [sorry Andrew, this is my feeble attempt at mimicking a South African accent – ek-sent!]. Hope things are going swimmingly and you've successfully negotiated some marvellous deals out there. Can we expect you to shower the UK in general and me in particular with an unbeatable Cabernet Sauvignon? Hope so, because my cellar is severely depleted at present, I'm afraid – even the Bolly is at risk. I thought of you the other day when I was in a wine bar in Knutsford. There I was dolled up in my Marianne Faithful motor bike leathers when this Bryan Adams double sidles up to me and asks, 'How do you get inside those leathers?' 'Well, a large G &T usually helps' I retorted, to thunderous applause. Really! This in a wine bar in Knutsford! Obviously the place needs your patronage to restore a bit of class. Anyway, what I'm saying as I splash around in this bath of anecdotes is that, if you get back next month as planned, do get in touch. And yes, I do solemnly promise not to touch the Bolly until then. Sally xxx

Three kisses, yes three but hardly charged with erotic tension and yet a little more intimate than 'Best Wishes'. With luck I should hear from him soon and perhaps add him to my trophy cabinet that is positively gleaming with my recent successes ... Hugh, Jonathan and ... and ... funny can't remember the rest!

Now, back to the emails. There was this Wayne from Blackpool, chancing his arm and really becoming something of a pain. That's the beauty of these sites though, I thought, with some comfort. Any threat can't achieve reality because it's all way out there in the swirling emptiness of cyberspace. Wayne's unsuccessful attempts at humour plummeted south into an endless stream of sordid innuendoes which I found increasingly alarming. Time to add Wayne to my 'Ignore' list. This would prevent him from emailing me again – let him share his *Readers' Wives* stories with someone else. I also had a speculative message from Dave but I'd been there, done that and wasn't going back for more, no matter how often that little devil with bright red horns in the right side of my brain reminded me how good he'd been in bed ... but, – ah, here's someone new, someone really quite striking – a god of ebony.

> THE MESSAGE: *Hello there, Sally. You know, your profile was something else. I had to ask my pal what Bulgari was because I thought it was a new Ryanair destination or something. Yep, all you girls always go for the Brad Pitt sort – sorry, but as you can see from my photo, we're not exactly identical twins! Must admit that sport is one of my passions,*

if you come to the gym where I work I promise you a full workout, free of charge. As for cooking, well all I know about Italian is spag bol but I'm a bit of a dab hand at gumbo. You see, my Auntie used to work at a really posh restaurant in Barbados where they specialised in more unusual West Indian cooking and her recipes from Guyana were always popular. Perhaps we could do some speed-cooking, my goat steaks and red pepper gumbo is a great favourite – think about it, an exotic dinner just for two, here in sun-drenched Stafford, rum cocktails with Bob Marley in the background, yes, I admit it, I'm a big fan. Now, this has to be an offer you can't refuse!

THE PROFILE:
Name: Clinton
Age: 45
Location: Stafford
Status: Divorced
Children: Three
Job: Manufacturing
Height: 6'3"
Build: Muscular
Appearance: Attractive
Eye Colour: Brown
Hair: Dark Brown
Religion: Pentecostal
Star Sign: Taurus
Smoker: No
Drinker: Moderate

INTERESTS: *Bodybuilding, football, music, animals.*

ABOUT ME: *Hi I'm Clinton. My job's on the production line in a factory but I also work part-time in my local gym. I look after my body and get a real rush from pushing myself to the limit. I love Reggae/Ska and my best mate is my dog, Winston. If you like the look of my profile, why not email me and let's see if we can get our adrenaline going together.*

MY PREFERRED REPLY: *You know, Clinton, I think meeting you could be fun, but the thing is I'm looking for something more than a few dates – long term probably wouldn't work out for us as we don't seem to have a great deal in common, although your sense of humour is a winner. And as for Barbados – well, it's a real pity you didn't contact my twitcher mate, Brian. He's desperate to see all the exotic birds in the Windies [feathered variety of course] and would have been with you like a shot! So, best of luck in the fitness centre of life and please give Winston a pat from me.*

Yes, sod it, I thought – I'll send what I thought of in the first place – bit of honesty won't do any harm and he seems to be a pretty mature type. So, there we go.

> *MY ACTUAL REPLY: As above*

Time for a coffee now – quick shot of caffeine needed in case I get any shocks. Ping! The computer's clarion call to action had me rushing back from the kitchen. From Andrew, hurrah! I thought we'd click. Bugger the coffee, let's see what the squire's got to say for himself. Weekend break over there perhaps, escorted tour of De Beers [not forgetting the goody bag], dinner on Table Mountain?

> *Hillo. Thanks ever so for the mail and yes, things are generally going well, better than we thought. They've been producing wine around here for centuries would you believe and they really know their stuff. The problem comes with the inevitable red tape – or should that be 'black tape'? Believe me, these guys in the export ministry revel in their recently acquired power, and you always need a few hundred Rand with you to grease their greedy paws to make any real progress. Mind you they've come on a lot. They even leave their spears outside the meeting room these days! So, yes, generally it's going well but the delays mean I'll be out here for longer than expected so it could be the end of September before I'm back. Endroo xx*

Hmm, I wonder. The confidence and warmth are still there but some of his throwaway lines such as 'black tape', 'greedy paws', 'leaving their spears outside' are a little worrying. What's all this about? Is he acting out the role of some colonial type to amuse me or is he a closet racist with life membership of the BNP? I need to be careful here. Still, perhaps some contact is better than none at all so it'll be a quick response to keep the pot boiling … perhaps he should be in it, bobbing up and down in the froth, surrounded by ravenous natives, gleefully wielding packets of Saxo?

Thanks for the prompt reply Andrew. Roll on September when you can exchange your colonial pith helmet for a deerstalker. Then you can entrance me with your tales of derring-do from the High Veld. Sally xx

---

7.15 pm. The pressing urgency of the mobile. It's Caroline, God, hope nothing's wrong.

'Cazi, where are you? Is everything OK?'

'Hello love. Yes, fine thanks – honestly, no major problems. Just wanted to pop round sometime and to talk to you about Internet dating. See, I've had time to think recently and …'

'Cazi,' I cut in sharply, 'I thought we'd already been through this? Don't even go there! Look, when I got going with it, it was you, remember, who pooh-poohed the idea with talk of acid bath specialists and hooded kinksters and, anyway, you've been married now for–'

'No, no – you've got it all wrong. You're jumping to the wrong conclusions – I'm not wanting to sign up to it, honest. Look, this is difficult, *Corrie's* on soon and his Lordship is ready for dinner – only wants salmon tagliatelle with mangetout, rocket salad and bloody Malvern water – yes, I'm not joking, Bob and *Malvern water*! And the kids are here arguing as usual – WILL YOU TWO JUST STOP IT! – look, can I pop round on Sunday morning?'

'That's fine love – I can assure you I won't be recovering from any electric shocks then, more's the pity – bye!'

Simply the best

Girl Guides' training had certainly left its mark on me. I reflected on those expensive courses I'd attended from work. Sometimes, I felt that they'd left less of an impression on me than those autumn nights in the draughty tent with the smell of damp earth, and the winds howling down across the Pennines. First rule in Guiding as in Scouting was one of life's immutable truths: 'Be Prepared'.

I was to deliver a training course in Coventry on the following day. This was an easy run; off early down the M6, use the new toll road [not even Lesley's hawk-eye would spot the £4.50 claim – then again, she probably would!] and into the city from the north. The course was due to end about four, and so I'd have the time to visit the cathedral. I'd never seen it and wanted to dazzle Hugh over a cheeky Merlot with my appreciation of its architecture. I began to work through the course. There was nothing too problematical here; it was much the same as I'd delivered in Durham some weeks before. I didn't bother checking out the standard corporate introduction section. That was Roy's responsibility and loath as I was to admit it, it was really impressive; he updated it from time to time but nothing too radical, so it should be all right.

Now, ten minutes checking out Dateandsee's finest in the picture gallery ... hmm ... Leonard from Liverpool. He was really quite nice, craggy good looks reminiscent of Harrison Ford at his best, but there was something slightly disturbing about men who posted a photo of themselves bare-chested or worse, lying on a bed bare-chested! Still, Harrison Ford was one of my all-time stars, so I ought not to dismiss Leonard quite so quickly. I'd put him in my Favourites for a message later once I'd exhausted my current crop of talent or, more likely, I thought, after they'd made me history.

Next, it was Ishmael ... gulp ... gorgeous, a positive god! Ravishing smile and lovely long eyelashes – yes, I'd definitely revisit him over the weekend; could be interesting if the Hugh/Andrew/Jonathan axis falls apart, perish the thought. Ah yes, Jonathan. I do hope golf is the only game he's playing in Spain. Actually, it wouldn't do any harm to send him a flirty text to remind him I'm around.

Dear Nick Faldo. Hope u playing well & missing me loads. B gd – my spies are everywhere! S x

As usual, the M6 had various sections coned off, so that in the haze of the summer air and exhaust fumes, the orange cones tailed off into infinity like some modern art community sculpture. Just then, a typically aggressive white-van driver, the equivalent of a New Guinea headhunting tribesman, catapulted me back from my daydreams to grim reality. He pressed hard on my tail, leering at me in my rear mirror and gesturing in a lewd fashion; this was par for the course, and nothing even remotely interesting.

He was obviously suggesting, in none too subtle a fashion, that 65 mph on a motorway was a bloody nuisance and a typically girlie thing to do. Whatever, at the first available opportunity, he careered out to the right, just grazing my side panel, mouthed the inevitable and familiar obscenity at me, and then streaked away; in doing so, he sounded his horn loudly – either to point out what I was missing or, more likely, to add insult to injury. Tosser! Eventually though, I reached the city; I had no difficulty finding a place to park and reached the venue in good time. Excellent. It was always useful to be there early to check on the training room and the facilities.

What a relief to see that everything was spot-on, even down to the jug of water and glass on the presenter's table. It was a bright modern room with an impressive suite of computers, one for each trainee. An enormous screen, worthy of UCI, almost filled the wall behind me. The list of attendees was on hand, together with their name, job and branch. I noticed too that the room wasn't one of those 'Mickey Mouse' efforts, i.e. a huge space capable of being separated by a divider resembling a huge concertina on runners. Things designed for two purposes rarely do either satisfactorily – it normally took the brute force of half a dozen burly men to jerk such dividers along the rusting groove. Secondly, there was sound proofing; all too often my courses had been ruined by gales of snorting laughter from the adjoining room, as some hapless senior manager was reluctantly persuaded to engage in the dreaded role play, acting out the part of a bemused Somalian refugee seeking advice on investments.

Proceedings were due to start at nine. Gradually the trainees drifted in and settled down to absorb my words of wisdom. Luckily the course was not one of the 'interpersonal' variety where the inevitable ice-breaker – usually employed by a lazy and ill-prepared trainer as a time filler – meant that you were required to 'share-your-most-outrageous-sexual-fantasy-with-the-person-on-your-right'. I'd endured one of these truly awful sessions some years previously. The 'person-on-my-right' turned out to be a lay [no, honestly!] Methodist preacher, and so the resulting conversation proved thankfully short.

Right, everyone appeared to be there. I introduced myself and reeled off the attendees' list; then it was time for action. First, the standard introduction as Roy's handiwork spiralled down from the ether onto the huge screen. Hmm, I thought, he's improved the layout, using more delicate colours; the music too was more than appropriate – I'd scolded him once because he'd pasted in the Beatles' hit *Give me money* when I was delivering an exit course to a particularly dispirited group – they'd only recently been informed of imminent redundancy. Then, as I glanced at my notes entitled 'FX, the possible repercussions on realisable assets', I became aware of laughter, restrained at first but then exploding as the trainees could hardly believe what they were hearing and seeing. Firstly, the music had suddenly changed as the audio treated them to *Simply the Best* and then, to my uncomprehending horror, on the screen, under the corporate heading and emblazoned in company livery was the startling instruction: 'Let's hear it for Sally, she's always Top of the Tit Parade!'

Bloody, bloody Roy, I growled to myself. Right. He's toast! Dead, buried, ancient history! Just wait till I get my hands on his scrawny little neck – I'll squeeze him so hard his pimples will burst! Duty called and I had to regain control of myself and set aside all thoughts of vengeance for the time being.

'Well, my friends.' A light touch here might just gain their sympathy. 'I'm sure I'm not the only one to suffer at the hands of those Data Services boys and their warped sense of humour.'

The trainees laughed.

'I think my friend back at base will have some irreparable problems with his joystick by the time I've finished with him.'

More laughter.

'Now, where were we, ah yes, FX – the weird and wonderful world of Foreign Exchange.'

I breathed a sigh of relief as the trainees' mirth evaporated when faced with the daunting challenge of Task 1. This was an exercise of such mind-numbing tedium that it made counting sheep interesting. By the coffee break, the unfortunate start to the day appeared to have been forgotten, publicly at any rate, and the course went on smoothly from there. At the end, the trainees thanked me warmly as they scurried off to the car parks to beat the worst of the traffic.

I gathered my things together, eyes still set in a steely gaze of determination and imminent blood letting. I couldn't wait to get back to the office and pounce on Roy so the appeal of Coventry cathedral would simply have to wait for another day. Unfortunately though, my grim plan was thwarted as a major pile-up on the M6 caused a two-hour delay. The only positive aspect was that this was close to Knutsford, Hugh's domain, and this gave me a warm feeling inside. As for Roy, he – without even being remotely aware of it – had secured a temporary stay of execution. But tomorrow was another day.

Every cloud has a silver lining

It was turned eight by the time I reached home. After a twelve-hour day, the embarrassment at the start of the session and finally the difficult drive back, I knew I wouldn't be able to raise the energy to rifle through the freezer for something to quell the nagging pangs of hunger. No, I'd decided to take the easy option and stop off at Mr Woo's – his sweet and sour pork with fried rice would fill the gap. Then, I'd enjoy a well-earned double snifter before my nightly séance in front of the computer. I really did enjoy conjuring up the spirits of phantom men as they roved, stalked and meandered along the superhighway in their eager search for a soulmate. Bingo! – Hugh. The traffic accident must have been an omen!

How are you tonight, my dear, and how is the frantic world of high finance? Do forgive the email approach but I tried your mobile without success I'm afraid. Here I am in a rather comfy Marriott in Harrogate for a trade fair. This is an annual event and a marvellous opportunity for networking which, as you would guess, is essential in my business, even though it can be rather dull on occasions. Still, there's the odd glass of Nuits St Georges to stimulate the proceedings. Now, enough about me – you

*could be forgiven for thinking I'm as stuffy as
one of those horsehair chaises longues I deal in
from time to time. Well, the real reason for my
contacting you is to see if we could possibly meet
up again quite soon? I remember that you're
a Virgo so your birthday must be in the near
future. I was wondering if the possibility of an
evening at the theatre followed by dinner might
be enough to entice you away from the delights
of spreadsheets and bar charts. Birthdays
are special events and must be celebrated
accordingly in my view. Do let me know if this
is a possibility and also the type of thing you
enjoy – I tend to go for the classics myself. I
hope to hear from you soon. With fond regards.
Hugh xx*

How was it possible for large vodka to disappear in
the blink of an eye? Must be the central heating, I thought,
desperately searching for an excuse for a refill – always
makes me thirsty. Just one more as I savour Hugh's
message. Mmm. That's nice. I smiled as I swirled the ice
cubes around the glass and, thinking of Hugh, felt genteel
sips were more appropriate than an unceremonious swig.
I liked the way he put things, that underlying refinement,
the warmth, the humour, the focus on 'you' were even
more intoxicating than tonight's liberal measure of
Smirnoff. Theatre plus dinner might 'entice… ', you bet
Mr Hugh; I'm looking forward to it already. Right, must

reply immediately – bet his diary has fewer windows than Wormwood Scrubs.

Hugh, so nice to hear from you. Sorry about the phone, I've been training all day in the Midlands and then got into a spot of bother on the motorway. It's very kind of you to ask me out again and yes, I'd love to come. As for my taste in the theatre, well, pretty general really. I've seen most of the musicals but I do like straight drama. I was in the dramatic society at school and we did some pretty good productions thanks to an inspired and inspiring teacher – we even tackled 'The Crucible' and some Shakespeare. So, I'll leave the choice of play in your capable hands, if that's all right. My birthday is September 13th, so a Saturday, the 10th or 17th, would be fine. Really looking forward to seeing you again. I so much enjoyed the Lowry evening. Has Edward offloaded my dear friend Arabella yet or, more likely, the other way round? See, I'm a terrible gossip! Lots of love. Sally xx

Ping. Off it went … oh dear, what have I done now?! I'VE OFFERED HIM TWO NIGHTS AND BOTH ARE SATURDAYS. He'll think I'm some sort of loser, little Miss Stay-at-home with her bottle of wine and box of chocolates. And 'Lots of love' – was that a mistake?

Too personal? Too warm? Too soon? Too late now, that's for sure.

A stay of execution

The combined effects of a hard day, alcohol and the inner warmth of being 'fancied' meant I dropped off to sleep easily. The next morning, I was refreshed, restored, ready for life, ready for action, ready for Roy! Because of yet another of Lesley's incessant demands I had to get into work earlier than usual and this on a Friday. Not surprisingly, therefore, I was already smouldering by the time I reached the car park.

As I bent over to the back seat to retrieve my briefcase, I was aware of a sudden movement on the second floor. I spotted the familiar red cap – Roy. Yes, there he was, safely, or so he thought, tucked away in his eyrie. He was watching my every move, and somehow I doubted he was simply admiring my choice of clothes for the day; I took an evil pleasure from the fact that he was totally unaware of his imminent extinction.

From the foot of the stairwell I heard a familiar screech.

'Roy, what the bloody hell are you gawping at? [He'd carelessly left the server room door open to allow air in]. I told you I want that Excel upgrade on my PC by ten at the latest! Just do it will you, just do it! And another thing – if you don't get rid of the silly cap, I'll chuck in the nearest shredder and you'll bloody well follow it!'

I chuckled and made my way up the stairs.

Of course it would have to be Lesley destroying his fantasies and consigning them to the shredder. Bloody bossy bitch, he must have thought, needs a good seeing to if you ask me but who would have the courage? To my shame I rather enjoyed the sight of him snatching off the offending headgear like a disciplined schoolboy. 'Oh yes, Lesley, sure, I've not forgotten – it'll be done in the next half-hour, promise.'

She didn't give him the grace of a reply but strode off, scowling, to her office, slamming the door behind her. The buzz in the office had been that she was supposed to be away all week on some management course or other. What could have brought her back, and on a Friday at that?

Lucy's face lit up when I came through into the office. 'Hello Sally, how did the Coventry course go? Oh, and thanks for the advice about those Far East reports. I've nearly completed the assignment, and Lesley doesn't need it until Tuesday. By the way, SHE is back – just what we need at the end of the week.'

'Well, never mind, we'll just have to cheer her up somehow won't we? Now, where did that hook-nosed, pockmarked, ferret-faced, evil-smelling apology for a human being called Roy scuttle off to? He and I need a little chat. I'll just get some coffee for us first.' Unfortunately, my hopes of delivering summary execution were dashed as Lesley's strident tones pierced the air, echoing along the corridor that led from the rest room to her office.

'Sally my office in five – about those expenses.'

For her, framing a request was synonymous with issuing an order. I made to reply but the Boss was gone, turning sharply on her heels and click-clicking her way back to her lair. I shook my head in disbelief but then caught sight of Roy, foolish Roy, who had been unwise enough to creep out from the security of his very own panic room, all for the sake of a Nescafé and a stale digestive.

'Hey Roy, come here you,' I snarled. 'What the bloody hell do you think you're playing at! What do you mean, "What do you mean?" YOU KNOW BLOODY WELL WHAT I MEAN! Tina Turner belting out her stuff and that "Let's hear it for Sally, always Top of the T ..." I wouldn't oblige him with the secondary thrill of hearing me utter his beloved T word.

And then ...

'And what's all this about?'

Lesley had suddenly appeared as if by magic, levelling her beady eyes, first at me, then at him.

'Well?'

'Oh, nothing Lesley, just a slight technical hitch on my laptop yesterday and Roy's just said he'll sort it for me by the end of the day, haven't you Roy, my dear little friend?' I replied with a truly saccharine smile.

'Er, yes, Sally, that's right'. His eyes were almost welling up with gratitude at this wholly unexpected – and undeserved – reprieve.

'I'm just about finished with Lesley's upgrade [he glanced at her for approval], then you're next on the list, definitely'. He beat a hasty retreat, mouthing a 'Thank you God' to the heavens.

'Wouldn't trust that tosser as far as I could throw him,' she snapped and then turned to me. 'Right, come on through.'

Promoting talent [1]

Lesley's office was entirely predictable, Spartan rather than minimalist. A desk, tidy and ordered, the computer at an angle to avoid the sun's glare and then, lined up as if for duty, her laptop, mobile, pocket calculator, her 'Holy Trinity' as she would often say at meetings. A decaying rubber plant sulked in the corner. The walls were bare except for the predictable printouts of flow charts, spreadsheets and bar charts. The only concession to individuality was a coaster, now heavily stained with more rings than the Olympic flag, bearing the fading motif 'The Great Caledonian Walk 2002'.

What followed was intriguing in the extreme.

She began by offering me some coffee then apologised for the delay over the expenses – 'a glitch in the system' – adding quickly that she had authorised a special cheque request so the money would be with her that week. Lesley offering coffee? Lesley offering an apology? Lesley offering to do a favour? All of this was as likely as George Michael going straight. Despite being pleasantly surprised, and not a little bewildered by her unusual show of magnanimity, I remained on the alert, being firmly of the belief that leopards did not change their spots; I instinctively felt that all of this was part of a softening up process, a pre-emptive strike. She was planning something, no question of it.

'As you will be aware, I've been away this week on one of *our* management summits. These seminars are really stimulating. We find that, away from the hurly-burly of the office, we can think outside the box, achieve the odd bit of social leverage here and there, and focus on straplines for the future. You do know what I mean don't you?'

Ignoring the slightly patronising tone of these opening remarks, I hesitated.

MY PREFERRED REPLY

'Oh yes, everyone gets plastered, and the married men desperately chase the   women all week.'

MY ACTUAL REPLY

'Yes Lesley, I do; I'm sure such occasions have several positive outcomes.'

Would she pick up the irony here? Apparently not. As she reached down into her briefcase, I glanced at my watch. What a waste of time – and I was being distracted from my principal task of the day, the public dismemberment of rancid Roy.

'Well,' she continued, as she theatrically placed an embossed folder on her desk. 'This time we've been analysing management structures. We've concluded that a degree of re-engineering is desirable with employee empowerment as its prime objective.'

Hmm. Red light! I can see more work coming my way, just wait and see!

'Yes, well, to be brief, we felt you were the ideal candidate for promotion. Take this folder away. Use it as background reading. You'll be able to download the actual application forms from the intranet next week. Any questions?'

The last phrase was uttered in a tone that signified none was expected.

I was momentarily stunned. 'Promotion? Me?' I stammered, knocked out of my stride by this totally unexpected development.

'Yes, you,' she replied, leaning towards me, with just a hint of menace. 'You've been here since you left school; you know the bank's systems, practices and procedures backwards. You're recognised as the most effective trainer in the north-west region. You-are-ready-for-fresh-challenges … [Dalek delivery underlining the implicit threat in all of this] … and a senior management position has to be the next step! Of course you can expect a considerable rise and you'll have a better car. This has to be right for you and right for the bank.'

She emphasised the apparently incontestable truth of this parting shot by tapping the desk fiercely with her yellow highlighter, rather like a particularly enthusiastic Morse code operator. Tap tap tap, tap tap tap.

Ping! 'Ah! At last, that miserable little toe rag has done something useful for a change; that will be my Excel upgrade coming through. Fine. This means I can now complete my interim Q3 report at last. Thank you.'

The meeting was clearly over. I left the office with my head spinning, walking, or rather stumbling, to my chair. The job news had been such a shock, I couldn't think straight. A shot of caffeine was called for. Ping! Oh what now? It's from Roy, just what I need. Wonder where's he's skulking, probably licking his wounds down in the basement with Dirty Dennis, the maintenance man who flogs dodgy DVDs.

Hi Sally. I always thought you were a star and now I know it's true. Thanks so much for bailing me out just then with She-who-must-be-obeyed. I thought I'd blown it big time. And as for the presentation, I'm really sorry – I honestly thought you'd pick it up when you checked it all out before the course started, hope it didn't cause you too much embarrassment [!] But that Tina Turner song you know, it's spot on – you're simply the best! Roy x

You clever little monkey, I thought, smiling, despite myself. You've emailed to avoid the more pressurised phone call or even a face to face where accountability really kicks in. Well, perhaps he could be forgiven ... but not immediately – he could stew for a bit! The day zipped by – it always did in a Lesley-free zone, better known as an LFZ; to universal relief, she was holed up in her bunker all day so everyone could get on with their own jobs, undisturbed.

In demand!

Friday night and the sweet taste of freedom inspired me to cook. Not much fun for one but the freezer would take the second portion. I'd conjure up a delicious chicken casserole, lots of herbs, tomato purée, new potatoes, vegetables and even cabbage out of homage to Mum. Then it was time for a quick chat with Caroline. The news was good. Bob was stronger by the day and there would be a full report at the Sunday conflab. I'd thought about asking her to go with me on the ball gown shopping trip but, truth was, Bob's setback had taken the wind out of her sails. Somehow, she wasn't quite the same girl, not quite as carefree, slightly more serious and certainly more focussed on home and family. No, I resolved to explore the unending delights of retail Utopia on my own. My Visa card would take a severe bashing but, hey, that's what credit cards were there for, wasn't it?

There was time now for a little cruising on Lake Dateandsee. Another hit. Ishmael, Dishy Ishie, that gleaming deity from the Indian sub-continent whose image on the picture gallery had been seriously tempting. He was a foreman in the textiles business and 'single'. But – and this was really odd – he had four children; there must be more to this.

THE MESSAGE: Hello Miss Sally. As you can see from my interests, my people's way of life is very important to me even though I am living here in Bradford far distant from my true home. I am praising Allah for His care of my four children, His gifts to me. I am wanting second mother for them, as it is that my wife died in childbirth last year. There are many Western women now who have interest in Islam because they are being impressed by the purity of the teachings of the Koran. Such a union will be helping Allah's dream of a world without conflict. I am believing that you are such a woman. I am respectfully asking that you consider me. Ishmael.

Well, what an offer! He might be 'dishy Ishie', but I was no Jemima Khan and things didn't work out for her and Imran, did they, in spite of the fact he's drop dead gorgeous with millions in the bank. But if Ishy's for real, I didn't want to offend him with some flippant response. This called for a sound, sober reply.

> *MY ACTUAL REPLY: Ishmael, thank you for your message and I'm so sorry to hear about the loss of your wife. I won't pretend to know much about Islam but I do know that family is important and it must be very hard for you to care for your children on your own. The fact is, though, I'm a Western girl through and through with no real desire to convert to anything else. Good luck with your search – I hope you find what you are looking for. Sally.*

Bzzbzzbzzbzz. The insistent tone of the mobile offered fresh hope. Ah, be still by beating heart, it has to be … it is! Hugh!

'Hugh, how are you and how was the trade fair in Harrogate?'

'Fine, my dear, fine – I'm surprised, nay, astounded to find you at home on a Friday night. I felt sure you would be enjoying a sumptuous dinner with some movie mogul after the latest premiere.'

'You flatter me, but don't stop! No, I'm not quite as young as I was and the closest I've been to a mogul is an Indian takeaway I know in Stretford, or was that a mughli?'

He laughed, perhaps appreciating my down to earth sense of humour, finding it a refreshing change to the shallowness of his business life.

'You know Sally, I'm inclined to think that you're wasted in banking; you should be in the media, advertising or writing TV scripts or something like that! Now, about that theatre trip. Can we settle on the eleventh do you think, if you're still available – forgive me, free – that is? We could go on to the Riad Marrakech again – you seemed to like it last time. Now, about the play itself – there's a drama festival on at the moment: Chekhov's *The Cherry Orchard*, Beckett's *Waiting for Godot* and Pinter's *The Birthday Party*. I plumped for the Pinter – do hope that suits?'

'Fine. I'm really looking forward to it.'

'Jolly good. I'll leave you to your beauty sleep now and, obviously, I'll be in touch before then. Goodnight, my dear.'

'Goodnight Hugh – take care.'

Hmm. Those plays. I sipped my drink and turned them over in my mind. Chekhov, isn't he one of those dire Scandinavians or Russians or something – you know, drama to commit suicide to? And Beckett. I'm sure we did him at school; something about two down-and-outs living in dustbins and gabbling on about the meaning of life – heavy or what! Pinter? – *The Birthday Party* sounds harmless enough – might be a comedy, you never know! Well, I'm still getting hits. It's operation ball gown tomorrow, can't wait, and, and, Hugh's been in touch – can't be bad. Er, and the job situation, well, I'll sleep on it.

A spot of retail therapy

The scent of the Selfridges *parfumerie* was as seductive as ever. This was my favourite shop in all of Manchester.

I was determined to look drop dead gorgeous for the ball and I'd booked an appointment with a 'personal shopper'. I generally trusted my own judgment when it came to clothes but it wouldn't hurt to get the opinion of someone who didn't know me – I might pick something completely different from my usual taste.

'Hello I'm Amanda, your personal shopper. Welcome to Selfridges.'

'Hello, Amanda, I'm Sally. I'm hoping you can do a quick Nicky Hambleton-Jones job on me and knock off the odd decade or do you think that's a case of mission impossible?'

'Why impossible? I'm sure we'll find what you're looking for.'

'Thing is, I'm looking for more than an outfit. On August 27th, I have to be the belle of the ball.'

'No worries. Let's apply some TLC to the process first by starting with coffee and croissants. You can tell me where you're going, the sort of thing you have in mind, what colours you like and then I'll get cracking collecting some things whilst you leaf through *Harpers*, *Cosmo* and *Vogue* for inspiration.'

'Sounds fabulous. Thanks.'

She left to sort out the coffee, and I idly flipped through the glamour magazines. Cazi's joke came to mind ... *Cosmo*, *Vogue* and *Woman's Weekly* all ran an article about female orgasms. *Cosmo* explained how to have one, *Vogue* explained how to have one with style and *Woman's Weekly* explained how to knit one! I was still tittering to myself when the beaming Amanda returned with coffee and a plate of dainty pains au chocolat and miniature croissants.

'Now, what is it that we're looking for today?'

'Right, I'm going to a summer ball at the Midland Hotel. It's for investment bankers from across the country. I'm going with Barclays' answer to Prince Charming and I've simply got to outshine every other Cinderella there.'

'Shouldn't be too difficult. You're really attractive and your hair and skin look fabulous. Are you sleek and sophisticated, hip and chic or hot and sexy?' Amanda smiled.

'Well, I'm thinking sleek and sophisticated with a hint of hot and sexy but I'll leave hip and chic to the under thirties.'

'OK, well, the most important thing is to feel comfortable in what you're wearing. That'll automatically give you confidence. Why don't I leave you for a while whilst I gather up a few things? I won't ask you what colours you prefer; I'll bring a selection and I ask only one thing … try them all on before passing judgment. My job is to help you try something you might not normally see yourself in. OK? Good. Now what size are you? A 12? And shoes? OK, a 6. Give me fifteen minutes and I'll be back with the first four. Relax and enjoy!'

Two hours, nine outfits and £585 later, Amanda carefully wrapped my 'goddess' apparel in tissue paper:

Ben de Lisi dress: £305

Kurt Geiger shoes: £140

Agent Provocateur body: £80

£60's worth of stockings, costume earrings, nail varnish and eye shadow. Jonathan had better be worth it and – note to self – tell Caroline this was what I wanted to be buried in if it all went wrong.

As I left Selfridges en route to The Blue Room for a celebratory glass of champagne, I saw Anne, my Internet catalyst, in the ground floor café bar stuffing herself with a huge portion of 'Death by Chocolate'.

'Hello Anne! Lovely to see you! Blimey, that's a doorstopper – are you hormonal or something?'

'Oh hello, love,' she replied with barely a smile. 'No, I'm not hormonal but definitely homicidal and possibly suicidal.'

'Oh no! What's wrong?'

'Oh, just the usual. Man trouble. That bastard Stuart, remember – that chef I was seeing? Well, he's been two-timing me, so I've dumped him.'

'No! You mean the one from that dating site?'

'Yes, that's the one. You know, I really thought he was different. We were getting on well then I find out he's been seeing some other dumb bird at the same time as me. And when I confronted him about it, he said, "Well Anne, I thought you knew what it's all about. The Internet is for fun, not for anything long-lasting." The bastard! I hope he catches his knob in the blender!'

I managed to stifle a guffaw.

'Oh, I'm so sorry but look, I can't believe they're all like Stuart, and when you're feeling better, I'm sure you'll be ready to try again.'

'I don't think so. At least not on the Internet anyway. I guess this has taught me the problem with these dating sites is that it's all TOO easy for men to be playing away. There's just so much choice, so many women to choose from. Anyway, enough of misery me and my troubles. How are things with you? You enjoying life?'

I considered telling her about my Dateandsee experiences but decided against it – in her present state, she certainly didn't need to hear about Dave, Hugh and Andrew et al. Instead, I played down how good life had been lately, and instead complained about work pressure; noticing the time, I said I needed to be on my way, and suggested that we got together for lunch or something soon.

Still, her experience did dampen my spirits to the extent that I passed on the champagne – a truly rare occurrence. By the time I was home, however, I'd managed to remind myself that two-timing had been going on since time immemorial – just think of Helen of Troy – it wasn't the technology at fault: it was people who remained faulty!

There's many a slip ...

The Fox was heaving when I got there; it was a lovely, warm summer evening and as the pub was one of only a few in the area with a beer garden business was particularly brisk. In between serving countless rounds, I was able to pick up on the news of the day from friends and acquaintances there but preferred to keep a discreet silence about my own adventures.

Sunday morning found me modelling my ball ensemble for an appreciative Caroline who kept up a suitable running commentary: 'And now, in a divinely sexy lace body, Heidi Klum sashays down the catwalk. My, oh my, what the average housewife wouldn't give for a body like that. And now she slithers into a deceptively simple satin sheath perfectly accentuating her trim waist and narrow hips. Fabulous! But can she walk in the diamanté sandals? Yes, she can! Cinderella you shall go to the ball!'

'Do you really like?' I asked. 'Please say yes. It cost me a fortune so it had better be worth a month on water rather than wine.'

'Darling, you look so heavenly, you could turn water into wine – it's gorgeous! Worth every penny. Now take it off before you spill something on it, then you can fill me in on your latest triumphs.'

We chatted away for another hour or so. It turned out that Bob's illness had really made her sit up and take notice of what was really important in life. She realised how much he and the kids meant to her and consequently was now all in favour of my quest to find my Mr Right via all means at my disposal, including the Internet.

Sunday evening promised to be quiet and leisurely. The site had few surprises. There was only a heartfelt plea from Dishy Ishie asking me 'please to reconsider'.

But there was a message on the answerphone from Jonathan. His plane home was delayed but he was hopeful of returning to the office on the following day.

Problem is all the girls in FX will be mistaking me for Enrique Iglesias but, of course, I'll only have eyes for you!

Dear old Jonathan, as cocky as ever but I couldn't help liking him … a lot.

The golf trip has been an outstanding success, even though I managed to win only three of the five trophies on offer. It's been tiring too but I'm sure that I'll be fully fit for our little soirée at the Midland Hotel, next Saturday, August 27th, in case it's slipped your mind Miss Bennet!

I texted a reply. *J, ball always in mind. Fab dress, shoes etc. Can't wait! S xx*

I was really tired and an early night seemed to be a good idea. Dring, dring. Dring, dring. 9.30 – on a Sunday evening; now who on earth could that be? Bet it's Jonathan affecting his Spanish accent; I'll get him sorted, pronto!

'Buenas tardes amigo,' I trilled – always thought that night school course would be useful sometime! – 'Dígame.'

'Oh, I'm sorry – oh dear,' said a bewildered but familiar voice. 'I was wanting to speak to our Sally but I must have made a mistake, so sorry …'

'Oh Mum, it's lovely to hear you – don't worry, that was me, just having a little joke. I thought it was a friend of mine. Now, how are you and how's Dad?'

'Oh I'm well thank you but Dad's not too good but I wanted to let you know that we've had to bring the family do forward because the pub got the date mixed up – they've got Debbie Smith's wedding that day – do you remember Debbie? Nice girl; she's nursing you know. I never thought she'd get married after that brush with …'

Bring it forward, I thought in alarm. Please God, not to the same day as the ball!

' … Anyway the pub said the end of August was OK and so we've booked for the twenty-seventh; it's a Saturday and I remembered you saying August was pretty empty for you so I said to Dad this won't be a problem for our Sally and we should be sitting down for tea about eight. Dad's even talking of getting some champagne; he's been bad with his back you know and the do's really given him something to look forward to and oh yes do you remember Mrs Burgess opposite? Well her daughter's … [I realised the futility of telling Mum about the ball; I could never put a social event before their happiness – I would just have to go up to the party.] ... just gladiated from Glasgow University doing them foreign languages I think and they're all going up there on that easyJet to see her get her decree so isn't that nice for them and ... and ... oh yes for the do I'm having a two- piece made and it should be really nice and ...'

No, there was no way round the problem. I'd have to trade the haute cuisine of the Midland Hotel for the Chicken Supreme of the Bricklayers' Arms. Now, what on earth was I going to say to Jonathan? Help!

Chapter 7

SORRY SEEMS TO BE THE HARDEST WORD

I slept badly that Sunday night. Even the coma-inducing properties of *The English Patient* failed to weave their customary magic and I wondered where I'd put that copy of Rushdie's *Satanic Verses*. The problem wasn't that the spending spree had grievously dented my credit card – already more abused than a boxer's punch bag – nor the fact that my finery would have to wait for another day. No, it was the prospect of having to face Jonathan. He'd seemed genuinely keen on me and he was obviously viewing the grand ball as a major tactical move in winning my affection, if not more. Still, I comforted myself with the thought that I would be even more restless if I let Mum and Dad down – they had to be my major priority.

And so, Monday came and with it a rather anxious drive to work. I passed Roy on the corridor, and for once there was none of the usual banter, slicked with all too obvious sexual innuendo; instead he struck a genuinely friendly and cheerful note.

'Hiya Sally – have a good weekend?'

It was as if in protecting him from the vengeful wrath of the ferocious Lesley, I'd acquired a new persona in his eyes. No longer was I a [highly desirable] sex object but rather a friend, a true 'mate' who had come to his rescue. Lust had been replaced by respect.

'Oh hello, Roy. Erm, yes, fine thank you – weekends go so quickly though don't they? See your lot did well down at Arsenal!'

Then, fearing that I was opening the door for a shot-by-shot account of United's rare victory over their arch rivals, I called over to Lucy. I apologised to Roy, now basking in the reflected glory of his team, explaining that I had to have a quick word with Lucy before the phones started. In fact, my intention was to contact Jonathan immediately – my firm belief being that you were halfway to solving a problem by tackling it head-on as quickly as possible. Lucy, though, looked thoroughly miserable, staring almost with incomprehension at her screen.

'Oh, just look at that for a start to the week. Great isn't it – just what I needed.'

NEXT TIME I ASK YOU TO DO SOMETHING, DO IT PROPERLY FIRST TIME INSTEAD OF FARTING ABOUT FOR A WEEK!

The aggressive style here and the lack of any opening greeting, produced the shock effect that had clearly been intended.

'Honestly, I did what I was asked to do. I've even been back to check her instructions but I seem to have messed up yet again. I'm beginning to think that she simply wants me out of here.'

'Look,' I said patiently, trying to soften the blow. 'We all know her bark's worse than her bite. I think she's due back in later today. Why don't you simply send her an email and ask to see her to find out what the problem is?'

'Oh thanks, that's a good idea; I'll do it right now and hope for the best.'

'OK, and Lucy, forward a copy of that email to me would you please. I can use it for one of my "How not to … " The real reason I wanted the email was that I'd had just about enough of Lesley and had decided to gather evidence in case I went head to head with her.

I moved over to my own desk, fired up my computer and saw exactly what my intuition had warned me to expect – an email from Jonathan.

And how is the worthy Miss Bennet on this perfect summer's day? You will be much pleased – nay, relieved I trust – to be informed that I have been assiduously practising the Military Two-step over the weekend so that you will not be tempted by some strutting Major! Now, I should be obliged if you would do me the honour of contacting me so that we might be able to discuss details such as timings, carriages, dance cards etc. Your obedient servant, Darcy.

I could have kicked myself. I realised now that I should have pre-empted this by mailing him from home on the previous evening, after the shock of Mum's call. But I always felt it better to speak to someone directly – email or texting was such a cop-out. Time to act; I phoned his extension.

'Ah, hello sweetheart – did you see my message?'

'Erm yes, Jonathan – thank you. That's why I'm ringing now to be honest. I need to speak to you urgently – the rest room will probably still be clear this early.'

'Sounds interesting! Always got time for a quickie with you, you know [unaware of me wincing at the other end of the line] – I'm on my way.'

Despite my use of the word 'urgently', deliberately chosen to give some intimation of impending disaster, he obviously had no inkling of any difficulty. This was going to be really awkward.

The rest room *was* vacant. I didn't waste any time. I launched into an explanation of why I'd have to miss the ball. I was totally honest in everything I said, and didn't seek to bolster my case by referring to the fortune spent on a stunning outfit nor by playing the family obligations card. I was sorry to have to disappoint him but hoped we'd be able to do something equally exciting in the near future. I was really, really sorry. There, it was done. I gulped and waited, eyes fixed on the floor. Throughout all of this he remained impassive, although I did detect a growing irritation, with all sorts of dire threats and grim recriminations screaming about in my skull.

'Well, that's it I suppose,' he said stiffly. 'Sorry it's turned out like this. I'd better get back to my desk; one or two *really* important matters to attend to.'

With that he was gone, leaving me to lick my self-inflicted wounds and to take in the full significance of the thinly veiled put down of his having 'one or two *really* important matters to attend to.'

Women!

In fact, I felt I'd got off lightly and breathed a sigh of relief as he swept out of the room. I quickly pulled myself together, and decided the best thing to do now was to plunge myself into my work. A year-on-year analysis of training courses and their respective take-up were sure to prove a powerful antidote to this less than blissful start to the week. In addition, Lesley would be descending soon – a chance to kill two birds with one stone. Ah yes – birds! From the corner of my eye I was alarmed to spot the determined approach of Brian, clutching what was bound to be an album of photographs from his epic adventure – *The Parrots of the Caribbean* or something like that; his hopeful, loyal sheepdog smile signalled a detailed commentary on the Rainbow Fantail or similar. Spare me – just what I need. I resolved to play it straight.

'Oh, hello Brian – and those must be your snaps. Look, you must let me see them sometime. Sorry I can't spare a minute now – important things to do for the boss. You know how it is!'

I continued to stare at the screen as I scrolled down a seemingly endless list of emails. The tactic worked, and Brian lurched reluctantly away, hoping to find a more willing audience elsewhere. I was determined to keep myself busy and worked throughout the lunch break.

Inevitably, though, by mid-afternoon the caffeine habit kicked in, and a quick visit to the rest room was needed. Scarcely had I taken my first sip of the steaming brew when Beverley [aka Miss Pricktease] came sauntering in followed by a gaggle of the FX girls from the second floor – Jonathan referred to them dismissively as his 'groupies'. Her miniskirt reminded me of the pelmet in Mum's sitting room: a similar colour and definitely the same dimensions. Her legs looked like an Immac advert. The girls' shrill laughter reverberated around the room as she continued her tale, flashing her gleaming teeth and tossing her flowing blonde mane like some rosette winning pony at a local gymkhana. She spoke louder than usual, making absolutely sure that I, obviously identified as her chief rival, would be left in no doubt about the reason for her euphoria.

'Yes girls, can you believe it – Jonathan mentioned it to me this morning as I got in – what a fantastic start to the week! Isn't he sweet; he told me that he'd been intending to invite me to the grand ball at the Midland for weeks now but thought an invitation nearer the time would be an even bigger surprise? Aren't I the lucky one! … She paused, her eyes locked momentarily on me in a steely glint of triumph. He's got absolutely everything arranged, including a limo to pick me up would you believe [chorus of oohs!!]. It should be fabulous: dinner first – silver service of course – then the dance, then some more champagne and then? And then? Well, we'll just have to see won't we?' This was greeted by squeals of laughter.

Beverley, if only you knew, I thought, determined to keep my counsel.

'So, girls,' she announced, 'If you do see his silver Mercedes whisking me off at the end of the day, it's because we're going for a drink after work to discuss the details.'

My mind numbed by this outrageous show of bravado, I quietly retreated to my desk. I couldn't deny envying Pricktease's good fortune at my expense, and I mentally speared Jonathan's groin with lethal barbs. I fantasised about different acts of revenge, each exceeding the former in its level of uncurbed savagery. It was then that I glanced across to Lucy. Her lower lip was trembling, and she raised a hand to her face in a vain effort to conceal her mounting distress.

'Come on now love, what's the problem?' I knew full well that the poor thing must have been injected with yet another shot of venom from her poisonous boss.

HOW BLOODY KIND OF YOU TO BE PREPARED TO SPARE ME TWO MINUTES OF YOUR PRECIOUS GOSSIPING TIME!! IN FACT I WON'T BE IN THE OFFICE UNTIL THURSDAY SO YOU HAVE UNTIL THEN TO DO THAT BLOODY REPORT PROPERLY. YOU SHOULD HAVE REALISED THAT I NEEDED COMPARATIVE DATA NOT JUST THIS BLOODY YEAR'S FIGURES – SO SORT IT!

'At least she's made it abundantly clear now. Look, Lucy, I'll be in early tomorrow before I leave for that course in London I talked to you about. We can do some useful preparatory work together then.'

She snuffled a pitiful thank you from the depths of her damp Kleenex. I could see that the kid's confidence was deliberately and gradually being eroded by Lesley's relentless demands and aggressive manner. Where would it end?

Planning ahead

What with one thing and another it had been a pretty fraught day. I realised that, unfortunately, I would simply have to put the Jonathan disappointment down to experience. Now, I had one or two important jobs to do, the main one being to contact several girlfriends about a night out to celebrate my birthday. Saturday the 17th of September wasn't far off, and I might need to book somewhere. So, drawing up a list, I texted them all in sequence, except for Caroline. I wanted to speak to her to see if she was any more settled after our emotional conversation of the previous week. But first the girlies!

Sat 17 Sept. La Tasca @ 8. R u up 4 it? Txt me asap. The b'day girl. X

La Tasca – the top tapas bar with a side order of Latin lovers.

Now for Caroline. 'Hello Cazi – thought I'd see how you're getting on. And how's Bob – back to his lovable old pestering self again and making the most outrageous demands on your exciting body?'

'Oh, thanks, yes, I'm feeling a lot better now. Things are a lot clearer and I've finally got my priorities right. And His Lordship? Yes, he's getting there – fed his salad to next door's tortoise – said he wanted sausages and mash pronto so I'm sure he's on the mend. In fact, he's here now, scratching his crotch watching beach volleyball from California! What about you?

'Well, I'm actually seeing a rather nice bloke at the moment – Hugh. Shut up, will you – I'm just about to tell you! Yes, Hugh, and he's as smooth as his name suggests. No, he's not a dodgy gynaecologist. What? Cazi! That's rude you naughty girl – wash your mouth out immediately! No, he's in antiques actually. No, that's *not* why he selected me you cheeky bugger. Had a great time last week – had a drink with him on Monday and then on Wednesday we went to an art gallery … yes, yes, go on, have a long yawn, very funny – you know that modern place in Salford? And afterwards we went on to a Moroccan restaurant. What? No I did NOT have sheeps' eyes poached in mint-flavoured yoghurt. Honestly, it was delicious AND I'm seeing him again soon – in fact, the week before we all go out for my birthday bash … what? … Yes, September 17th; I've just texted the girls. Yes, La Tasca again, but this time, please spare us Uma Paloma Blanca and don't summon the waiter with, "Hey Juan, get your cute Latino butt over here."'

And so it went on. She was very much her old self now, full of life, joking and swearing, much to my relief after the distress and worry of recent weeks.

From Liverpool with Love

Sparky Dave was history, Andrew a million miles away recolonising South Africa, and Jonathan, sadly but definitely, a no go area; still, there was Hugh: kind, considerate, charming Hugh; he was so entertaining and such superb company but not yet ticking all the necessary emotional boxes. Perhaps a brief foray into the undergrowth of Dateandsee might flush out some interesting specimens. Ah yes, I've noticed him before – he's quite good-looking actually and now he's contacting me; that's it – Leonard 'Call me Lenny' from Liverpool. Kop that – love it!

> THE MESSAGE: *Hiya Sally, I loved your posting on the site – a Mancunian with a sense of humour and obvious good taste as well [most of my mates think Bolly is a starter at the local Indian]. It'd be great it if we could meet up, perhaps here in Liverpool; the 'Ferry across the Mersey' is still chugging away you know! Hope to hear from you. Lenny.*
> *P.S. So you're a Virgo too. That has to be a good sign, geddit?*

THE PROFILE:
Name: Leonard
Age: 43
Location: Merseyside
Status: Divorced
Children: Three
Job: Film Technician
Height: 6'1"
Build: Medium
Appearance: Attractive
Eye Colour: Hazel
Hair: Brown
Religion: Christian [non-practising]
Star Sign: Virgo
Smoker: No
Drinker: Moderate

INTERESTS: Football (Everton FC), cinema, home movies, Internet, Travel, especially Thailand.

ABOUT ME: Successful, solvent, sober and sartorially elegant Scouser – honest! I like to think I'm a bit unusual, not one to follow the crowd but more interested in finding my own approach to life. Individual, a bit eccentric possibly. This means being dead straight with people, with me it's definitely WYSIWYG. My three children have just

> *about flown the nest now. The oldest is married, the middle one's in the Army, in Iraq actually, and the youngest bless her is at university. We got married early, the kids came quickly – I don't know, perhaps this led to the break-up. But that's life. As for my second marriage, well it was one of those on the rebound jobs and I think we both realised soon it wasn't going to work out. So, that's my story – love to hear yours. Lenny*

> *MY PREFERRED REPLY: Well. Lenny it's quite refreshing to meet someone as open as you. Actually, I do know Liverpool quite well as I worked in the Bootle branch for a short spell – nearly died of sheer boredom, nothing to do all day because Scousers and loan repayments are mutually exclusive. Whoops – sorry, just that awful sense of humour you referred to. You know, we might just hop on that ferry sometime. Regards, Sally*

In fact, after some thought, I decided not to send a reply for the moment. I had quite a lot on my plate already in the immediate weeks ahead but I mentally registered Lenny [the long-haired lover from Liverpool] as a 'probable' for the future.

Ah, here's someone else – my God – a foreigner! Henrik from Stockholm. This has got to be worth a look.

Time to go global?

THE MESSAGE: Hello Sally. Your obvious sunny personality is really pleasing to me. I consider that you have an open approach to life and to the world, which is very much the manner we Scandinavians are. If you would like to read my particulars, you might extend your horizons to Sweden; I hope certainly that you will. Henrik.

THE PROFILE:
Name: Henrik
Age: 46
Location: Stockholm, Sweden
Status: Divorced
Children: One
Job: Civil Servant
Height: 5'11"
Build: Medium
Appearance: Attractive
Eye Colour: Blue
Hair: Dark Blonde
Religion: Christian
Star Sign: Aries
Smoker: Yes
Drinker: Moderate

Kelly Carter

> INTERESTS: Winter sports, jazz music, theatre, books by English writers, the natural world.

> ABOUT ME: All nationalities have their stereotypes. Most people think that every person in Scandinavia is the same. That they all drive Saabs, live in Ikea homes, meet for village Abba Parties and retreat into their igloos at the fall of the first snowflake. You, I feel sure, will find it of interest that I do not fulfil any of this. I am very outward looking. I prefer the open land to the city. I enjoy – how do you call it? – yes, the 'buzz' of winter sports. Also I love observing God's creatures in their natural habitats. But as you can see I enjoy culture as well. Books by John Grisham and Ian McEwan are special favourites of mine. Company in all of this adds to the experience I find. To glimpse a pair of sea eagles sweeping high above the archipelago or the seals slipping off the rocks into the waters is wonderful – but even more so with a close companion. Are you perhaps the English lady who could become my 'close companion'?

MY PREFERRED REPLY: Henrik, I must come clean. I have to confess that I fell straight into the open pit of conventional thinking when I began to read your posting. Visions of flaxen-haired babes in multicoloured Abba outfits with the dazzling snow reflected in their spandex, trudging valiantly through raging blizzards on nine inch platforms – sorry about that. It was really interesting to read about you and what you find important in life. It was all very refreshing. I hope to contact you again in the not-too-distant-future as I have a particularly heavy workload at the present.
Best wishes. Sally
P.S. I'm a regular at IKEA – love the meatballs.

I read through my preferred reply again and decided that it would fit the bill, so off it went. I was really quite excited by this. I did have a lot of work on but going global would be a real change – quite an adventure in fact. I made a mental note to check out Ryanair for cheap flights to Stockholm.

Who needs promotion?

I spent most of the following morning with Lucy, poring over acres of data. She had been right. Lesley's instructions had been vague and woolly – it was as if the kid had been set up to fail. Still, we made sound progress, and I was able to leave her in a much more confident frame of mind, cheering her up even more with the promise of that shopping day out sooner rather later.

For a change, I'd decided to go to London by rail – much more straightforward and relaxing; I could open up the laptop to add some final touches to the presentation. I was pleased but not surprised to see that, this time, Roy had played it by the book; his input was impeccable – he was well and truly forgiven.

With a string of social commitments in the offing, I was glad of some time on my own. The hotel near Euston was nothing special but it was clean and secure. There were several good restaurants nearby as well. The training courses themselves went like a dream and, with Jonathan most definitely in the 'jobs pending' file, I felt reasonably content with life. And then, just when I thought it was safe to open my emails ... on the return journey to Manchester, I picked up the latest missive from Lesley. Typically, it was terse and to the point, but without the venom that tended to characterise her style.

I see from your diary that, because of the 'trainers' summit' you won't be in the office until Friday afternoon. Are you sure you need to be there? I find these summits are generally a waste of time. Anyway, I need to see you about that promotion. Time is getting short and the deadline is approaching fast. My office at 3.30 prompt.

'3.30 prompt': bloody great – doesn't his woman ever give up? Just when I was hoping to skip off a little earlier to beat the worst of the traffic on the M6. As far as the promotion opportunity was concerned, the truth was that, as yet, I hadn't so much as glanced at the details. I simply had no interest in applying for the job. As far as I could see, promotion at the bank meant more money in exchange for a shed load of additional responsibilities and allied pressures. Not exactly a fair swap. Still, I could at least download the information from the company's intranet. This would provide the basis for what I was determined would be a brief meeting with Lesley on the following afternoon.

The most cursory perusal of the advert confirmed my decision against applying.

Post: Client Relationships Interface Manager

The job title itself had the same deterrent effect as two free tickets to a Des O'Connor concert.

Location: North West

Reward Structure: Negotiable but within MMS parameters

We are on the cusp of implementing a radical realignment of the company/client interface. To achieve our goals, we are replacing the ladder of progress by a climbing frame of opportunities …

What the bloody hell is all that about?

Recognising that the assets of our key personnel will grow exponentially with our clients' pressing need for a comprehensive and exciting product range …

Hmm … are our clients aware of their 'pressing need'?

… It will be your challenge in this provider/consumer nexus to meet, indeed exceed, company/client expectations …

Initial expressions of interest must be with Central HR no later than Friday 2 September.

Into the lioness's den

The trainers' summit, contrary to Lesley's and, it must be admitted, my own scepticism, proved really useful; the group developed some innovative ideas about virtual classes and online training, supplemented by tutor-led sessions. It was all really good stuff. At lunchtime I grabbed a sandwich and a bottle of spring water before reaching the office at 12.30. Lucy wasn't at her desk; this was most odd because she was a creature of habit and always went for lunch at one as regular as clockwork. Perhaps she'd left early to get some last minute shopping done before the holiday weekend.

I just had a moment to switch on my computer. 'URGENT!' from Roy. What's he up to now, I wondered. Hope it's not a peace offering by way of tickets to a Man U reserves match. I read his message – at first in a bored, rather detached manner, but then with increasing alarm, if not fury.

Sally, for God's sake, watch it when you get in today. Lesley is on the warpath big time. She sacked Lucy this morning in the rest room would you believe just after eleven when it was still pretty full, had to be deliberate timing. Bawled her out something shocking. The poor kid just burst into floods of tears and ran out. Please delete this immediately! Otherwise Lesley will have my bollocks on toast if she finds out I've told you all this, especially as I was pretty close to the chop last week! Roy x

It was as if a sledgehammer had hit me; I sat motionless. So many thoughts were racing through my mind that I found it difficult to concentrate. I remembered that first 'drop in meeting' with Lesley when she dished out a number of tasks with the trickier ones going to the prettier, younger women. And, yes, since then, her demands on Lucy had been increasingly onerous and when fulfilled, as they invariably were, they had been acknowledged with a sour comment rather than the fulsome praise they deserved. Lucy had been spot-on. From day one Lesley had wanted rid of her, and she had succeeded. The afternoon session was likely to be somewhat more than an informal chat. The bitch was going to get it, like it or not!

It wasn't until four that she buzzed me to join her – an innocent delay or deliberately timed to disrupt my holiday plans just that little bit more?

'Ah, Sally, nice to see you – do sit down. Coffee?'

'No, thank you, I won't.'

'OK, fine, right, now – down to brass tacks – how's that application of yours coming along for that marvellous promotion opportunity?'

'I won't be applying – I'm not interested.'

'What do you mean, "not interested"? This is a godsend – this sort of thing doesn't come up every week you know.' She obviously saw my lack of interest as mutinous, a challenge to her position, to her authority.

'It doesn't matter – I've got other priorities at present.'

'Other priorities? Ah, yes – you mean men. Well if you're putting your sex life ahead of your career, then I for one think …'

This coarseness mingled with the still-seething sense of injustice at Lucy's fate was the seismic rumbling that triggered my volcanic eruption.

'What the bloody hell are you talking about? "Men", "sex life" – my priorities are *my* business, not the bank's and certainly not yours. Do you understand? *Not yours.* You owe me an apology – now!'

169

The air crackled with tension. She looked daggers at me.

'Who do you think you're talking to? I'm the boss around here remember, not you and I don't …'

'I couldn't give a toss about that Lesley – I'm past caring; you've insulted me and I want an apology!'

She was speechless. Like all bullies, she hadn't reckoned on retaliation and when it came, it knocked her off her stride. She became more and more fidgety. gulping down her coffee and fiddling about on her keyboard – ploys to gain time as she fished around frantically in the deep, murky pond of her malevolence for some piranha-type response. None was to be found. A decoy move was the best she could manage.

'Ah, I get it. None of this is really about the promotion thing is it? How foolish of me. You must have picked up on this Lucy business from some loudmouthed twat in the office – probably that miserable little turd Roy. He's got his cards well and truly marked I can tell you. And as for that snivelling little loser Lucy. Well, for your information a report she'd produced for me – I'd given her ages to do it – was total crap! Then the little shit tried to stand her ground in front of everybody. If you must know why I got rid of her it was for "infringement of business procedures" – got it?'

She was becoming increasingly agitated and ever more foul-mouthed because I just continued to look at her impassively, unperturbed, in control as much as she was out of control.

'And, oh yes, she can run off and whinge to some bloody industrial tribunal as far as I'm concerned but so what? Probably won't have the guts to do it – and anyway, if she did win, a few thousand quid compensation is a drop in the ocean to the bank.'

I fixed my eyes unblinkingly on her. The noise of the traffic was clearly audible. Despite that, here in the grim HQ of Lesley's domain, you could hear the proverbial pin drop.

'Now look,' I began, in a steady, unwavering and, frankly, threatening tone. 'You must know that your behaviour is totally out of order. It's utterly unprofessional. Just for the record, I'd decided long since that the promotion route wasn't for me – that's got absolutely nothing whatsoever to do with Lucy's problem. But I'm telling you now [finger wagging to emphasise the point] if she does go legal on this one – and I for one certainly hope she does – then she'll have my 100% backing at the tribunal, do you hear?'

Lesley was now completely at a loss; her bluff had been well and truly called. 'Hang on a moment Sally; things are getting out of hand a bit – all I meant was ... ' But just as she was blurting out a pathetic apology, her office walls shuddered as I slammed the door behind me. Do your worst, you bloody evil little woman!

Chapter 8

Home sweet home

To intensify my fury with Lesley, a serious accident had shut the motorway northbound. I phoned Mum to say I wouldn't be able to make it up there until the following day because of this serious accident. This wasn't a problem for her as she was under the impression that I wouldn't be coming until the Saturday anyway. Predictably I was still preoccupied with Lucy, a sweet, young innocent impaled on the merciless spear of Lesley's jealousy. Other phone calls, the dating site, even Caroline would have to be put on hold. All I could think of was Lucy right now.

Lucy's mum breathed a sigh of relief when she recognised my voice. The girl was in her room, in a state of shock. The dismissal had proved traumatic, and it was the first major setback in her albeit short working life, her first exposure to malevolence. She added philosophically that it might be for the better because she'd been unsettled ever since Lesley's arrival at the bank. She'd lost weight, slept badly and was no longer the settled and contented youngster she used to be. In recent weeks she'd even been talking about looking for a new job. She'd sobbed her heart out, saying that if I rang, would I mind contacting her in a few days' time as hearing my voice would start off the tears once more. I understood perfectly and ended by sending my love and saying I'd be in touch again in the near future.

The day's events, deeply distressing though they were, could not be allowed to cloud the weekend with Mum and

Dad; this was their time. I reached their trim little bungalow for morning coffee and, although I felt immediately felt at home, I was more than a little troubled. The front garden was relatively unkempt. The lawn hadn't been mown to its usual high standard, and coarse grass was springing up liberally. The flowerbeds were arid, the plants were wilting and the normally startling red of the geraniums and blazing yellow of the marigolds had faded badly. The cracks between the flagstones on the pathway up to the front door were choked with ugly weeds. How dispiriting all of this was. Gardening – along with cricket – had been Dad's consuming passion – he'd even won prizes in the local horticultural shows. Did this sorry neglect point to a lack of interest or, worse still, the debilitating impact of his advancing years?

Mum brought the coffee through on a tin tray with a garish, autumnal picture of the Lake District. Her movements – when compared with Dad's – were still nimble. She was slightly built; her hair, tied back tightly in a bun, had stayed surprisingly dark though it was traced now with filaments of silver. Her face was small and round, her cheeks and forehead lined but far from wrinkled. There was a quickness and vitality in her eyes, which danced with glee now that her beloved daughter was at home.

'Dad won't be a minute love. He's just popped out to get the paper. You know what he's like with his cricket scores.'

Moments later the key turned in the lock and I leapt up to greet him. I caught my breath. I hadn't seen him since the Easter visit and he seemed to have aged so much since then; he was *so* haggard. What little hair he had was now pure white. He was slow in his movements and slower in his reactions. Once tall and erect, he had visibly shrunk. His grey cardigan hung limp about his chest and seemed several sizes too big for him, as did his trousers; he hadn't fastened his leather belt properly, and it drooped down over his thigh like a lolling, black tongue. His watch hung loose around his scrawny wrist, as the strap had run out of holes to fasten it securely. Nevertheless his eyes lit up as I kissed and embraced him warmly.

'Oh love, it's great that you've found the time to come and see us isn't it, Margaret', he said, squeezing his wife's hand. I could have choked. 'You see, I've not been too good sweetheart, fell in a heap in the middle of the Wichita Waddle at the club last week. Didn't quite catch what the caller said – my hearing you see. I knocked over the tea trolley and sent the cups and saucers flying all over the place – the hall looked as if a bomb had hit it. Only good bit was that we were allowed to keep the broken biscuits, weren't we Mam?'

'Now, love – no need to go on about it so much; you'll be on about Dunkirk next. Let's have some coffee and those nice Jaffa cakes I bought specially.'

As she poured the coffee from the old-fashioned dark brown teapot, my eyes swept around the room. She had obviously been tidying up as she always did when they had 'company'. She always took great care with the 'ornaments' – mainly small horse brasses, figurines of animals and gaily coloured Toby jugs. An enormous TV dominated the room; 'it's got one of those new fangled plastic screens you know', she'd said proudly, 'but it's so difficult to work – really complicated you know'. The set had been an anniversary present from friends and relatives who had clubbed together to sustain Dad's interest in sport. The two familiar photographs were on top – one, in black and white, was of their wedding day. They both stared grimly into the camera in the style of the times. Mum looked lovely in her wedding dress, which was fringed with lace, and Dad was impressive in his army uniform. The other, in colour, was of me in my christening robe, a little bundle of cherubic perfection in the arms of a doting mother. *The Laughing Cavalier* hung alongside the old windmill plaque on the chimney breast. The dark green suite was showing distinct signs of age, and the castors squealed in protest when the settee was moved. The fireplace was made of white and brown tiles. This overall outdated aspect though was radically changed whenever the gas fire was lit – its spiralling jets of orange and scarlet flames lending a welcome cosiness to the room. The set of brass implements was still on the hearth: tongs, a brush and miniature shovel – their usefulness now long gone.

Over coffee the conversation inevitably turned to a catalogue of the dead and the dying which was a central topic whenever we got together. Most of the names meant nothing to me but I was content to play along. I didn't find it odd that Mum still got the *Manchester Evening News* simply to read the obituaries.

'Oh he's gone – didn't think he'd last long after his big op last year.'

'You remember Cissy don't you Dad – been a creaking gate for years she has.'

Perhaps this is what happens when you reach their age. Would I ever be lucky enough to exchange news with anyone in my later years? To reverse the mood, I popped back to the car for Dad's birthday present. Finding something suitable had been something of a problem. What on earth do you buy for a man who reaches eighty-four? All the usual material possessions are in place; clothes are a bit dull; the usual daily cocktail of tablets rules out alcohol. Then, I'd had brainwave, and had even sought Roy's advice, before surfing through *Amazon* to find what I needed.

'There you are Dad! Many, many happy returns!'

As he carefully removed the wrapping paper, his eyes positively gleamed with pleasure. *An Illustrated History of English Test Cricket.* The tome was beautifully produced and promised endless hours of enjoyment. He was absolutely delighted with the present – it was as if I'd given him the Crown jewels.

As the day wore on some friends and relatives turned up, and they all left in convoy for the evening venue. Mum had changed her mind about the 'catering'; the steak meal had been supplanted by a cold buffet. 'Everyone can help themselves you see and it'll be easier to clear things away for the disco later.'

My ears pricked up in alarm. 'Disco'? I had worrying visions of septuagenarians – and these were the younger ones – hauling themselves up onto the dance floor to strut their stuff under the glittering, revolving globe, itself a relic of a forgotten culture; I sensed trouble ahead.

'Well love if you have a disco it works out cheaper,' Mum explained, obviously chuffed that she'd been able to strike a bargain with the management. All of my financial training couldn't quite work out how something priced at £18 a head could actually be cheaper than the initial quote of £15. But there was nothing to be gained from questioning Mum's business acumen.

Strictly come dancing

French windows opened from the car park into the function room. Trestle tables there were groaning under the collective weight of endless platters of sandwiches, filled rolls, vols-au-vent, 'fancies' and trifles. It all *looked* quite appealing but I did wonder how long it had been standing there; I suspected that the salmon might already be suppurating. The chicken legs too – their tops blackened through reheating – presented a real challenge, even though the waxen pink of their underside made for a pleasing contrast of colour.

Later in the evening the perky DJ appeared; this was 'Willy the Wally from Wallasey'. He was about 5'2" and as broad as he was tall. His open-necked shirt betrayed an upper chest with a crude tattoo of an armed soldier crouching under a defiant 'No Surrender' slogan – perhaps an emblem of some youthful affiliation. A silver earring in his right ear balanced the miniature gold bolt through his left eyebrow. He was as bald as a coot and his skull was already streaked in sweat owing, no doubt, to his constant moonwalking. Every now and then he paused to mop his glistening brow with a used serviette, blissfully unaware that it left him smeared with tomato stains. And, as to his performance, well, although an objective critic might have gently suggested to him that his best days were over, he clearly felt he was at the apex of his career, modelling himself on Peter Kay; sadly, his repartee and timing were not quite up to Peter's impressive standards. This actually didn't make that much difference because most of the guests were hard of hearing, and the music reached a rate of decibels unequalled since the Live8 concert.

I did my very best to get into the swing of things, even shimmying a little with Uncle Bob whose lecherous eye was undimmed by the passage of years. I smiled and chatted away amicably with everyone, even if they clearly knew me, and I didn't have a clue about them. The opening bars of *Is this the way to Amarillo?* hinted at impending disaster. Sure enough, before you could say Tony Christie, there was Dad in the middle flanked by his friend from bowls, Norman, 'who should have known better' (at seventy-three, he was the junior partner) and close neighbour Albert (ably supported by a knotty walking stick). Their showmanship earned a tumultuous applause that grew louder as they sought to gyrate in time with the pounding rhythm. Then, at the very first 'Daa di daa di daa di daa daa' Albert's stick slipped from his hand and went skittling into a radiator on the wall opposite. Dad, losing his support, felt his knees buckle under him and with a sorry cry he ended up in a crumpled heap.

The DJ sought to make light of the situation by observing smartly, 'Hey up, someone's overdone the Boddington's over there,' as we rushed to his assistance, propping him up on a chair. He apologised profusely, saying that he'd better stick to the Kentucky Kickalong in future. 'At least I know all the moves to that ...' Beneath the forced humour though he wasn't at all well – he'd turned ashen and was still gasping for breath. He had just about enough energy left for the parting *Auld Lang's Syne* before being gratefully helped along to the car for the journey home.

We spent the rest of the weekend quietly as he was still not at his best. As we did the washing up together, Mum gently asked about my 'new friend', but I swished the tea towel and laughed it off saying that my job with its sixty hour week left little time for romance.

On the Monday afternoon, I gave them a particularly warm hug and left for home, whispering to Mum to keep me posted on Dad's condition. As I drove away, I gave them a cheery wave through my rear mirror but felt sick at heart; Dad's frailty was now becoming a major concern.

World news

A quiet evening in – just a few hundred thousand Dateandsee hopefuls and me. Yes, messages from Alderley Edge Andrew and Stockholm Henrik.

Hillo. Endroo hee-are! Sorry my dear, can't sustain this curious accent any longer. You'll have me grunting like the blacks next and that would be a disaster. Just a note to let you know that we've had a severe setback on the business front, bloody red – or should I say – black tape again I'm afraid. These people seem more interested in getting revenge than in getting on. Talk about turning the screw! Anyway, the thing is I'll be out here until January now, 'I'm dreaming of a black Christmas' as it were. Is the Bolly still unbroached? Yes? You're a real star! Andrew xx

This sort of thing was really beginning to annoy me now. I'd been inclined to overlook his earlier crass asides but this was just too much. The imposing Cheshire mansion – if it existed at all – was no compensation for life with an overt racist. I was tempted to give him a piece of my mind but decided it would probably be a waste of time; instead, I settled on a different approach.

Hello Andrew. Thanks for your message. I'm sorry things have been difficult for you. In fact, my life has undergone some changes recently. I've started seeing someone, from work actually, not the Internet. I guess dating, like most things in life, is all about timing. Hope you find what you're looking for on Dateandsee. Best wishes, Sally

---

Right, that's Africa sorted – now off to Scandinavia and my Viking; what news from the tundra?

Hello Sally. I felt I wanted to write to you quickly in order to thank you for your kind reply. Your sense of humour is most definitely English. I don't always fully understand the irony and so you will have to educate me when we meet. I will leave you now to your files and spreadsheets. I hope to hear from you again when the work pressures are alleviated. Best wishes. Henrik

---

Dag Henrik. See I'm already half- fluent in Swedish. I'll be in touch soon. Sally

News of the grand ball

Given the tumult in the office of the previous week I wasn't at all relishing the prospect of returning to work. To my amazement there was an email from Lesley to say that she'd decided to take some leave due to her; she would be off walking in the Lake District for a few days and we would talk further on her return. Well, this *was* welcome news – perhaps the ongoing feud would soften to the point of peaceful co-existence after all, and, who knows, there may be hope for Lesley yet – she does have an interest outside work! Yes, I concluded, it was no bad thing that she was out of the picture for a spell; this would help things calm down.

Taking the almost statutory mid-morning break in the rest room was a big mistake; I reproached myself later, realising that I should have known better. Beverley was there with her posse of young admirers, giving a colourful and almost intimate account of the proceedings before, during and, most tantalisingly, after the ball.

' ... And as for Jonathan, well I've never known a man with such energy [pause for dramatic effect]. He plays golf all day, spends the entire evening bopping away until two in the morning – couldn't take his eyes off me; nor his hands for that matter!'

Howls of laughter.

'Anyway, one nightcap followed another and … well, before you could say king-size [...more inane howling …] there I was in this enormous suite: the business – plasma screen TV, drinks cabinet with everything you could want, two bathrooms but we only needed one shower! His and hers bathrobes – not that we had any use for them! Well we finally got to sleep – about four it must have been – I thought, well done girl – you've really cracked it this time – mind you, I could scarcely walk straight when I did get up about midday.'

The further frenzy of shrieking laughter that followed proved to be the last straw, and I quietly made for the door; but eagle-eyed Beverley wanted her final pound of flesh.

'Oh, hello, Sally, I didn't see you sulking in the corner over there. By the way, Jonathan did say how nice it was to be out with a younger woman for a change – just thought I'd let you know.'

The other girls did their best to stifle their laughter but Beverley's magnetic personality carried the day, her eyes now positively shining in triumph. I gave her a withering look and made a mental note – come the revolution, Beverley and Jonathan would be the first lined up against the wall for summary execution.

A dramatic evening

I hadn't forgotten Lucy. I phoned and was pleasantly surprised to find how composed she was. She said that that she'd slept well for the first time in weeks, and also had three job interviews to attend; there was a boyfriend on the scene as well. No, an industrial tribunal wasn't a real option; she said it would simply be too upsetting. She wanted to erase Lesley from her life and start afresh.

'Lucy, that's great news! Job interviews *and* a boyfriend eh? Look, how about doing that shopping trip this weekend? See if we can get the perfect outfit for your interviews and of course something drop dead gorgeous for your new man?'

'Brilliant – I'd love to. Where shall we go?'

'Oh, let's think big and make a day of it. How about the Trafford Centre then an early dinner in that Mexican place in the food avenue? I'll pick you up about ten this Sunday. Can't do Saturday I'm afraid – I've got a date but at least the shops will be a bit quieter on Sunday.'

'No prob. Sunday's great. Thanks Sally. I'm soooo excited. See you soon.'

As I put the phone down, I heard Lucy shouting … 'Mum, guess what?' and I was delighted to hear her sounding so happy.

Heartened now by Lucy's more promising news and thoroughly relieved about Lesley's absence, I was able to shift mountains of work. Later that night more of my friends replied about the La Tasca evening. Mad Janey wanted us all to wear outfits. Perhaps it was the relentless passage of time, or the unstoppable extension of the waistline, that caused restraint: bunny girls' costumes, nuns' habits and nurses' uniforms had all lost a bit of their daring. The fact was that, whatever the girls' attire, swarthy waiters, tapas and vino tinto would still have their appeal.

The 'Hugh Saturday' was now in sight. I'd let Marie know in good time that I wouldn't be able to do my regular stint. There was just one irritating fly in the ointment. Stomach cramps had clenched me with their customary fury, and I had slept really badly, well, scarcely at all on the Friday night. I did manage a nap in the afternoon but was still feeling weary by the time I got to the theatre. I hoped that Estée Lauder would mask my heavy fatigue; despite my stylish escort it was going to be a long evening.

Hugh was there to greet me as I made my way to the Actors' Bar. True to form he had reserved a table, and a waiter scurried over immediately with white wine and canapés. We exchanged news; his business was booming … had I ever thought of a change of direction? [In recent weeks, absolutely!] He'd been to view a dilapidated Georgian town house on the outskirts of Knutsford and felt it would be a sound investment. Restoring it would be a challenge but great fun as well … for a fleeting moment I felt there was more than a hint of a job offer here.

'So, Sally, what have you been up to recently?'

I told him about the situation at work, mentioning the trip to Coventry but omitting the Tina Turner incident, feeling it would be too salacious for this rarefied ambiance. As I went on to tell him about my trip up north and, in particular, my father's declining health, he listened patiently, patting my hand.

'Ageing, my dear, ageing. It comes to us all in the end I'm afraid. That's why I believe we must live life to the full – *carpe diem*, as the Romans used to say.'

My sojourn in the ancient world had been relatively brief, and distant memories of Latin lessons chanting '*amo, amas, amat*' in a cold and draughty classroom occasionally resurfaced in nightmares even now; my reply to Hugh was the social utility phrase of 'Oh yes, absolutely, absolutely.'

The bell for curtain-up interrupted our conversation, and we took our seats in the central stalls, some rows from the stage.

'I'm not totally familiar with Pinter's work I must confess,' he whispered as the lights went down, 'but it's sure to be stimulating.'

Bloody hope so, I thought in a moment of irreverence – I need something to keep me awake! The play became something of an ordeal. People laughed and I wondered why, and when I wanted to laugh, they didn't. I tried desperately to stay conscious and prayed for the time to go more quickly. I spent most of the interval in the Ladies, and back in the bar turned down the offer of champagne in favour of ice-cold mineral water. I felt decidedly unwell. In the second half, my worst fears were realised. My general weariness, the endless verbiage from the stage, the absence of any detectable narrative line and the lack of action – all of this conspired with the heat of the lighting and comfort of the seat to send me off to sleep. Hugh's gentle squeeze on my arm restored me to consciousness but staying awake required a monumental effort – my eyelids seemed made of lead; my head kept nodding forward until a marionette jerk returned me to an upright position. Then a spread of surprisingly loud applause echoed around the theatre. It was over. Thank God for that! Next time, I thought – if there is one! – it's got to be a musical.

We soon found ourselves at 'Mr Folker's most liked table' in a discreet corner of the Moroccan restaurant. I had no real appetite but did my best; I felt rather like a vegetarian at a barbecue, picking over the food and using the remains of the salad to camouflage the neglected meat. Luckily, there was lots of water. Over a strong coffee I apologised for not being my usual self, I felt I'd ruined the evening for him and was mortified at having dozed off midway through the performance. I prayed to God that I hadn't been snoring 'like a factory hooter' as one former boyfriend had somewhat uncharitably put it. Hugh, ever the gallant, waved my apologies away, lifting my spirits by assuring me that I hadn't been the only one to find the piece heavy-going.

'That's the problem with so much modern theatre – so little to hang on to really; sort of minimalism of the mind.'

I wouldn't have expressed it in such profound terms myself but agreed entirely with the sentiment behind it. With a parting embrace he saw me off safely, and we agreed to be in touch soon.

I got home shattered, dissatisfied and really cross with myself – he'd been the perfect host, but I'd been a less than perfect guest; I resolved to make it up to him somehow. I felt I could sleep for a week and really hoped I'd recover in time for the shopping trip with Lucy; the last thing I wanted to do was to let her down.

I needn't have worried though because I really did feel so much better on the following day. Fortified by a strong Mocha Latte in Caffè Nero, we trawled every single one of the chain stores in the Trafford Centre. It was a pleasure to be with her, and I wasn't immune to the girl's almost hero worship of me. The way she took my fashion advice on board, her doubts about this new boy being 'only after one thing' and the way she laughed and hung on every word when I regaled her with amusing stories about my own love life. It was a hugely enjoyable day for both of us even if it did serve to remind me, yet again, of all I'd missed out on as a mother. Still, Lucy wasn't going anywhere in a hurry, and I really hoped I could continue to encourage the girl's ambitions and watch her grow into a confident, successful young woman.

Viva la vida loca!

An email came in from the persistent Lesley who wouldn't let the promotion issue drop, steadfastly refusing to take no for an answer; she felt a further meeting would help.

'*A one to one would in all probability be conducive to an amicable resolution of the issue – a way forward aligning corporate need with individual aspiration.*'

Oh dear, Lesley, you know you really should have been a member of Alastair Campbell's entourage – this sort of guff would have made you a superstar of spin!

No, my real priority was to finalise arrangements for my birthday night out, only a few days away. Everything was in place. Saturday came, and by 8.45 we were all gathered in La Tasca, enjoying the first of many glasses of sangria. The Latin rhythms were already throbbing away, the waiters flitting expertly from one table to another, the prevailing mood one of relaxation, pleasure and self-indulgence. All the girls had made it. Caroline was the first to arrive, dressed up to the nines in a fetching little number, very boho chic. Anne as well – she had entered the restaurant munching a Mars bar.

Karen was there, quite soberly dressed despite the occasion but alert, as ever, for a possible husband. Janey, in contrast, had donned an outrageously skimpy top that signalled a clear intention to seduce or, as she more directly put it 'to pull'; unfortunately, her clumsily applied eye shadow gave her a sinister rather than a sultry look – more Morticia than Madonna.

There were one or two others from the 'outer circle'. By midnight our bubbling conversation had given way to raucous shrieks, and every tapas bowl was empty. The waiters hovered at some distance as if fearing for their safety and the table displayed a long line of [empty] wine bottles like sentries on duty. From some unsavoury source, Janey, still suffering from arrested development, had purchased for each of us the most disgusting earrings shaped like male genitalia but thoughtfully painted in Spain's national colours. She was more than a little miffed when we all refused point blank to wear these hideous accessories; needless to say, she wore hers out of sheer bloody-mindedness. They bobbed obscenely from side to side with every swig of her sangria.

The wine waiter, Angel – 'Ankell the angel' as he was dubbed – was the night's clear favourite. He joined in the fun, persuading me to don a mantilla and click a set of castanets to a mock flamenco number, to roars of 'Hola, olé'. By one-thirty ours was the only party left and Carlos, the proprietor, whose dark menace hinted at membership of the Spanish Inquisition in a previous incarnation, enquired if there was anything else the 'layidiz want before they go, *now*.'

Like footballers' WAGs, we staggered, tottered and shuffled out half an hour later. The cold air of the early morning hit us like a right hook from Sylvester Stallone with a sobering effect on all of us – all, that is, with one exception.

'Lo Stile', some doors along, was a chic bar of some repute. As we congaed along the pavement, hair let loose, skirts bundled up, screaming at the top of our voices, Hugh emerged from the restaurant with a ravishing young woman on his arm, holding her close as he hailed down a taxi.

'Hugh, my dear', I roared, unthinkingly, flushed with excitement, Rioja or both. 'Girls, this is Hugh, the man I told you about – the man of my dreams!'

'Oh, yes', shouted Janey with a manic grin on her face, 'and who's that with you mate – one of your antiques?'

Hugh and his companion did not share in the general mirth. His stare almost turned me into stone. Hatred? No. Disdain? Possibly. Disappointment? Certainly. I took a step back, cringing with embarrassment, looking on in miserable silence as he helped his companion into the taxi. The girls' attention was diverted as Janey focussed her dilated pupils on a young Community Police Officer whom she immediately caught in a tight embrace. As Hugh's taxi sped away, he didn't look back. I felt my throat tightening, oblivious now of the noise and high spirits around me. I recognised that this was entirely my fault. How totally idiotic of me to let out an unseemly yelp when I spotted him – indeed I shouldn't have greeted him at all, given the situation; this, together with Janey's unfortunate observation and the general disarray of the group, would have convinced him that he was facing a feral pack of Kappa slappers. Hugh, I feared, was lost.

It was Sunday morning, or to be more accurate, Sunday afternoon. I had a splitting headache. I crawled out of bed and staggered to the bathroom; bleary-eyed, I felt for the cold tap. I downed a gallon of water and threw back the curtains; the early autumn sun streamed in, momentarily blinding me. I blinked uncomprehendingly into the searing glare, the memories of the previous evening and, in particular, its sorry finale, flooding into my mind. Somehow, I knew my time with Hugh was over. I wasn't exactly distraught because there had been no deep passion or real love there but I had enjoyed my time with him, and he'd certainly extended my horizons. No, it was regret rather than anguish that was the overriding emotion. Later in the evening, I plucked up the courage to log on to the dating site. Sadly, my memories of him would forever be scarred by that final glacial stare. Not surprisingly, there was an email from him; its terse message was predictable.

> *Sally, I hope you do well in your chosen career and enjoy success and happiness in your life generally. Best wishes. Hugh*

Given its distanced formality, this was by no means the most brutal of rejections I had experienced but it was disappointing nonetheless. There was no way back from this. He must have thought about it and rapidly concluded that the Sally he'd got to know and value was not the Sally as encountered outside the restaurant in the chilly small hours. Which of the two he may have asked himself, was the true *objet d'art?* Was he angry with himself for what he might have considered an error of judgement about me in the first place? Had his professional eye for real quality well and truly let him down on this occasion? Whatever the truth, I took some smidgeon of comfort from the conclusion that if he couldn't handle me letting my hair down occasionally then he wasn't the man for me, irrespective of the stylish life he had to offer; it was time to move on.

Chapter 9

SCOUSER'S HONOUR

Wednesday night. A quiet evening in. Where was I now? Jonathan was undoubtedly still wallowing in the ample bosom of the obliging Beverley [bitch!] and, as for myself, well, Hugh had blown me out. It was high time to visit the Aladdin's cave of Dateandsee.

I'd stored the hirsute Lenny from Liverpool in a special 'probables' file and re-opened it now for a further appraisal. He was quite good-looking and seemed younger than his stated age. The naked-to-the-waist photo bothered me but at least there was no medallion and excess chest hair. He appeared to be free of emotional baggage as well. He had enjoyed/endured a series of relationships – nothing wrong with that. One major plus was that he had clearly imbibed Liverpool's famed sense of humour at his mother's breast. Also, there was no reference to a criminal record. You may laugh but on these sites, subscribers often post up the most amazing things. He actually had a job! All of this pointed in the right direction – talk about breaking the mould! A Scouser in gainful employment; some would say this was a documentary maker's dream – not unlike a pigmy becoming a world basketball star. No, no this won't do! If Scousers were an ethnic group as some anthropologists claim they are, then I would be rightly hauled up by the Thought Police and prosecuted under the Race Relations Act. I was indulging in the unkind stereotyping that continues to blight Liverpudlians, despite the global success of The Beatles, Liverpool FC and the truly stunning regeneration of the city thanks to its selection as European City of Culture 2008. The famed local humour was immune to social change. 'How can you spot the bride at a Liverpool wedding?' ... 'Don't know' ... 'she's the one wearing the white shell suit.' Jokes like this flourished, becoming almost part of the folklore, and the unsurprising truth was that the main culprits were the Scousers themselves.

But, back to Lenny. I was puzzled by his job as a film technician – did he operate the projectors at the local fleapit or did he have a more artistic involvement? Was he a director in the making – a budding Guy Ritchie to my Madonna perhaps? Well, there was only one way to find out! Ping! Off went my previously drafted reply.

Next, it was the customary forage in the freezer – please God, not lasagne, again – before alighting upon something edible, healthy and interesting – a rare combination in the dull world of single eaters. Scarcely had the 'Chicken Risotto 4One' completed its monotonous circuits of the microwave when I caught the familiar ping from the computer. Lenny – it had to be him. I scampered over to my chair, plate in hand; I could imagine him there, sipping Merlot and perusing *The Financial Times* in his designer loft, high up in the minimalist fortress of the refurbished Albert Dock. Of course, it could just as easily be a can of Foster's XXXX and *The Sun* in a squalid bedsit on the Scottie Road – you just don't know with these dating sites; they're not yet into virtual tours of subscribers' homes [thought for the future: must log on to 'Contact Us' and suggest this enhancement].

Hiya Sally – thanks for the reply. Do people in Liverpool repay heavy debts? Heavy Debts? Round here they think that's a pop group. See, you've got me having a go at my fellow Scousers now, must be the instant hold you have over me. Well, how do you feel about meeting up for a drink and a chat, bite to eat perhaps – time, place, of your choosing, of course. I don't mind taking out extra insurance – certainly life, probably car as well – and driving over to Manchester, or you could come my way and visit some of your old haunts such as Bootle-super-Mare. We could settle for somewhere in between but not Warrington please as I'm barred from every pub there after a mate's stag night got out of hand. I got the blame for it and all I was trying to do was UNTIE the barmaid from the optics – honest! Love to hear from you soon. Lenny

Yes, there is something here; he really has got a terrific sense of humour – hope he's joking about Warrington though. I concluded that Liverpool would be the safer bet; it would be good to revisit my old stomping grounds. I mailed back suggesting we met …

> *Outside the Plaza Hotel on Liverpool's famous waterfront, close to the Liver Building. How about a Saturday night, around 8 in a fortnight's time? But Lenny, please be on time because I don't want to be hanging around on my own. Thanks.*
> *Sally*

His reply was immediate. It was as if he was poised by the keyboard, ready to respond the minute he got the green light.

> *Wow, that's terrific, thanks very much but there's just one slight snag over the date. I need to be up in the North East that weekend, some event at my girl's university and I don't want to miss it obviously – already got the new film for my handycam – how about the Saturday after that? The 15th of October. And yes, I promise on Cilla Black's deathbed not to be late. Lenny*
>
> *Fine, Lenny, not a problem. I hope you'll recognise me from my photo, I didn't doctor it too much, promise, although I did put in my best set of dentures and cropped my hooked nose a bit. Sally*
>
> *It's a deal, and I'll have on my favourite Batman cape. Lenny x*

Some progress there, I thought, although I did find the reference to the Batman cape a little strange; I hoped he wasn't a member of Fathers4Justice or some outlandish sect: probably not – probably just the usual pinch of Scouse humour to sign off with. The full significance of the Batman cape would be apparent in due course. I phoned Caroline between mouthfuls of the Chicken Risotto – a worthy contender for referral for prosecution under the Trades Description Act. Even a Geiger counter would have had trouble locating the microscopic atoms of chicken seeking refuge under the piles of sloppy, steaming rice.

Growing pains

Caroline had phoned with further positive news about Bob. He was now back at work – just a couple of days a week to start with. He was still off the fags, had cut his drinking by half [the local brewery would be facing bankruptcy] and, unbelievably, he'd even managed to walk around the park a few times. It was not all positive, though. He was seriously worried about his sex drive and his allied performance – 'limping home' was how he graphically described it with his customary black humour. Caroline also shared her worries about Louise; she'd always been a model pupil but a recent letter from school had drawn their attention to 'a marked and alarming decline in both her work rate and attitude'.

'It's all because she's got involved with one of the many deadbeats at that place – he's called Toby and yes, Bob does call him jug head just to rile her … but no, I'm serious.

I saw him in Sainsbury's last weekend where he's got a part-time job – he had more piercings than a dressmaker's pin cushion and his Bob Geldof "hair style" was streaked with all the colours of the rainbow! He looked a real bloody sight altogether. Why does the school let him in like that? What are his parents doing about it? Tell you, if my Richard ever, ever, ends up like that, I'll march him straight down to the barber's for a number one. And there's our Louise mooning over him like some bloody pop star – wouldn't surprise me if they were having it off. I'd kill her if anything went wrong I really would – I'd –'

'Caroline,' I cut in firmly. 'Come on, your imagination's running riot. Teenagers are always mad about their image – what about you in your Farrah Fawcett Major days? Your hair was like a haystack after a hurricane. You must get some sense of proportion here. You'd be just as worked up if she was going out with some boy as smart as a bank clerk, wouldn't you? Have you actually sat down and talked to her?'

I sensed that in the previous months all of her attention had been focussed on Bob and his needs; this was of course entirely understandable, but the children had undoubtedly been neglected to some extent.

'You're probably right there. I'm just terrified of her making the same mistake I made – remember I was only a year older than she is now. Yes, I will sit down and talk to her; I'm just praying to God that she won't make a mess of things like I did.' We agreed to get together soon for coffee, but already I could hear warning bells sounding; I felt sure that, however diplomatically, I would need to become involved as umpire, intermediary or peacemaker in the never-ending and never-new problems of the generation gap.

Promoting talent [2]

For once I didn't get into the office early on the Monday morning. I'd been reading a really disturbing article about high cholesterol levels and had made an appointment at the doctor's. To my intense alarm, a blood test was necessary. Now, as I felt faint at the sight of a pair of knitting needles let alone a hypodermic, it took me half an hour or so to recover from the ordeal which I ranked a close second to a heart transplant. The injection had left an ugly, purple blotch on my right arm – it must have been as big as … oh … a 5p piece; I didn't try to conceal it but wore it with pride – rather like an infantryman returning from the front, face pitted by shrapnel. But no one at work had time for my medical condition …

Even as I stepped into the office I was aware of a warm buzz, a sense of excitement. The adrenaline was almost palpable. Roy and his crew were clustered around the water dispenser, indulging in endless rounds of whooping high fives. What could this be about? News from on high about a 0.3% wage rise? Or was it an instruction to all female staff to go topless every Friday in an extension of dress-down day? Neither was the case, although Roy's boundless euphoria certainly suggested the latter. But there *was* news. A copy of the intranet message had been pinned up on the wall, underneath a screaming 'Happy Monday' headline picked out in red and yellow. There was a God! The message read as follows:

Following her spectacular success as your branch manager in recent months, the Board has decided to transfer Ms Lesley Dunsmore to the Dudley branch where a managerial vacancy has arisen due to the sudden illness of the current incumbent. It is not anticipated that she will return to the Manchester branch until January.

The Board wishes to record its thanks to Ms Dunsmore for her readiness to support the bank and its Dudley branch in this problematical period.

As a consequence of her temporary absence, the Board has appointed Mr Jonathan Wilson, currently Manager of Foreign Exchange, as Temporary Manager of the Manchester branch.

The Board feels sure that all members will echo their good wishes to these colleagues as they face their new challenges.

Ah, so that's it. Roy and co. were not only delighted that Lesley would be out of the frame for some time [the changes would come into effect on October 3rd] but were positively elated that 'one of the boys' was to replace her. The office already suffocated in a clammy testosterone-fuelled fug, and this change would only makes things worse. But of the alternatives, which was the less intolerable? Was it the known severity and malice of Lethal Lesley or the hoped-for depravity and bonhomie of Jonathan 'special FX', his favourite nickname – especially with the ladies. I had to agree with the consensus for the latter, despite its possible repercussions. Whatever the forecast, it wouldn't all be plain sailing and experience had taught me the cruel truth that, in life, a new problem so often springs from the solution to a previous one.

After this wholly unexpected start, the rest of the week flew by with training sessions in Norwich, Exeter and Stockton. Years of driving had made me an authority on the road system. I knew the motorways, the A roads, the B roads, the toll roads, the highways, the byways, the spurs, the rat-runs, and the bypasses. Such comprehensive knowledge often proved of no avail, however, late on a Friday afternoon when the nation's roads invariably suffered from what one analyst had labelled DVT – 'deep vehicular thrombosis.'

I was both shattered and frustrated when I got home about ten. Surprise, surprise - a scrappy note from the neighbours asking me to feed their 'little treasure'; this time it was an unmissable hotel offer in Wales. The brazen cheek of it! A shower and suitable beverage restored life to my aching limbs, as I settled down to catch up on calls and messages. One was from Janey whose outburst on the party night had contributed to the premature and hurtful end of the liaison with Hugh. Her tone was placatory in the extreme.

'Hiya Sally, me I'm afraid – no don't put the phone down, please! Look, the girls have told me about last Saturday night. I don't remember a thing 'cos I must have hit the Breezers big time! Is there anything, anything I can do to help, like surrendering my near-maidenly body to Hugh as a kind of peace offering perhaps? No, better not – might actually make things worse I suppose. Still, you'd think he'd have a sense of humour about it wouldn't you; after all you are – were – going out with him and you've never been Miss Po-Faced or little Miss Lah-di-dah have you? Anyway, what I was going to say was that me and ...'

And so it went on; by turns – overtures, self-examination, contrition with just a touch of defiance, and regret, all delivered at a torrential rate, and all intended to cloak the embarrassment which lay at the heart of it.

I texted her to say she was forgiven – after all, within myself, I knew full well that there would be nothing long term with Hugh.

From Stockton to Stockholm

To divert me from this dismal introspection, Dateandsee had a treat in store in the form of an email from Henrik, inviting me to Stockholm. In a way I felt this was fated; only a day earlier, one of the trainees on my course in Stockton had turned out to be Swedish, and during the coffee break he'd raved on about the beauty of his capital city, Stockholm. Henrik's email certainly lifted my spirits. He had visited England several times, for both business and pleasure, but perhaps Sweden was new to me? A whole new experience was sorely tempting. He added that if I could make it over there, it would be good to go before the end of the month as the bad weather tended to set in then. I mailed him back to thank him for his kindness, saying that already the work pressures were reducing and I would really do my best to accept his kind offer. Then, ping! A further approach! A striking man, with a mop of thick black hair and soft brown eyes smiled invitingly at me from the screen.

Matters spiritual

THE MESSAGE: *I'm new to all this, a bit nervous to be honest and already possibly out of my depth. All I can say is that your irresistible sense of humour and lovely photo made it imperative for me to contact you. You wrote about 'humour' being your 'favourite drug' – well, believe it or not religion was once mine but is no longer. My addiction is now Life with a capital L. Perhaps we could meet up, talk and share our approaches to the world? Dominic.*

THE PROFILE:

Name: Dominic
Age: 42
Location: North West [Lake District]
Status: Single
Children: None
Job: Writer
Height: 6'2"
Build: Well Built
Appearance: Attractive
Eye Colour: Brown
Hair: Dark Brown
Religion: Roman Catholic
Star Sign: Pisces
Smoker: No
Drinker: Moderate

INTERESTS: *Church architecture, philosophy, the organ, church music.*

ABOUT ME: *Hello there. I'm Dominic. I earn my living these days as a writer, producing articles on philosophical and ethical issues for magazines, including the Sunday supplements. For many years I was a Roman Catholic priest but as the years went by, I realised I could no longer cope with the strict rules on celibacy. I had to renounce my vocation but not my personal faith, which remains very important to me. I know full well that mine is an unusual profile but I remain hopeful that, with God's help, I will find a kindred spirit for a long relationship based on deep mutual respect.*

MY ACTUAL REPLY: *Hello Dominic, the RC angle is an interesting one as this is my background too. In fact I have a cousin who is a Catholic priest. Apart for the religious aspect, I have to be honest and say that I don't think we have that much in common. I very much hope however that you will find your 'kindred spirit' sometime and that you find lasting happiness with her. Sally*

Hmm. Ex Roman Catholic priests too! The home page for the dating site was certainly not exaggerating when it claimed, 'all human life is here'.

There may be trouble ahead

On the Monday of the following week, Jonathan informed everyone in a lengthy email that he proposed to hold a staff meeting at the end of the day. After several paragraphs alluding to the current harsh financial climate it ended in a rather peremptory manner … 'and I expect everyone to be present'. Hmm … I reflected on the tone and tenor of the message ... were we to witness a new Jonathan now that he'd been elevated to the peerage? The message after all was remarkably businesslike, lucid, well phrased and to the point. This seemed out of keeping with his character – after all, I had some personal experience of this – and also with his reputation as the office Casanova. Perhaps he had realised that a golden opportunity had fallen in his lap and he was now determined to exploit it to the full.

His manner and bearing at the meeting matched the impersonal style of his message. He spoke with clarity, forcefulness and immense self-assurance. I wasn't aware of even momentary eye contact with me or with Beverley who had arranged a prominent seat for herself to his right. His message was blunt. As Branch Manager [albeit temporary] he would be under intense pressure 'to deliver' and was therefore intending to hold one-to-ones with all budget holders within the next fortnight.

My meeting took place a few days later. He occupied Lesley's office. It was now lighter, warmer and dotted about with individual items. It had a personal stamp with a calendar of 'The Most Challenging Golf Courses in the World' and photographs of him and his friends at squash or golf matches; on his desk stood a framed photograph of Monty, an adorable golden retriever, purchased by his section after a sponsored golf tournament and now busy as a loyal guide dog. There was also a map of England studded with different coloured drawing pins. From their location and clusters I felt sure they were the bank's various branches across the country. I hazarded a guess that the different colours represented the current profitability of each; our own branch was a rather insipid and uninspiring green. This was disquieting.

'Ah Sally; yes, nice to see you. Do come in and sit down please. Tea, coffee? No? Fine. Look, I've been studying the figures relating to training income over the last few months and I need your help with one or two associated issues.' [i.e. you've not been bringing in enough money. Why not?]

Yes, he was focussed all right, perfectly civil and friendly, but without the smallest trace of the familiarity I might have expected given our recent history. He did betray a slight touch of emotion – a repressed snort of indignation actually – when I explained that the alarming drop in training revenue had resulted from continuing delays in the release of the latest software; the beta version had been available since Easter – since then all my enquires about progress had been greeted with a deafening silence.

'Bloody Karl, I knew it!' Jonathan banged his knuckles on his desk. 'He's a decent golfer but as an IT Project Manager he's total crap! Leave this one to me!'

On this warlike note, the one-to-one meeting ended. There was no lingering eye contact, no social chit-chat.

The next interviewee was hovering by the door. I needed some water; I felt I'd been grilled and was certainly relieved to have the necessary cogent explanation at my fingertips. How would other senior colleagues fare?

Last Tango in Toxteth

One week on and my attention and interest turned to the date with Lenny. He'd contacted me again, initially to keep the soup on the boil as it were but also to ask if I could get over to Liverpool a little earlier than planned. He explained that it was the final day of a *Hollywood Greats* festival, and there was a film showing that he simply couldn't miss; he was sure I would enjoy it just as much too. What about meeting up at four? The screening would be at the Liverpool Tate within walking distance of the Plaza Hotel where we had agreed to meet, and there would be time for a drink before going into the cinema. Why not, I thought – I'm always up for a good film and given Lenny's professional interest and expertise, it might be of particular interest.

In fact the closer the date came, the more I was looking forward to it. When Saturday did arrive, I spent some time on the dress ritual. What should it be today? Drinks, film, and probably a bistro – so nothing dramatically elegant; haute couture could be dispensed with for once – and anyway, I might get mugged! Eventually I settled on black jeans and a vivid jade-coloured kaftan top sprinkled with a few sparkly bits – well, I was going to Liverpool where sequins were de rigueur even for morning coffee.

He was certainly attractive with his mop of really dark hair, hazel-brown eyes and a warm smile that relieved the narrowness of his features. More than that – and to my delight – he was taller and slimmer than I had imagined. He was dressed in contemporary style – informal and relaxed. He was chirpy and bright, clearly animated because the first stage of the encounter had passed successfully.

'Do you go to the pictures much, Sally?' he began.

'Not that often to be honest – maybe two or three times a year at the most. I tend to wait and see what the Oscars come up with. I went to see that *Atonement* thing but found it hard work – have you seen it?'

'Oh yes,' he replied, leaning forward and warming to the topic, 'the thing is, most of these really successful films like are technically very good – so's the acting and the script. But, for me, most of them don't have any real passion, any deep feelings to grab me. Just think of those great Brando films made over … what was it? Yes, fifty years ago.'

'Fifty years? You got me there Lenny, I thought it all began with *The Godfather*.'

'Oh no, not at all – his breakthrough was *On the Waterfront*; this was amazingly modern for its age. I've always been a big fan of his – seen all his films like, read all the books about him – he really is one of *the* greats.'

Well, he was clearly an enthusiast. Now, I'd never actually seen *Last Tango in Paris* but I was aware that, on its release, it had enjoyed certain fame – or was it notoriety? *Groundbreaking, Hugely brave, Truly challenging* – these and similar garlands of praise garnished the central portrait of 'Brando' on the front cover of the festival programme.

We took our seats with Lenny eagerly leading the way, like a schoolboy attending his first Premiership match. Was it my imagination or did his leg deliberately brush against mine during that delightful scene showing the heroine sitting on the loo? Charming. And later, during the infamous lovemaking scene, when Brandon reached over his partner's naked body for the butter, I watched transfixed. My God, this is raunchy and it's from twenty-five years ago! At one point I simply had to avert my eyes, stealing a glance at Lenny who continued to stare at the screen in almost reverential awe; I practically had to pinch him back into consciousness.

'Oh, sorry, I do get wrapped up in these films like – sixth time I've seen *Tango* to be honest.'

Six times! Maybe you need to see it that many times to grasp what it's all about? I smiled to myself, realising that my initial hopes/expectations of seeing *The Queen* had proved seriously wide of the mark.

'Right love, time for a quick bevvie!' I noted the use of the word 'quick' and wondered whether this suggested the imminence of a further equally murky experience. Over a glass of wine he asked me my opinion of the film. What could I say? That I'd never eat butter again? That I was soundproofing my bathroom walls? That I'd spent half the time with my eyes closed and the other half trying to understand Brando's primeval grunting?

'Well, to be honest, psychosexual drama really isn't my thing – I mean he was a bit mixed up, wasn't he?'

There, Lenny, ball in your court; I soon wished I'd said something slightly more non-committal. For the next half hour he delivered a blow-by-blow account of the Brando character's anal fixation, which, apparently, 'struck to the very roots of his sense of isolation and estrangement from society …'

' … Well, you might be right, Lenny, but I'm starving – how about you?'

'Spot-on, love – now you mention it, I'm pretty peckish myself.'

A growing relationship

Entering Liverpool's Chinese quarter was like stepping into a different world. We passed beneath an enormous pagoda-type arch, vividly painted with preening peacocks, their luxuriant tails fanning around the sides. Two columns supported the arch itself, each decorated with warring dragons, breathing out sulphurous flames, their razor-sharp claws curved into menacing hooks. The Chinese people around, though, generally dressed in Western clothes – T-shirts/jeans/trainers – were true to their race; they were short, slim and small-framed, their oval eyes darting left and right as they chatted away in lively conversation. As we strolled along the main street, I wouldn't have been at all surprised to see a rickshaw trundling by. Lenny seemed to know the area well – perhaps he'd filmed one of his documentaries there?

The street was lined with shops of every sort – specialist tattoo parlours, several herbs and medicine stores, each fronted by an image of the human body pierced by flashing needles. A curious sort of strident, oriental-influenced techno pop added to the vibrancy of it all. And of course, food shops and restaurants were in abundance; the air seemed condensed, thick with the unusual odours of exotic dishes. He claimed to know all the best restaurants and chose the 'The Pink Lotus'. He expertly guided me through the bewildering range on offer, and we eventually settled on the 'Lucky Feast for Two' – spring rolls, spare ribs Peking style, satay chicken, scallops in bird's nest – the list was endless but fortunately the portions were small. On his advice we simply drank water; this, he assured me in true connoisseur fashion, would refresh the palate so that we could enjoy the different and competing flavours to the full. We had fun too as he attempted, with only limited success, to teach me how to use chopsticks. Crunching through his spring rolls, he almost breathlessly gave me a detailed description of the entire *Emmanuelle* series, clearly knowing off by heart the actresses' names, dimensions and favourite positions. 'It's funny you know, but each film like is more artistic than the previous one.'

Perhaps he'd spotted a glazed look in my eyes because he then changed the subject, beginning to talk at length about his background; his father had been in the merchant navy, had sailed off to the Far East when Lenny was a toddler and had never been seen or heard of again. Life had not been easy for him and his two brothers, but, thanks to their mother's determination, they had won through. He was keen to hear about my life and family. I noticed how polite he was when talking to the waiters – 'never trust a man who is nice to you but not nice to waiters.' This had been one of the guiding precepts of my relationships' history.

Thankfully, there was no pressure from him for more drinks or a 'nightcap' at his place. He escorted me to my car, and gave me a swift hug and a peck on the cheek. Oddly though, as I slipped on my safety belt, he seemed to be peering inquisitively into my car. Distinctly odd. No matter. As I drove home, I went over the date in my mind. I had actually enjoyed his company and was only mildly disconcerted by his choice of *Tango* and his extensive knowledge of *Emmanuelle*. He seemed genuine enough and was pleasant and humorous. Another date was certainly possible but who would make the first move? This question was answered when I received an email from him on the following evening.

Hi Sally! Thanks a lot for yesterday, I really enjoyed it. Sorry if I gabbled on a lot about this and that, must be the Irish blood in me to be sure. I wonder if you'd like to come to a party with me. A bloke I know from a band I played in some years ago is having a birthday bash for his fortieth on the 29th of October. He's got this lovely big house, a mansion no less – see the sort of folk I mix with? It's on the outskirts of Chester, ideal for a big do. Things won't be getting underway until about eleven but there'll be loads to eat so please don't go filling up beforehand. Lenny xx

Hmm ... eleven's a bit late and Chester's not exactly on my doorstep. No, come on – you're in danger of becoming an old maid. Your car won't turn into a pumpkin at midnight and one really late night won't do you any harm. Go for it!

Yes, Lenny, that's fine, although I would have you know that I already had several celeb social occasions to choose from on the date in question, such as a ball at the Manor House to celebrate the opening meet of the local pack, the premiere of 'Star Wars X11'

> *at the Odeon, Leicester Square and a hen weekend of debauched drinking in Prague, but, see, I have rejected them all just for you – never let a good Scouser down I always say! Looking forward to it already. I'll be in touch nearer the time for directions etc. Sally xx*

The agony aunt

No sooner had I lifted my finger from the 'Send' button than the phone rang. Caroline.

'Cazi, how are you love and how's Bob the Builder? Being a good boy is he? Ten mile run every morning before gorging himself on the muesli and dry toast?'

'He's doing OK; I'm really pleased with him. He had me in stitches last night – he'd had one too many I suppose – saying he'd been reading about property prices in Florida in the *Daily Mail* and thought that if we tightened our belts a bit, we could afford to buy a condom.'

'A condom? You mean–'

'Yes, I'm not kidding; that's what he said – buy a condom. What a bloody scream! When I patted him on the hand and pointed out you could buy a three-pack from Boots round the corner for a fiver he began to see the funny side of it too. "Oh yeah I meant condominium didn't I? Must be this health food stuff affecting my brain or the six-pack I've just demolished." Louise? Well, things are a bit less fraught. She's still seeing Worzel Gummidge but seems to have knuckled down to her schoolwork again. But when I started to broach the sex bit, she got all defensive and said she wasn't some silly 14- year-old with a crush on the nice boy who lives next door. I said "no, you're a silly 16- year-old with a crush on a New Age Traveller." And the school, well, they don't help either, even dishing out the morning-after pill like Smarties. But what about us – don't parents have a say in all of this? Makes me bloody hopping mad it does!'

It was clear that she wanted to talk, offloading her worries. I listened patiently, trying now and then to strike a positive note in the conversation, saying that Louise was fundamentally a sensible girl and that teenagers' sex lives were just headline fodder for the papers.

'I hope to God you're right – you know how worked up I get about this sort of thing and ... RICHARD WILL YOU GIVE THOSE BLOODY DRUMS A REST FOR FIVE MINUTES! ... Sorry love, like living in a jungle here sometimes! Anyway, I'd better get the tea on now – I'll catch up with you soon.'

Orgy, orgy, pudding and pie

The second date with Lenny was on my radar. In the background I continued to receive messages from Henrik in snowbound Stockholm [stereotypical thinking, must cut it out, I reprimanded myself]. So, it was going to be big party in a big house. Now, the question – as ever – was what to wear? This was something of a problem. 'Mansion' suggested manicured lawns, marquees and evening wear but I just couldn't see Lenny going for that. Play it safe. Simple black dress.

The mansion was set some distance back from the main road. As my car crunched along the long, winding drive, floodlights sweeping across the night sky and throbbing music signalled that the party was already well underway. Lenny was standing by the steps, glass in hand, ready to greet me. I was a little disconcerted to see him stripped to the waist; the end of October in the north of England is hardly Ibiza. Maybe he'd spilt something on his shirt? But next to him was a much taller man, much broader too, also half-naked. As he turned to go back in the house, I made out an enormous tattoo that covered the whole of his back, featuring two women, with breasts that were positively pneumatic, cavorting with a single male. I HATED tattoos – I was even put off by 'MUM'.

As I got out, I noticed several young women also displaying lots of flesh. Micro skirts, brightly coloured tops with plunging necklines and a black bra occasionally peeping through. Obviously a progressive lot, I thought, not without a smidgeon of discomfort; I had the distinct impression of being overdressed in every sense of the word, feeling like a nun shipwrecked on *Celebrity Love Island*.

Lenny greeted me warmly and offered me a glass of champagne. We went inside, along seemingly endless corridors, through rooms that were for the most part decorated in a faux Balmoral style. The heavy reds and gloomy greens formed a brooding backcloth to the faded sets of antlers and grim fox masks that adorned the walls in the absence of imposing portraits. Dark, solid furnishings completed the gothic effect. A sumptuous buffet had been laid out in the Billiard Room, the baize protected by a highly polished tabletop. I was in fact delighted to see this; I was really hungry by now, having had nothing since a runny yoghurt and rock-hard apple in the afternoon. The food was of exceptional quality and obviously the work of professional caterers. Bottles of wine were freely available; the labels were new to me but they certainly looked impressive. It was pretty clear that no expense had been spared on this event.

Lenny introduced the host. I immediately recognised Mr Tattoo who turned out to be Derek from Fazakerley, quite obviously an unreconstructed Scouser. Thirty years out of date it might be, but he still sported an Afro and a long, drooping moustache à la George Harrison. His sole concession to modernity was a single earring in his right ear, the gold hoop reflecting the flickering light of the candles.

Derek, apparently, had started out as a joiner but he'd always had a shrewd eye for business. Countless TV programmes promoted the new, fashionable look for the home and, quick to spot the huge potential of decking and laminate floors, he'd made a fortune. There were no airs and graces with him. He was down to earth, warm and friendly. With an odd smile he asked me if I'd been entertained by Lenny's home movies yet ... and when he promised us both a guided tour of 'the establishment' later when things got going', I noted they exchanged conspiratorial glances. There was more dancing, more food, and even with a single glass of wine I was enjoying myself.

I had a bit of a shock to see it was already nearly two, and just then Derek re-appeared, his speech noticeably slurred; he was determined to honour his promise of the guided tour. I had noticed other guests pairing off; well, sometimes it was in groups of four or five. As we climbed the baronial staircase, I caught the acrid smell of cannabis, a further worrying sign … then, as Derek led me and Lenny into a side room, I caught my breath and felt my eyes widening at the sight that greeted us. On the wall was what was obviously a one-way mirror. Through it I could see an enormous bed on which a threesome, stark naked and glistening in oil, were kissing, fondling, licking … rolling about in athletic paroxysms of passion. The next room offered more of the same but this had more of a community feel to it with several beds and knots of guests indulging in carefree, energetic group sex.

'Nice to see people enjoying themselves, isn't it?' remarked Lenny in an easy, matter-of-fact tone over the pulsating beat of Cream in the background. He slipped his arm around my waist, making to steer me to one of the rooms.

'Sorry Lenny but I really don't think so – got to be up early tomorrow to visit my mum and dad – they're just back from the Dominican Republic with really bad food poisoning. Derek, thanks for inviting me, it was a real eye opener. Lovely house but it's definitely time for me to go now.'

I shot a withering look at Lenny, virtually hurled myself down the stairs and reached the security of my car in a breathless lurch. He caught up with me just as I was reversing.

'Oh, I'm really sorry you've got to go just when things were livening up – hope your parents are OK – safe journey home, I'll be in touch soon.'

I smiled weakly. My wheels skidded over the gravel, scattering pebbles into the air, as my car spirited me away to the dull but secure homeland of suburbia. On the way home, I had visions of Lenny, shrugging off his disappointment and returning to that den of iniquity, comforted by the prospect of easier pickings within. All the jigsaw pieces fell into place. How utterly, utterly stupid of me … 'film technician' … Thailand … handycam … *Last Tango in Paris* … *Emmanuelle* … his unconventional attire and then the brooding mansion with its dark secrets. Yes, the evidence was incontrovertible; with Lenny you had your standard pervert. No danger at all to the vulnerable and quite content to lead his life with like-minded hedonists. I was most definitely not one of these. Dateandsee, I concluded, should introduce a guidance rating for subscribers.

An unwelcome visitor

My sleep that night was far from restful. Nightmares of leering vicars, naked but for purple posing pouches, licking their lips, as they frenziedly tied screaming virgins to a makeshift scaffold. A leering Derek stood by, brandishing a B&Q chainsaw and wearing only his red Liverpool FC scarf. Next to him was Lenny, sweating profusely under his Batman cape, peering into his handycam and yelling 'legs wider, legs wider and give me some *action!*'

Not surprisingly, there was an email from him on the following day with its normal everyday tone, as if we'd been out to see *Lord of the Rings* the night before and suffered a puncture on the way back; a simple, everyday occurrence.

> *Really sorry you couldn't stay over last night. Perhaps I should have mentioned to you that I'm into these swingers' parties. They're really great fun you know and everyone loves the*

> *movies I make of them – hope you'll agree to*
> *come to one we've got on New Year's Eve. In*
> *the meantime I was thinking of a weekend in*
> *Amsterdam for Saturday week, any chance of*
> *you making it? Lenny x*

No fear! I'd rather chew razor blades than share the same air with him again, but I chose not to reply immediately. I'd need to have my strategy neatly formulated in order to deal with this one.

On the following Wednesday night Anne popped round for a chat. Ringo, now more of a lodger than a neighbour, was stretched out contentedly on the sofa, paws akimbo, revelling in the extra attention as she stroked his glossy coat. She was gushing, eager to tell me that, despite her earlier disappointment, she had in fact renewed her subscription to the dating site; more than that, she'd struck lucky! She'd had a date with 'a really nice bloke' who lived near Stoke-on-Trent and loved everything about Italy – she'd met his son too, a nice lad but painfully shy ... I couldn't believe my ears but decided to keep a discreet silence; I'd work out how to avoid the 'dinner date for four' later.

To change the subject, I offered her coffee and scuttled off into the kitchen. At that very moment the doorbell rang.

'Get that for me please, Anne, there's a love,' I shouted above the piping kettle.

When I came back into the living room, I nearly dropped the tray in shock. Standing there, in front of me, as large as life, was ... Lenny. Worse followed – before I could say a word, Anne, understandably misreading the situation, felt as if she was intruding and made an excuse to beat a hasty retreat. Even a mountain of chocolate biscuits couldn't entice her to stay. Now what? So, there I was, alone, in my house, with Lenny.

He clearly felt it would be impolite not to help himself to the coffee and settled down on the sofa, taking everything in. He wasn't at all threatening, but I felt uncomfortably exposed. How on earth had he got hold of my address? What had happened to the much-lauded Fort Knox style security of the Internet site?

'Mmm, this coffee's really good – is it Alta Rica? Lovely flavour ...'

'Oh, well, I'm glad you like it but – '

' ... And, oh yes, before I forget, you know that Amsterdam trip I mentioned to you? Well Derek knows this bloke like who can get us tickets at a reduced – '

'Lenny, look,' I said quietly but firmly, trying to keep my voice under control, 'how on earth did you find me?'

'Oh that, yeah – it was no problem really. Remember, I walked you back to your car after that Chinese we had and I caught sight of some junk mail on your passenger seat like and I suppose your address must have stuck in my mind.'

[Damn it, I was furious with myself for my colossal stupidity].

'Hope you don't mind me just dropping in from the blue like this – I thought if you're free, we might ... '

But he didn't, couldn't, finish the sentence ... I noticed Ringo rubbing against his legs. Lenny began to splutter, spraying biscuit crumbs onto his lap and coughing violently. His face turned scarlet and the whites of his eyes seem to bulge out – ready to explode – leaving his pupils as Mongoloid slits.

'Hang on, I'll get you some water,' I volunteered, rushing into the kitchen. He drained the glass gratefully and held it out for a refill. From the kitchen I heard him splutter something like 'sorry – it's this allergy to cats and dogs I've got.'

'Oh no!' I said, seizing the opportunity. 'Good job there's only the one of them here; I've actually got four of the little darlings you know!'

In the present dire circumstances, the lie was definitely forgivable. He started to reply but hesitated as Ringo peered inquisitively round the door, ready for an encore.

Lenny spotted him and shuddered. 'Sorry love – I've just got to go; I really can't risk it.' And with that, he was gone.

I couldn't bolt the door fast enough. The truth was that this unexpected and unwelcome visit had truly scared me. Strengthened by a large brandy, I decided to contact him, making it clear that there would be no more dates. Next day, true to my resolve, I mailed him to apologise for having failed to mention that I was a great animal lover, claiming that puppy walking was another of my interests, but regardless of that, I didn't think we were well suited. In due course, he did reply, wishing me well for the future.

I was shot of him. Last Tango with Lenny. Thank God!

Chapter 10

THE ART OF MANAGEMENT

Back at work, Jonathan had not wavered an inch from the moment he'd taken up his new appointment. Although he lacked Lesley's venom, he was just as ready to upbraid people for their failures, but, mercifully, in the privacy of his office rather than the open-plan area. On the other hand, he made a point of handing out praise publicly if a particularly lucrative deal had been struck or valuable suggestions made about streamlining office procedures. He seemed to get the best out of people, especially Roy, whose work rate had increased noticeably. Jonathan had sent him on a web designers' course. Roy couldn't believe that people were actually spending money on HIM! He'd come back full of confidence, bursting with new ideas. The standard of his work had improved significantly. The office, in general, was altogether a much more harmonious place under Jonathan's leadership. True to his word, he'd contacted the IT Project Manager and – lo and behold! – within ten days, the first release of the new software was available. Some branches had elected – or rather 'been selected' – to be 'early adopters' – that gaggle of enthusiastic techies who seemed determined to threaten their own and everyone else's sanity, and jobs, by being the first to install and run the latest programs. Needless to say, our branch was among these intrepid pioneers.

But Roy rose to the challenge manfully. Under his guidance and with his technical insight, the new software was pronounced 'fit for purpose' and was then rolled out to other branches in the north-west. My training diary was consequently crammed full for the immediate future.

As regards my love life, Jonathan was professionally and therefore socially strictly off-limits. Lenny was undoubtedly spending his pocket money in Ann Summers. There had been lots of interest but no chemistry. Was I being too picky? There were millions of men out there, and I only wanted one of them but, hey, the Swedish option was still available. My mind was made up: it was time to cast my net beyond UK waters and see what the wider world had to offer.

Stockholm beckons

Hello Sally, I do hope that you are not letting your job dominate your life. I have decided to write to you because I have some time free from work in mid November and I am hoping that this is a good time for you to visit Stockholm. Would you consider my proposal please? I have lots of space in my apartment and you would be my honoured guest. Kind regards. Henrik

This sounded like the sort of offer I couldn't refuse – new bloke, new city, new country, new adventure. And you have a genuine local as your personal guide and protector, just in case those muscular types with long beards and horned helmets get a bit fresh. But no way was I staying in his apartment. What if we didn't get along? No, my own room was essential and I'd find a polite but firm way to put this to him.

> *Dear Henrik, it's really very kind of you to invite me and yes, I'd love to take up your offer. But you must promise not to force me to eat whaleburgers while frolicking naked at midnight in some frozen fjord. I should be able to catch a plane towards mid November but Henrik, as this will be the first time we meet, I'd much prefer to have my own hotel room if that's OK with you – I hope you're not offended.*
> *I'll get back to you with flight details. Sally x*

His reply flashed back.

> *This is truly wonderful news and, yes, I do understand why you prefer your own hotel room. This is not a problem. Just let me know the details when you have made the booking. You have my word that 'whaleburgers' will not be on the menu but have you tried our rollmops? They're really delicious with aquavit, our local 'brew' – as you English would put it. Kind regards. Henrik*

Right, time for action. I logged on to the Ryanair site. Fantastic! £4.99 going out on the Friday and £1 coming back on the Sunday! How did they do it on those prices? The taxi fare home from La Tasca had been £22 [mind you, the driver might have charged extra for stopping twice when Janey threatened to throw up over his furry seat cover]. The low airfare meant I was able to book a better quality hotel right in the city centre and it was convenient for everything.

I mailed him to suggest that we should meet in the lounge of my hotel on the Friday afternoon at about four. I added that I was really excited by the chance to meet him and to visit Stockholm; I promised to brush up on my Swedish, which was getting a little rusty these days. Time was when I could follow a Bergman movie word for word ['Honest Henrik, this is true – mind you, the film was dubbed'] and I promised to acquire a level of fluency needed for those everyday but important social encounters such as 'hello', 'goodbye', 'please', 'thank you' and 'I'm awfully sorry but my left ski has just become trapped in your zip fastener.'

Doesn't it come round so quick!

Mum had been on the phone about Christmas. 'Yes doesn't it come round so quick and all the shops have had their lights on and everything for ages now and Dad needs a new cardigan so I'll use them Marks and Spencers vouchers I got from Auntie Betty last year and will you be staying over until New Year's Eve only with Auntie Betty and Uncle John here it'll be difficult with the beds and …'

I always saw my parents at Christmas; it was something of a ritual. The prospect of an extended stay though was a little unappealing as I was hoping to get a bit of winter sun somewhere – after Stockholm, I'd need it this year more than ever. So, I promised Mum that I'd definitely be with them for Christmas Day and Boxing Day and would even help with the washing up!

'Dad will be so pleased he's still not right since that fall at the do and keeps on calling me Mildred and that was his mother's name you know and so it's all a bit strange really ...'

I did my best to reassure her, saying that the years were flying by and it was not surprising that Dad's memory should be playing tricks on him like that. After all, he was turned eighty-four now and even he would have a bit of trouble winning *Mastermind*, wouldn't he? This was his favourite TV programme, and the joke cheered her up considerably.

Playing politics

My computer, even when inactive, still retained some sort of quiet, magnetic pull. I thought half an hour's surfing might be worthwhile. Ah here's someone new: Reginald from Worcester, who was heavily and learnedly [yawn, yawn] into mock Civil War battles and a fervent monarchist to boot. Next please! Here was Rory, a fierce-looking Highlander with a shock of red hair and a bristly beard; his admitted predilection for, and intimate knowledge of, malt whiskies was not a bad start but he was destined for the delete button because of puerile references to ' the caber beneath ma kilt.' Oh dear. Next please. Hmm ... this one's by far and away the best-looking of tonight's clientele ...

THE MESSAGE: Hello Sally. I've just finished reading about you and I have to say I'm impressed. 'Smitten' might be premature perhaps but there's time. Seriously though I did enjoy your wholly original sense of humour – so many of these Internet postings are predictable and a bit tedious don't you find? You obviously like the good things in life too, which is terrific. No blue blood in me I'm afraid and as for money, I've got none at all, neither old nor new, and most of it goes on the kids' university fees, but that's life. But I do share your interests in the Arts and I think we'd get on. Read a bit about me and if it doesn't bore you rigid, especially the references to politics bit (sorry!), then what about getting together for a drink some time? Best wishes James

THE PROFILE:

Name: James
Age: 44
Location: Southport
Status: Divorced
Children: Two
Job: Administrator
Height: 6'2"
Build: Slim
Appearance: Attractive
Eye Colour: Brown
Hair: Brown

Religion: Christian [non-practising]
Star Sign: Gemini
Smoker: No
Drinker: Moderate

INTERESTS: Good food, good wine, travel, politics (local/national), cinema, jazz.

ABOUT ME: Hello, I'm James. Wow! Are you still reading this? There's hope for me yet. The very mention of the word 'Politics' directs most ladies unerringly to the delete key. There are aspects of my life that I take very seriously but I can relax and enjoy myself as much as the next man. Politics can be fun as well you know, just ask Bill Clinton. Why not read my personal manifesto and let's get a focus group going, well, a focus duo preferably.

Yes, distinct possibilities here, I thought, looking at his photo on-screen again. He seemed to have been honest in his details. He *was* attractive and, though turned forty, hadn't piled on the weight too much. He was something between the [literally] heavy presence of Tony Soprano and the beguiling fragility of James Blunt. His hair was swept back from his forehead showing off his eyes and strong eyebrows to best advantage. His features were clear-cut. He had neither glasses nor facial hair. But was there just a suggestion of arrogance in his half-smile, I wondered, before correcting myself – I didn't descend to the uncomfortable beggars-can't-be-choosers zone, and, instead, recalled that the Internet site was inhabited by real men and not teenage fantasies. A positive response was called for – Downing Street here I come!

> *MY ACTUAL REPLY: James, you are obviously silver-tongued and very persuasive. I've met members of every profession from brain surgeons to bouncers but I've never actually dated a Prime Minister. Yes, I agree, let's meet up for a drink. Only problem is that between business and family commitments, I'm pretty well tied up until the end of November, but unless you've got a G8 conference scheduled for then, what about it? Now at this point James, brace yourself – I'm going to take a very deep breath and ask you a very personal question [no, relax, not of the Cosmopolitan variety – promise]. The thing is, I'm not very politically minded but most Tories I've met recently have been closet Fascists – do you break the mould? Lib Dem or Labour perhaps? Best wishes Sally*

His reply came on the following day.

Hello there and many thanks for your entertaining message. Now, let me put your mind at rest IMMEDIATELY. The odd four-letter word has been known to escape from my lips – only under the most severe pressure you understand – but T-O-R-Y never! This is the most obscene word in the colourful thesaurus of the English language. No, my fault, I should have been clearer about my job. I'm an administrator for a national trade union. So, do relax, I'm Labour through and through and, for the record, New Labour at that. Do reply reassuring me that I've got a least one foot in the door, even if it is my left. Regards. James

James, your nomination has been accepted! I'll contact you in a couple of weeks so we can finalise details, where, when etc etc. Best wishes Sally

I thought/hoped that this date could prove to be HUGELY interesting; he might have lots of scandalous stories and amusing anecdotes to tell about politicians in the public eye. He may even have met Alastair Campbell, top political eye candy! Who knows, he could – after a few drinks – divulge the full lurid details about that John Prescott business; now that would be entertaining!

Come fly with me

Things were beginning to fall into place nicely – it was as if someone up there liked me. The training course at Northampton, for example, postponed because of staffing problems, had been rescheduled for Thursday November 17th, the day before I was due to fly to Stockholm. A glance at the map confirmed my hunch. Northampton was more than halfway from the north-west to Stansted and so I'd be able to deliver the training, and then drive on to the Stansted area where I knew a small, comfortable B&B with safe parking; I'd then be set for the flight on the next day. Yes, on paper it was easy. In the event, however, dreadful traffic along the M10 coupled with the lashing rain made it a difficult journey. It didn't help either that the B & B was out in the sticks but the landlady was always welcoming, and the rooms spotlessly clean and comfortable. I drained the bottle of spring water and devoured the chicken sandwiches, purchased in haste at the petrol stop, had a long refreshing bath and then lay back. Yes, everything was now in place for 'Operation Viking'. The next morning the landlady drove me to the airport 'All part of the service dear'; the plane was on time, the flight perfect.

As I retrieved my bag from the overhead locker, I felt a growing sense of excitement as I joined the other passengers shuffling along the central aisle of the plane towards the exit; I noted their heavy coats and thick scarves and realised with a sigh that my pre-flight research had not been thorough. What I hadn't prepared myself for was the truly piercing cold. Picking my way gingerly down the steps, the sudden chill hit the back of my throat like the blast of a blowlamp fuelled with particles of ice; the handrail was thick with frost, leaving a glistening streak of icy crystal on my black leather gloves. Despite the canopy of blue above, it was positively arctic and I broke into a trot to reach the security of the shuttle standing just a hundred yards away. It was only an hour's journey into the town centre, and I soon found myself relaxing in the modern, airy lounge of the hotel. With Swedish precision, Henrik, the Viking, appeared, right on time.

'Oh dear' was my immediate thought and 'thank God I booked my own hotel room' was my second. 'Florid' didn't quite describe his curious complexion. Nor did 'follicly challenged' quite describe his pate. He was, quite simply, a snooker ball with ears and a red one at that. His Internet photo was clearly ten million hairs out of date – a fact that he'd chosen to keep to himself.

Nevertheless, I was determined to make the most of it now that I was there, and he was soon proving to be a gracious host. He planned to show me 'his city' including plenty of time for me to explore alone 'if that is what you are preferring.' And now Sally,' he continued with a flourish, 'I think we should drink Aquavit and eat herring, the best appetiser in the world.'

But the problem was that I really didn't like fish. I'd spent most of my primary school days sitting next to Ronnie Dodd, the fishmonger's son. Poor Ronnie. Such a curious smell always hung about his person, and his nickname of 'Dodd the Cod' haunted him way into adolescence.

The bar we went to sold nothing *except* Aquavit and herring. The herring buffet, despite its truly comprehensive nature, remained totally unappealing. I didn't want to appear unappreciative so I gamely took a small piece of 'Herring studded with Juniper Berries' together with a slug of the prized potion. The liquor scorched its way down to the pit of my stomach but at least I couldn't taste the herring.

'Mmm Henrik, I think this must be an acquired taste but I guess the aquavit really gets things going on New Year's Eve.'

'Try the aniseed herring which is the most perfect of food.'

'Oh, no thanks – I don't want to spoil my dinner.'

'Good idea for we will go to The Fish House – this is one of Stockholm's most famous restaurants.' More fish ... oh dear ... weren't the Swedes supposed to vary their diet from time to time and indulge in the occasional elkburger?

'Oh, I'll look forward to that – thanks,' ... resisting the urge to add '... and will you point out where I can get a burger on the way back?'

'The Fish House' entrance was fashioned like the mouth of a whale, and, going in, I felt like Jonah. From my point of view the meal was instantly forgettable although I did enjoy the wine; to help things along, his English was first-class and so conversation was easy. First up on Saturday was some essential shopping – earmuffs the size of frying pans, mittens as big as boxing gloves and several pairs of extra-thick tights – all of this would surely help combat the marrow-penetrating cold. We moved on to tour Stockholm. Actually, it was quite an attractive city – small, compact and incredibly clean – but it was hideously expensive. We stopped for coffee and cakes; the bill came to something like £23 and I resolved to pay for Henrik's dinner that night as the last thing I wanted was to feel beholden to him in any way.

'Now, I am sure that you find excitement in shops.'

I perked up immediately, my eyes alive with consumer zeal.

'I propose to take you to one of the city's most famous establishments.'

I dipped into my handbag, caressing the visa card.

'Over there, next to the pharmacy do you see the name? Systembolaget.'

The very name … 'system' something … had a strange almost totalitarian ring to it, and the drab exterior strengthened this feeling. He explained that it sold nothing except alcohol; indeed alcohol could *only* be bought there.

I listened in uncomprehending horror, and thought nostalgically of my local Morrisons or the paper shop, with their shelves straining under the weight of beer, wine and spirits. I gratefully took him up on his offer to 'leave you to your own pursuits' whiling away a couple of hours in the shops.

The best thing about Saturday night was Lars, the Volvo area manager who was sitting alone at the next table in the restaurant. We got chatting when Henrik went to the Gents and Lars leaned over to say 'I am hearing you are English; welcome to Stockholm.' He had a cheeky twinkle in his eye … he was great fun and I could have easily lost my head were it not for the forbidding presence of my host.

Sunday morning passed quickly. Late lie-in, lazy breakfast alone in the hotel, and Henrik was there at midday to run me to the airport.

'Thank you so much for looking after me.'

'It was all my pleasure and I would hope that we meet again soon.'

'Well Henrik, we do live rather a long way apart – long-distance relationships are not easy.'

He dropped his gaze, and was silent for a moment. He seemed disappointed, and I regretted my observation, realising I just couldn't bring myself to give him the 'Dear John' lines after he'd been so kind.

'That is true but when the desire is more the miles are less.' He moved in closer to me, his pate shining under the strong airport lights.

I touched his arm and gave him a quick peck on the cheek 'Look, there's my boarding call. I'll be in touch and, once again, thanks so much for showing me Stockholm. Bye.'

The plane was filling up fast. I soon found my seat and sat back in relief. Phew! My first global venture would most definitely be my last; only home-grown talent from now on, thank you very much.

Redundancies

Jonathan had summoned a staff meeting for nine o'clock 'sharp'. He was stone-faced. We began to feel uneasy, suspecting that something was afoot. He waited for total silence. Only when satisfied that he had our full attention, did he impart his news to the sullen gathering. It was devastating, encapsulated in the chilling word 'Redundancies'.

He did his level best to put a positive gloss on impending disaster, but we drew scant comfort from his words. He explained that the redundancies were not a reflection on the branch's performance, not on his and certainly not on ours. It was, rather, a logical response to the realities of

modern banking. He pointed out that whilst in the last
decade the banking sector had lost thousands of jobs at
all levels more banking than ever was being done. This did
little to alleviate the prevailing gloom which had settled on
the staff like a heavy autumn mist. He added that there
would be no immediate action and that further news
would be available after Christmas. He made a valiant but
unsuccessful attempt to raise morale by urging us all on to
greater efforts ... Nothing for it, I decided – I'd just have
to get stuck in; the approach of Christmas and the need,
now more marked than ever, to maximise revenue pointed
to an extremely busy month ahead.

From Stockholm to Southport

Within the space of three days, Henrik sent several
emails; all were very friendly '*I do hope you enjoyed your
first taste of Scandinavia*' and very hopeful '*are there any
major cultural events in London in the near future?*' In other
words, he would welcome another visit from me ... and,
rather more worryingly, welcome an invitation from me.
Decisive action was needed:

*Dear Henrik, yes, I did enjoy my time in
Sweden and thank you once again for your
kind hospitality. However, I do not think
that we have enough in common, to make for
a lasting relationship. Every best wish for the
future. Sally*

Ping! Off it went. I wouldn't open any further messages from him; to do so would serve only to protract something that was doomed to failure.

Among my emails was one from James, the political animal and resident of Southport, a sleepy resort on the Lancashire coast. I knew the area really well – as did Jonathan, who often spoke enthusiastically about the golf courses along the coast. Somehow, I didn't think James would be a sportsman. He was politely asking whether the work pressures had eased off at all and, if so, whether we could meet up for that drink that we'd spoken of and perhaps a meal as well. Yes, this seemed a good idea, Southport wasn't far off and the date would be an insight into a different world – politics – and anyway, he was really quite good-looking albeit in a conventional way – probably someone to like rather than to lust after. I contacted him, and we agreed to meet in a fortnight's time.

Getting ready for the date, I wondered, not without a touch of irritation, whether men ever really bothered to prepare for such occasions with the same care, the same intensity as most women did. From my extensive personal experience, all the evidence suggested otherwise. Oh yes, they were perfectly clean, tidy, smelled nice – that'll do! Perhaps it was a cultural thing or was it something deeper in the female psyche as women, consciously or not, strove to find a suitable mate. Finally, I opted for trousers and an attractive fuchsia kaftan top. The forgiving style hid the evidence of a recent bout of comfort eating that followed Beverley's double-edged admiration of my dress: 'a really good shape for bigger girls' – the bitch.

I met James at the restaurant he'd chosen – a small, intimate bistro in the better part of town. This was light years on from the fish and chips cafés of my childhood with their stewed tea and heaped rounds of bread and butter. The menu was varied, original and not terribly expensive. Minimalism had certainly hit the Lancashire coast as well. Laminate flooring, concealed lighting, highly polished tables, beautiful linen, stylish cutlery, inviting cream sofas in the lounge area and plain walls for the most part but enlivened here and there by a Matisse print or a vividly coloured Spanish dish. The music too, thankfully, was discreet and so a real conversation was possible without the patrons having to run the risk of an aching neck the following day from craning forward the entire evening. He was already there, sitting on one of the sofas, idly leafing through a glossy Sunday supplement. He recognised me immediately. He was casually but fashionably dressed. His winning smile made me feel very much at ease.

'Sally, hello, nice to meet you. Thanks for coming over,' he began, planting a modest kiss on each cheek. 'I've taken the liberty of ordering you a small glass of wine – Sauvignon Blanc OK? Didn't think you'd want a large glass because of driving home later.' Tasteful, considerate – things were getting better by the minute.

'Here's the menu. If we can't go mad with the wine, then at least we can indulge on the food side.'

The food was exceptionally good, and my initial doubts about the much-vaunted 'Britisserie Promotion' were ill-founded. We chatted easily.

'Yes, my marriage ended up on the rocks about three years ago; my fault – I was the guilty party, as people say ...' [I began to hear alarm bells ringing] ' ... I'd been spending far too much time on my job and politics and neglected the family I suppose. My wife, Sheila, put up with it all but when I cancelled our Caribbean cruise to rescue the local MP from some scandal, well, as you can imagine, that was the final straw.'

'Oh that's sad, James – these days, twenty-one years is quite an achievement and what about the children?'

'The girls got through it all pretty well really – kids can be amazingly resilient. They're both at uni now; one doing Geography, the other Political Science – perhaps the only good influence I've had on them. After the divorce I was working flat-out for the local MP.' 'The problem was,' he added a little wistfully, 'the expenses scandal proved his undoing. Luckily we were able to find a good replacement and went on to win but by a much-reduced majority, so in the end, it was worthwhile. I must confess, I felt a bit deflated after the election was over, despite our success. There was this … sort of enormous vacuum in my life and this was when I started to use the dating site.'

He paused.

'And have you been using the net for long?' I asked him, trying not to be too inquisitive.

'Not really – eighteen months or so max I suppose. I've met quite a few women, all pleasant enough, but I think it's fair to say that no fires were lit on either side. Now, you must be fed up with 'me, me, me' all the time. Your turn now: what's been going on or rather *is* going on in your life?'

I warmed to him. It wasn't often that men spoke openly and readily about their personal failures, not least when they were at fault. I laughed his apology away because I'd found it all so different and interesting. I also liked the way he focussed on me throughout the evening and tried ever so gently to winkle out a few details about my own life.

'As regards my own marriage, that's a long story, for another time maybe. We were both too young and, in the end, wanted different things out of life. As for education, I wish I'd gone to university. A degree seems to give people a passport to life. Still, I've got my professional qualifications so that's something.'

He seemed genuinely concerned and supportive, pointing out that the OU offered a whole range of courses from diploma through to degree level and beyond, adding that he still had the necessary prospectus at home from the time when he had followed a course in Industrial Law.

'Yes, Industrial Law,' he laughed. 'I know – not exactly thrilling is it? Not like Painting in Renaissance Italy or Modern British Drama ... [I shivered at the painful memory of the Pinter play] ... but my fees were paid for by the TUC and so it wouldn't have been fair really for me to study something that really fascinated me.'

Inwardly, I was actually quite taken with the idea of furthering my education, although OU-style courses would not be my first choice. I'd prefer something less cerebral, reviving my school interest in Art perhaps or moving into ceramics or design. Food for thought certainly.

He ordered coffee, noting with approval that it was 'fair-trade sourced'. I didn't have a clue what this meant but was reluctant to ask, fearing my ignorance might prove as shameful as quaffing brandy with a starter. It was time for me to go. He was the perfect gentleman, seeing my safely to my car. He gave me a warm hug and kissed me briefly.

'It's been great – hope we can repeat it soon.'

I drove home in high spirits. He'd made quite an impact. I really did like him, his humour, his conversation, and I was already looking forward to our next date. I awarded the dating site nine out of ten, minimum.

Things developed quickly. We met again for dinner, and there was also a trip to the cinema – Syriana proved easier viewing than Last Tango in Paris – and a trip to the Liverpool Tate. We managed to cope with the distance between us by reciprocating journeys or meeting somewhere halfway. It was all going well, and I told Caroline all about him. We tried to organise a foursome but had some difficulty in finding a suitable date; there was so much going on with the approach of Christmas. He suggested that we should spend Christmas together. He would pay a perfunctory visit to his children at their mother's, but other than that he had little on. I apologised, saying that I would be spending Christmas with my parents. I sensed a certain huffing annoyance in him, as he muttered something about 'families being the cause of so many problems in society'. I countered this quite firmly by declaring that I wasn't seeing them out of a sense of duty – I wanted to spend time with them. He read the signals correctly and immediately backed off, realising he'd overstepped the mark. He could see he wasn't getting very far on this one – well, what about New Year? Yes, that would be fine, I thought, relieved at the prospect of normality when he promised to book a high quality country hotel. Perhaps, he could really unwind there.

Chapter 11

Jingle bells

At his final staff meeting before Christmas, Jonathan, now somewhat more relaxed, said he hoped his brief 'window' of management hadn't caused too many sleepless nights! This was met with nervous laughter as the redundancies were still on the agenda. He was really sorry he wouldn't be able to join everyone at the staff party as he was using up the last of his leave to go skiing in the French Alps; 'After all, I have to defend my slalom trophy.' Oh, Jonathan, you big poser, you've not really changed, have you, I thought – beneath the sharp suit and business jargon you're still the same irrepressible fun-loving bloke I nearly ended up in bed with. I wonder...

As people returned to their 'work stations' [another 'Lesleyism'] Jonathan caught up with me in the corridor. To my immense surprise, he kissed me furtively and whispered 'The old Jonathan will be back in January you know – will the old Sally still be around? Please? – affecting an almost doe-eyed expression of need and dependence. 'Well, that's up to the bosses now isn't it, darling,' I murmured in mock vamp style, but not without sensing a ripple of interest coursing through my veins. A blast of perfume signalled the approach of leggy Bevvy ... with a conspiratorial wink, we went our separate ways.

The office party, at a restaurant in the town centre, was set for the Wednesday evening; the bank was to close at two on the Thursday afternoon, Christmas Eve. As I normally staggered from the office party with sore feet and a sorer head, I'd booked the following morning off as leave, giving me the chance for some last-minute shopping and ample time for a leisurely drive north. As usual, many of the women – certainly the younger ones – would take the afternoon off BEFORE the party 'to get ready', a female ritual that left the men shaking their heads in disbelief.

As regards presents, I'd been exceptionally well organised this year, with my parents' gifts purchased some months before. This really left just Cazi's family, and I was pretty sure about them; James, though, was a bit of a problem.

For Caroline: some of her favourite perfume – 'Ami' by Gaultier – and a faux fur thong.

For Bob: giant size earplugs to combat Richard's, aka Phil Collins, drumming, together with a glossy guide of Florida.

For Louise: CD tokens and a voucher for Tony&Guy – this, I subsequently discovered, had been a real hit.

For Richard: the latest Kaiser Chiefs CD plus a Jordan calendar – sure to be confiscated by an outraged Bob...

That left James. Yes, James. This was something of a problem. He'd never shown the slightest interest in sport; he did tend to be a little pernickety and so was the type who preferred to buy his own clothes; drink – yes that was the solution and a bottle of malt whisky would certainly do the trick. Now, how on earth could I find out if Talisker was 'fair-trade sourced'?

I hadn't joined in the usual Christmas debauchery at the party, managing to slip away quietly towards midnight, well before the illicit groping began. I got up early – and unusually clear-headed – the next day and my resolve was rewarded. In under an hour I completed my mini shopping expedition; by mid-afternoon, I was putting my feet up in my parents' living room which was decorated now for the festive period. On the walls were dozens of Christmas cards affixed to long strips of pink tissue, miniature bells of crepe paper and chains of mini red and yellow hoops criss-crossed the ceiling. By the TV stood a small Christmas tree; on top of it there was a tiny angel, hands clasped in reverent prayer, her red, expressionless eyes flashing intermittently.

'Mum, the room looks really nice but how on earth did you manage to put it all up?'

'Well, it's Mr Neal next door – he's divorced now you know – he brought his stepladders in and got the decorations up for us otherwise we'd never have managed it what with Dad's back and everything anyway it's lovely to see you love I'll get the tea going soon then we can all watch *Coronation Street* mind you I'm losing track of it what with all these new faces in it and all these divorces and people going off with one another and God knows it gets me all confused and …'

I realised how much my parents meant to me, and at one stage in the evening just jumped up and gave Dad a big hug.

'What's that for?' he asked in amused amazement.

'It's for you, you silly old devil – it's your Christmas box – all I could afford this year I'm afraid.'

Just then, my mobile rang, and I made my excuses as I went off into the kitchen. It was James. 'Look Sally, I know you're with your mum and dad and I'll only be on a minute – just to let you know, I'm missing you very much and loving you more.'

'Oh, this is really sweet of you but are you sure you've not been at the Christmas sherry too early?' I suppose I often used humour to camouflage my feelings and was in fact quite touched by his thoughtfulness.

'No, not at all – I'm really looking forward to seeing you next weekend, and do say Merry Christmas to your parents from me won't you?'

Well, that was unexpected. I felt a warm glow – after all, it was nice to be missed and to be loved and, yes, I was really excited about the New Year break with him. I just hoped against hope that it would be light, frivolous and self-indulgent and wouldn't involve a cheerless sit-in at some godforsaken nuclear plant or something similar. I passed on his good wishes to Mum and Dad; Mum's ears pricked up at the phrase, 'from James, a friend of mine,' but she had been schooled to enquire no further.

The bitch is back

Tea was just about ready when my mobile rang again. Damn – probably Caroline; could do without it right now – I'd have to keep it short. I hurried into the kitchen once more. Now, this was odd – Brian from work. I silently cursed myself for being incapable of managing separate mobiles for business and private use.

'Oh, Sally, I'm so sorry to be phoning you like this. Look something awful's happened.'

'Something awful?' For a split second I thought of Jonathan – perhaps he'd been badly injured skiing or something. 'Awful, Brian, what do you mean?'

'Guess who came into the office with just ten minutes to go today? Only Lesley. [I relaxed – good, Jonathan's safe.]

She strolls in, heels clicking like a velociraptor walking on tiles, and finds Roy in the server room, bottle of whisky in one hand and an FX girl in the other – '

'Don't tell me Brian – I can imagine the rest; Lesley – '

'Dead right – she fires him on the spot for "unacceptable and unprofessional standards of behaviour"! And then he's virtually bundled out of the building! Happy Christmas! What a nasty piece of work that woman is!'

After thanking Brian for letting me know and wishing him a Merry Christmas, I explained I'd have to get back to my parents. Office politics would mean nothing to them. They still found it hard come to terms with even the idea of a woman being in charge. I wouldn't let the toxic gloom of the news from the office seep over a cosy evening at home so I said it was just Caroline, sending them the season's greetings.

Mistletoe and wine

After tea and *Corrie*, we settled down to watch Dad's favourite video; they could just about manage this – DVDs were as yet a little bit too new and complex. The video was my Christmas present to him, a boxed set of the 2006 *Mastermind* series. Although, Dad complained a bit that 'this new boy John Humphreys isn't a patch on Magnus McManaman.' There was some confusion here between the iconic presenter and the Liverpool footballer but never mind. Dad had a paper and pencil at the ready, and every time he recorded a correct answer he would shout triumphantly 'Got it! Got it!' Whilst he was delighted with his gift, Mum was equally thrilled with her boxed set of expensive soaps and sprays, which I'd bought in Debenhams. I burst into tears when I opened my Christmas present from them. It had been carefully wrapped, and I guessed it contained a small box. It was an antique wedding ring, gold but studded with tiny diamonds.

'It was my mother's you know love and I've always worn it but the arthritis in my fingers won't let me any more and it'll be nice if it stays in the family.'

Christmas Day passed in this relaxed style though my parents were disappointed because our relatives from the north-east hadn't been able to make it after all because of illness. 'None of us are getting any younger,' said Dad philosophically, as he carved the succulent turkey with all the relish of a hunger striker who had changed his mind. The Queen's Speech punctuated the afternoon and he felt obliged to propose a loyal toast. This was either because the Queen's appearance had re-awoken his dormant patriotism or simply because, by then, the combination of sherry and wine – 'Yes, we always have wine at Christmas these days' – had achieved their inevitable effect.

Boxing Day lunch saw the remains of the still-tasty turkey and a healthy portion of Christmas pudding. I'd intended to leave after lunch but changed my mind – much to their obvious delight – and stayed over until the following day. This worked a treat. Dad seemed positively rejuvenated, the television was switched off and instead we played Whist and other family games.

Back home the next day, I had time for a long and intimate conversation with James. He hadn't phoned me again, explaining 'I respect your wish to focus on your family.' A kind thought but, it seemed to me, an odd way of putting it. He was eager to let me know that he'd found a really classy hotel on the Internet. It was in the Lake District. Bracing walks by the lakes, roaring log fires, delectable food and drink and the company of the first man I'd felt really close to for years. He would pick me up on the morning of New Year's Eve.

Caroline phoned in the evening and soon had me in hysterics describing how, when the kids were out of the way, she'd donned the faux fur thong; this had sent Bob crazy with lust.

'Hang on, I thought, there could be problems here. If he recovers his piston-driven sex drive, he could have a heart attack again and then we'd be back to square one – on the other hand if I take it off he'll see this as a further come-on and it'll make him absolutely bloody rampant' – 'No, listen … ' she added, trying to quell my howls of laughter '… it gets worse; there I am cavorting round the bedroom like some slapper in a Soho strip joint when Richard only turns on that bloody CD you bought him. Honestly, I thought the bloody ceiling was going to come crashing down on us. Well, that put an end to the orgy-for-two I can tell you! Bob thought the earplugs were a better alternative so we just ended up on the bed, him watching golf on Sky and me flicking through *Hello!* That bloody Paris Hilton – her tits get everywhere!'

I chuckled an apology for the CD that had suddenly doused the raging fire of Bob's rediscovered libido.

'Oh, don't worry, love,' she replied with a laugh. 'Probably for the best anyway – I had visions of riding side-saddle for a week! Tell you what, give me a ring after New Year – we'll have a drink, and you can update me on you and James – the four of us must get together soon so I can check if he really is good enough for you.'

A lakeside romance

A bottle of champagne, swishing gently in an ice bucket and an enormous bouquet of red roses stood on the small table in the centre of our suite. Alongside was a tiny, scarlet casket opening to reveal a pair of pearl earrings. Tears welled up in my eyes. It had been so long since I'd been spoiled like this. We ignored the New Year's Eve party and went to bed. Our lovemaking was passionate; it seemed as if I was releasing years of pent-up emotion. This first day and night typified the weekend that passed all too quickly. I'd sorely missed this kind of intimacy and it wasn't just about the sex. We talked about anything and everything, AND I felt sufficiently confident to tell him of the real reason for my marriage break-up. In fact, he gave me the opening.

'You know I'm really glad that I've managed to maintain a relationship with my girls. Somehow it all seems so much easier now they're growing up. I can relate to them much better as young adults than I ever could when they were little. I'm enormously proud of them and really enjoy the odd time we spend together even if it does usually end up with me dragging out my cheque book. But, can I ask you something? Is there a reason you never had children? And don't answer if that's too personal a question.'

I sighed heavily and looked away slightly.

'Well, the short answer is that I always did want children; would have loved to be a mother but I've got a problem which means I'll never be able to carry a child full-term. We went through every possible test, spent thousands on private consultations but it wasn't to be. IVF wasn't an option, the idea of surrogacy was only just starting up and my ex-husband was completely opposed to the idea of adoption. Oh yes, he wanted kids but only if we were *his* kids. He wouldn't even discuss adoption. So that was it. I couldn't get past his total disregard for me and my feelings and this – and his obstinacy – finally drove us apart.'

'Oh darling, I'm so sorry. That's a terrible story. What a selfish bastard! It must have been awful for you. I won't say something trite like, children can be a blessing as well as a curse – I'll just say that I'm glad you left him because that means we can be here now.'

He pulled me towards him, kissed me tenderly on the forehead and wrapped his arms around me as if he never wanted to let go. We left the hotel, sharing the buoyancy of a new year and a new love. He resolutely declined my offer to 'pay my way': 'if you've enjoyed it even a half as much as I have, darling, then I'll be really delighted.'

A new year, a new Lesley?

Like lambs to the slaughter, people assembled in the main office for Lesley's first staff meeting since resuming her duties as Branch Manager. I looked over to see Jonathan; he was bronzed and better looking than ever … and he returned my glance with just a hint of a mischievous smile on his lips.

Her opening words were to welcome everybody back and to hope that we had all enjoyed a well-earned break. This was *Lesley* speaking … what a surprising and disarmingly human prologue! She then went on to say that following Roy Palmer's sudden decision to leave just before Christmas – what a brazen cheek! – the bank had secured the services of Mike Preston, as temporary IT manager. Lucy – as well as Roy – flashed into my mind, but I realised I couldn't fight everyone's corner for them. Lesley said the new man would be starting immediately, but requested that people 'should not burden him too much straightaway until he gets to grips with everything.' Another uncommonly kind thought from this erstwhile ogress and how sensitively worded – what on earth was going on here? She was unusually open with everyone in fact – there was more positive eye contact, cheerful greetings and seemingly interested questions about the Christmas break and how things were with our families.

The week went by and there was no mention from her of the promotion issue – not even when she asked me into her office; its former harsh aspect softened by some beautiful blue hyacinths in an elegant bowl and a Highlands Calendar on the wall. She needed my advice on a training course for the new IT man and I was happy to oblige. Curiouser and curiouser.

James, the political animal

Friends of James lived on the outskirts of Manchester and had invited us to dinner on the Saturday evening. He had often spoken of 'Ian and Val'; clearly they'd been part of his life for many years and he was anxious for me to meet them. They had a spacious, modern detached house. The garden was trim and tidy though lacking much colour because of the time of the year. Most driveways in the road displayed fine cars; Mercedes or BMWs were the norm or one of those fashionable 4x4s that comedians mocked as 'Chelsea Tractors'.

The evening was going well. We seemed to hit it off, surprisingly so for a first meeting. Before having her children, Val had worked as a bank clerk, and this was a useful starting point for conversation. We chatted easily about our jobs and recent holidays, the usual topics over a suburban dinner. Ian and Val spoke enthusiastically about a recent month's holiday in Australia to celebrate their silver wedding; they'd loved the country, the weather, the spectacular scenery, the wildlife.

Ian was an educational psychologist by profession and let slip that they had contemplated moving out to Australia but had concerns about the standard of education out there. I thought of 'St Thug's' as Cazi so damningly referred to her children's secondary school, and wondered whether state provision in Australia could be any worse than here at home.

Val began to speak gushingly about their daughter, Jackie. She was attending the 'local girls" high school; she'd performed brilliantly at GCSE and the outlook for A-level was equally promising. 'It certainly needs to be,' she added, 'because she's got her sights firmly set on medical school. And, of course,' she continued as she replenished our glasses, 'we've got our wonderful James to thank for all this, haven't we Ian?'

Ian readily concurred. I glanced at James ... he looked uncomfortable.

'Yes, without his intervention, our Jackie would have ended up at the local comp with all those layabouts.'

I knew that the girls' high school was semi private and so could be really choosy about admissions.

'Yes,' Val blithely carried on, 'James was on the Board of Governors at the time and – let's say – used his influence

… [she giggled] … well, pulled a few strings actually, to make sure she got in.'

Throughout all this, James had the look of a guilty man – for all the world like a light-fingered shopper apprehended by a store detective. He kept his eyes firmly fixed on the table, as if determined to avoid my gaze. Luckily for him, conversation moved on to other subjects before, at midnight, it was time to go. They had been wonderful hosts and I was happy to agree to a dinner out with them sometime. Beneath my relaxed demeanour, however, something was nagging away like a toothache. For the moment, nothing further was said.

Marching for justice

Some days later, I received an urgent call from James asking if I was free during the day on Saturday week. He hoped so because he'd already lined up a friend who lived nearby to pick me up and drive me over to Southport. It was a rally in support of Bob Geldof's Live8 initiative, intended to heighten people's awareness of the 'problems of world debt and the intolerable levels of poverty in Africa'. I reluctantly agreed; I was due to see him over there in the evening anyway and didn't want to alter the arrangement he'd made with his friend. Inwardly, however, I was annoyed, miffed at the presumption on his part. I wasn't *that* politically minded and resented the fact that he simply assumed I shared his view of the world. Furthermore, he'd compromised me by fixing something up with a friend. The business of the school still rankled. It was clear that he had used his public position to advance a private agenda, thus ensuring that 'our Jackie' would be spared the fate worse than death of attending the local 'comp'; the Waynes and Jodies of this world have no such champion: where, I wondered, was all his idealistic talk of 'social justice' in this situation?

So, reluctantly, I found myself side by side with him on the day of the event. Little did I suspect then, however, that my worst fears were to be realised. Sadly, but not altogether unsurprisingly, the rally turned nasty. In a provincial version of the anti-capitalist riots normally reserved for capital cities, 'Temples of economic and social repression' – banks, building societies, the ubiquitous McDonald's – were targeted. To begin with, the usual suspects were to be seen gathering for the march; anarchists, skinheads and hoodies mixed in with serious devotees of Marx and Trotsky. The latter were all the more recognisable because of a messianic gleam of a fairer society in their eyes, hand-rolled cigarettes drooping from their lips and a copy of *The Guardian* tucked securely under their arms.

It was a bitterly raw day, and the slate-grey sky, with billowing black clouds, was a bad omen. James was at the head of the column, struggling to keep aloft a TUC banner that was being heavily buffeted by the wind, sweeping in from the bay. I watched anxiously as the surging crowd formed some sort of semi-military order to the deafening accompaniment of whistles, hand sirens and drumbeats. I could almost smell the heady rush of imminent combat. The police had already been deployed in force and were now in serried ranks, with their riot gear and black, menacing helmets. It was alarming to see their horses, even though they were protected by huge metallic blinkers and voluminous folds of chain-mail aprons. They snorted restlessly, their breath – rising in thick, white puffs

– mingled with plumes of steam as they sweated heavily beneath their armour.

Yes, I was scared – bewildered too. What had I got myself into? What on earth was I doing here? I wanted out, there and then. The central square was already packed so that escape wasn't easy. Luckily, though, I knew the area quite well, and muttered something to James about not feeling too good and needing the Ladies. I managed to slip away, along a side street. From there I reached the station. Two hours later, I sat at home, trembling with delayed panic, waiting for the inevitable phone call from James. But the call never came – not on that day, not on Sunday, nor on Monday. On Tuesday I decided to act. By now I'd convinced myself that he'd taken the proverbial huff, seeing through my feigned illness and was now sitting back, determined to let me do the chasing, whilst proffering some derisory excuse. I phoned his mobile. A female voice answered. Ah! I was quick to establish myself as 'Mr Charlton's partner'; this was not strictly accurate but the kernel of truth would enable me to get the information I needed. The story then gradually emerged.

The speaker explained that she was a nurse at Tall Pines, a BUPA hospital some distance from Southport. James had been admitted late on the Saturday apparently suffering from severe concussion from a heavy blow to the head. He was still under sedation; the nurse allayed my worst fears by saying that there would be no permanent damage – the doctors were confident of a complete recovery and, in fact, he was to be discharged on the following day. I was numb.

That damned rally. I remembered the TV news footage of it on the Monday morning with the protesters, chanting their slogans as they streamed forward, perilously close to the police lines. I thanked the nurse, asking her to let him know I'd called and that I'd be in touch again very soon.

On Wednesday evening, I found myself in his flat – or 'apartment' as he preferred to call it – ministering to his needs. He was feeling really sorry for himself and, though still a little groggy, told me the tale.

'We were marching peacefully down the high street when suddenly, without the slightest provocation on our part, the police attacked. In the confusion I felt this crunching blow on my head. I must have blacked out immediately, because the next thing I knew I was in A & E at Southport General. It had to be a truncheon blow from one of those fascist twats we recruit as policemen these days – bastards. I'm telling you, I'm going to sue them for every penny I can get.'

I made the usual reassuring noises but remained perplexed. 'But, I don't quite follow. You went to A & E but when I phoned you were in that BUPA place.'

He reacted violently to this. 'Southport General, bloody NHS shithole that is,' he sneered. 'Yes, I did end up there on the Saturday night; desperate place, bloody desperate – drunks staggering around, pools of vomit on the floor, junkies sprawled over the chairs, tattooed louts with blood streaming from their noses. When I complained, the nurses got really shirty, saying what did I expect; this was a normal Saturday night after the pubs had emptied. I told 'em straight: I wanted a taxi immediately, and off I went to Tall Pines – that sorted 'em!'

It was obvious from his language and vehement, truncated speech that he was probably still recovering from the shock of it all. It would have been unfair of me to challenge him about how he squared his principles, so loftily aired at dinner parties and the like, by paying for private treatment when the local hospital was on his doorstep. By now he was visibly tiring, and I felt it was time to return home. But he wasn't quite finished yet, saying how maddening it all was, as he was representing the TUC at a Pan-European congress in Paris in the week ahead. He felt sure he'd still be able to make it but obviously we wouldn't be able to get together for the next week or so. Hmm ... his priorities hadn't changed...

Second thoughts

I drove home, my mind in turmoil, my feelings mixed. What was it with him? I had become really fond of him – in fact, some weeks earlier, I'd begun to think he was the fabled 'man of my dreams'. Increasingly, however, his star was fading. I remembered his explanation for his marital problems, how he had relegated his married life to second place behind politics. Then there were those uncomfortable contradictions. The problem was his double standards. His friends had openly described how he'd used his influence to help their daughter, and then his passion for the NHS had quickly been exhausted by his personal experience of it. He had compounded all of this by viciously condemning the local hospital. He could, by all means, have his political beliefs – I had no problem with that. But, there was a key issue here of integrity; I felt deceived and disappointed, and this worried me deeply. The future now looked uncertain and, for the moment, I decided against arranging the proposed evening with Caroline and Bob.

St Lesley's Day

Lesley had organised a staff meeting first thing on the Friday morning. People trudged into the main office, downcast, displaying all the pessimism of Tory candidates seeking electoral success in the Welsh valleys. The energising aroma of freshly made coffee immediately lifted our spirits, and our eyes feasted on an appetising array of pains au chocolat and pains au raisin. Lesley was scarcely recognisable. The forbidding black trouser suit had disappeared and with it the daunting manner. She was wearing a dark-blue skirt – not exactly pencil tight but sufficiently narrow to emphasise her contours and certainly short enough to disprove the oft-repeated allegation that she had a dragon's tail. A smart, fresh light-blue blouse, sapphire necklace and attractive hairstyle enhanced the overall pleasing effect. The tinted glasses had been discarded, replaced no doubt by contact lenses. Sitting within fondling range of her was Mike, Roy's replacement; she was exchanging pleasantries, smiling contentedly and looking so relaxed and at ease with the world. I continued to stare in disbelief. Where was the Lesley of old? She rose to speak.

'And now, colleagues, I have an update on the redundancies situation.'

The casual chatter came to an immediate halt; we all exchanged anxious glances: suddenly, the coffee and cakes became stale and tasteless. We thought we'd seen through it. The refreshments, the new-look Lesley, the easy pre-amble – all of this, we were sure now, was a sham; simply the empty facade to the crumbling structure of our security.

'You will all remember,' she began, 'that before Christmas we got news from head office about the possibility, the likelihood, of job losses. The full picture is that, nationally, the bank has to lose 2000 jobs.'

A sharp intake of breath.

'Since there are some 300 branches, this means in broad terms that each branch will need to let six or seven colleagues go.'

A sharper intake of breath.

'However, as one-third of the branches are in London in a relatively confined area, amalgamations down there mean that that is where the brunt of the losses will be.'

A murmur of hope around the room.

'Our quota was set at four. However, the unexpected departure of Roy just before Christmas and the sad loss of Lucy in the autumn ...' [You two-faced cow!] ' ... Means that we're already halfway there. Additionally the husband of one of the cashiers has a job move to North America, and two of the girls in the Foreign Exchange section are soon to take maternity leave ... ' [At these words, I noticed that Beverley shot Jonathan a venomous look – he stared resolutely at his feet.] '... And they've said that if they do come back, they would be more than willing to go part-time and share one post. And so colleagues – dramatic pause here and an imagined fanfare of gleaming trumpets – I am now in a position to tell you that my branch, your branch, *our* branch will not be exposed to any losses at all! We will certainly have to work that bit harder, go that extra mile, but our jobs are safe.'

With a contrived flourish she gathered up her papers, neatly folded them, and placed them carefully on the desk to her right.

'Thank you all for your kind attention.'

At this point she glanced at Mike for his approval. She was not disappointed. Their eye contact was warm and lingering.

At first the staff couldn't take it in but then, as the truth dawned, what began as a gentle ripple of applause from the back of the room swelled into a tidal wave, accompanied by a flurry of high-fives and American-style hooting and hollering. People then moved off to their 'work stations' in groups of four or five, talking animatedly. I spotted Mike unobtrusively following Lesley into her office. Hmm ... perhaps he was installing an upgrade for her ...

St Valentine's Day

February was now close and James, fully restored to health, was back from France. 'Marvellous experience, absolutely marvellous; these European socialists – they really know how to fly the red flag high – they make us lot seem like wimps in comparison.' He went on to say that for St Valentine's Day he'd booked dinner at a restaurant of some note in one of the region's premier hotels. As usual, there was no consultation, no enquiry about my movements, about my availability. I agreed to go, thinking that it might repair some of the recent damage to our relationship but deep down I harboured severe doubts.

Then, on the tranquillity of a sharp, frosty February morning I suffered a real shock. One of the tabloids had picked up on the riot in which he'd been injured. 'Greedy Councillor – Sow Sorry', shrieked the headline. There was a photograph of him as well, looking utterly dejected. The story maintained the pig metaphor, by describing how, immediately after the incident, he'd been 'squealing for £100,000 in compensation' for 'this wanton act of police aggression'. The report described how, once the violence had erupted, CCTV coverage had recorded a drunken lout, sporting a Mohican haircut, cracking down a bottle on James's head. There was some speculation as to whether the bottle was Guinness or Newcastle Brown. As regards the assailant himself, however, the footage was unambiguous; the youth stood out all the more clearly because he had dyed his Mohican tartan – perhaps a relic of the 'Walk on Edinburgh' some months before to coincide with the G8 meeting at Gleneagles. James, shamefaced, had been forced to withdraw his allegations against the local constabulary and issue a 'profound apology'. Why on earth hadn't he explained all of this to me in person instead of leaving me to read of it in the papers? I was hurt. What sort of relationship did he want?

He'd phoned me, saying, rather curtly, that he'd be a little late, and would meet me inside the restaurant. After an hour or so, there he was, striding in with a face like thunder. He was untidy and dishevelled; his jacket was creased, a button was missing from one of his shirt cuffs, and he hadn't shaved – tiny bristles were sprouting from his chin. This dismayed me, considerably. He knocked back a double whisky and complained bitterly that he had failed to win the nomination for Regional Party Organiser.

'After my years of loyal service this is my reward – the bastards – and they've given it to a bloody snotty-nosed armchair socialist – Dr, yes, *Dr* Damian Grant straight out of Oxford bloody University! I'm telling you, he only clinched it because he's queer and has been sucking up to the right people or in his case sucking them off – perverted little twat! And to think I even turned up for his Civil Ceremony only a few weeks ago!'

He drained his glass again in fury and slammed it down. I winced at his behaviour. 'James, please cut that out and keep your voice down,' I hissed, eyes blazing.

He fell silent and seemed momentarily penitent. Luckily, a waitress then appeared to take our order. As the meal progressed I could see him drinking more and more – perhaps the fact that he'd booked a room for the night made him think he could act with complete abandon. His voice rose again. Food slipped from his fork onto his shirtfront and then onto the plush carpet beneath; he didn't seem to notice this.

As he talked endlessly and volubly about 'necessary changes to the party voting system', I sighed and felt my eyes glazing over. Not quite the romantic dinner *à deux* that he'd promised. To emphasise a specific detail of his 'Manifesto for Change' he swept his hand across the table spilling a glass of red wine. He glowered at me, yelling that I was 'Bloody stupid for leaving the glass there in the first place!' The other diners looked over at us in disgust.

I was incandescent with indignation, and was just about to get up and leave when a pleasant young waitress scuttled forward to clear up the debris.

'No doubt you'll try to sell me another bottle of this crap won't you, you silly little bitch,' he shouted.

The waitress froze, helpless. At this point the manager marched forward, his face dark with intent; he was accompanied by two of the hotel porters. They were stocky, silent, intimidating, and each took up a position on either side of their quarry. 'It is time for you to leave, sir– now!'

261

As the porters half dragged, half lifted him to his feet I asked them to call for a taxi. My final view of James was as he stood there, swaying: a crumpled, stained and sorry mess. Thoroughly embarrassed and humiliated, I mumbled for the bill.

Chapter 12

RESPITE
PART 1 CHILLING AT CHEVERNY COURT

Discouraged, disappointed, dismayed, disconsolate, dissatisfied, just how many words beginning with 'dis' accurately described my disillusionment [there's another] with men in general and Dateandsee in particular? I'd had a bellyful of it, and decided to abandon dating for a while and concentrate on having fun without any male input.

First up was a three day/two night break with Caroline at Cheverny Court. This was a luxurious and proportionately expensive health and leisure spa in Northamptonshire. Until a few years previously it had been a handsome hunting lodge, but the owners had clearly seen which way the wind was blowing and had sold it off to a leisure industry group. Yes, it *was* expensive – hideously so – but where else could you slob around in your dressing gown for days on end AND still expect to look and feel fabulous at the end of it? We arrived at 10.30 to be greeted by 'Miranda'. Her hair was bouncy and shiny, her make-up was subtle, perfect, and her body was slim and firm. Also, she was irritatingly prim. I hated her on sight.

'Why is she wearing a nurse's outfit?' whispered Caroline in alarm. 'We don't have to have colonic irrigation do we?'

'Shsssshhh. Good morning, erm, Miranda. I'm Sally Johnson. You should have a twin room booked for me?'

'Hello ladies. Welcome to Cheverny Court,' she chimed. 'Let me check for you … ah, yes, a twin … a *superior* twin in fact.' She emphasised 'superior' as if complimenting me on my innate good taste in shelling out a further £35 a night each simply for the dubious benefit of brocade scatter cushions on the beds and glistening jars of toiletries in the bathroom.

'Now, if you would sign in please, I'll explain a little bit about Cheverny Court, give you your bathrobes and a porter will take you to your room.'

I signed the register noticing the names of two 'Z-list' celebrities further up the page; one of them, Rebekkah, was the page 3 model girlfriend of a footballer, the other, Luna, a Big Brother contestant.

Miranda smiled sweetly, cocked her head to one side and began the finely crafted but utterly predictable corporate introduction.

'Thank you. Now, ladies, here at Cheverny Court we like to take a holistic approach; therefore, we offer our patrons a comprehensive range of treatments guaranteed to pamper mind, body and soul. Everything from meditation rooms to fully equipped beauty salons and fitness centre, with fascinating lectures on subjects such as yoga and reiki. Naturally we also have a wonderful spa area, swimming pool, sauna, steam room, jacuzzi and even a thalassotherapy centre!' She paused for effect before raising both hands heavenwards in the manner of a TV evangelist and saying, 'We want you to leave here relaxed, refreshed and rejuvenated!'

Both 'ladies' wore the fixed dazed smile of the utterly bewildered. We collected our bathrobes and information packs and followed the porter to our room. 'Blooodddyyy hell!' said Caroline. 'What are we doing here? Meditation? Reiki? And what's that bloody lassoo therapy thing all about– it sounds raunchy to me. I'm getting worried – I told you we should have taken easyJet to Palma!'

'Now don't be so hasty. We both agreed that this place would be something completely different for us and I, for one, am really looking forward to it. Now pass me that information pack and let's have a look at what's on offer.'

'What time's lunch?' Caroline growled. 'I haven't had anything since one or two chocolate croissants early this morning.'

'That's your problem Caroline. You never eat anything with any goodness in it so you feel hungry all the time.'

'Ooohh, listen to Dr Gillian over there. As I recall, your local Thorntons had to sack someone due to a loss in profits the last time you went on a diet.'

'OK, so I'm not perfect, but I am sick of eating junk and I'm hoping this break will kick-start me into something healthier.'

A little later we joined the tour of the 'resort'. Samantha, a Miranda clone, took us first to the spa area.

'Here we are ladies … the Cheverny Court Spa and Thalassotherapy Centre.' The changing area was beautiful – cleanser, toner, shampoo, conditioner, etc. all provided; the underlit pool and bubbling jacuzzi were equally inviting. There were a few other people around including, I noted, a solitary male. And not a bad-looking one at that. Blimey! What a great place for a man to meet a woman! He'd be outnumbered at least thirty to one; all he needed was the confidence to go in the first place. After all, a health resort is still considered a predominately female preserve.

' … And soaking in the mineral salts is an excellent treatment for cellulite which makes it very popular with our ladies. If you would like to experience thalassotherapy, I strongly recommend you book a session well in advance as we can scarcely keep pace with the demand.'

Caroline nudged me. 'I think I'll have some of that – my cellulite doesn't exactly enhance that thong you gave me.'

'And here's the coffee bar, lounge area and restaurant.'

The lounge area was filled with squashy sofas and comfortable armchairs. There was no television and no music playing. Books, magazines and newspapers were scattered around. About two dozen people [including another two men] were lounging around in their bathrobes reading or chatting quietly, drinking coffee or fruit juices.

'Erm, where's the bar?' I enquired politely.

'Bar? Bar?' replied Samantha in wide-eyed astonishment, as if asked to spell Czechoslovakia backwards in two seconds flat. 'Oh, there's no bar. We don't encourage drinking alcohol, although you can order wine with your meals so long as you drink it in the restaurant.'

We stopped dead in our tracks, looking at each other open-mouthed. Surely we had misheard?

'No bar?' I asked, incredulously.

'No bar,' Samantha solemnly replied, shaking her head to reinforce the truly grim and immutable nature of this unwelcome information.

'But, but …' Caroline spluttered. 'What do people do after dinner if not have a drink?'

'Well they go to bed of course. Most people are up *very* early. The fitness centre opens at six and many guests are keen to work out for an hour or two before breakfast.'

I attempted to lighten the mood. 'Oh, right then. Well I hope they close their bedroom doors quietly on the way to the gym because on holiday I don't open my eyes before nine!'

'Later than that if she copped off the night before,' Caroline sniggered.

I pinched her hard and smiled apologetically at Samantha, as if seeking understanding for my friend who was so obviously a Tourette's sufferer. The tour continued for another ten minutes before finishing [surprise, surprise] at the souvenir shop.

'So ladies, that's it. Do take the time to familiarise yourself with our facilities and remember, if there's a treatment you really, really want to have, book for it as quickly as possible. Lunch is being served. There's no need to reserve a table for breakfast or lunch but Leone the restaurant manager will ask you to book a time for dinner.' She glided away, her Birkenstock sandals slapping gently into the deep pile of the Cheverny Court monogrammed carpet.

We flopped down on one of the many sofas dotted about the place.

'No bar! No bar! You didn't tell me this place was part of the Betty Ford franchise!'

'Relax, Cazi, relax – don't forget I was in the Girl Guides for a spell, remember? "Be Prepared" and all that – and in anticipation of just such a catastrophe, I've brought a box – please note a box, not a bottle – of wine!'

'*You* are a *star*!' cried Caroline in relief, giving me a big hug.

A male guest sauntered past, a flicker of hope fading from his eyes, as he labelled us as dykes and therefore out of scope.

'Let's have lunch – then at least we can order wine. Save the box for those long lonely evenings.'

'But we're only here for two nights. You make it sound like a six months' stretch in Holloway.'

The dining room was spacious and modern. The diners, in their spotless bathrobes, resembled born-again Christians waiting to be dunked in the waters of eternal peace and harmony. The almost monastic silence was broken only by the occasional clink of cutlery against crockery and the tinkle of water pouring into wine glasses.

'Why do we have to share a table?' said Caroline. 'Why can't we sit on our own?'

'I don't know. Let's wait and see where "Leone" is taking us before we say anything.'

Fortunately, there were only single places left at the larger tables so we were allocated a table for two by the window. This overlooked the Japanese garden in which six people were bending themselves into positions which could be construed as pornographic were it not for the fact that the beating rain and howling wind did little to suggest an orgy was taking place.

'Hello, ladies. My name is Helena. Lunch is served buffet-style so do please help yourself. May I bring you something? Evian or fruit juice perhaps?'

'Err, could we see the wine list please?' I replied sheepishly.

'The wine list? Err, well, yes of course. One moment please.' Helena looked taken aback, but recovered to remark pointedly, that she'd have to go and search for one because there was *rarely* any call for wine at lunchtime. The wine list was short and expensive – around £25 per bottle; curiously, though, the house champagne was a positive snip at £33.50. That settled it.

'Might as well be hung for a sheep as a lamb,' I said cheerily. 'Let's have a bottle of bubbly.'

'Oh, great!' said Caroline, clapping her hands in delight – she had really perked up now that she was within spearing distance of lunch.

We placed our order with the clearly disapproving Helena, and walked up to examine the buffet table. A veritable banquet of beans awaited us. We recognised the broad beans, runner beans, string beans, white beans, black beans and bean sprouts but as neither I nor Caroline were gifted in the kitchen, some of the beans were a mystery. We did however recognise the bean accompaniments – more familiar fare such as lettuce, tomato, onion and cucumber. There were no dressings and certainly no mayo. Only plain cottage cheese was on hand to add 'colour' [white?] and 'flavour' [huh?] … we progressed to the hot table. Ah, now this was more like it. Plain pasta and rice admittedly, but the chef *was* whipping up tasty-looking sauces to order. We could have hugged him! We joined the long queue – obviously no one was interested in the beanfest – and filled our bowls to the brim with assorted vegetables and meat. We returned to our table each with a steaming plate of freshly prepared pasta.

'Excuse me, Helena. Do you have any cream please? This spaghetti carbonara looks lovely but I bet a drop of cream would improve it.'

'Sorry, no,' replied Helena, '*Dr* von Palach, our resident nutritionist, says it's far too high in fat.'

'Umm … how about some Parmesan then?'

'Ditto, I'm afraid.'

'OK, salt then?'

'Good heavens, no! Far too bad for the heart!'

'Pepper?'

'No.'

More negatives than an amateur photographer.

'Ketchup? brown sauce? soy sauce? Have you got any condiments at all?'

'Certainly, madam,' she replied. 'Just one moment.' She returned with a small cellar of what looked like chopped seaweed and placed it on the table with a flourish. 'Organic chopped herbs, ladies. Wonderful! The complete accompaniment and sooo aromatic!'

'Thanks,' we muttered in unison, eyes heavy with depression that was increasing by the minute.

'I'm so glad I brought some Pringles just in case,' whispered Cazi to relieve the prevailing gloom. 'And I've got a block of Fruit and Nut *and* I've even remembered the emergency Hobnobs. Remind me again how much we're paying for this "holiday"?'

'Actually, this isn't too bad,' I said, tucking into my mushroom pasta. 'It's not up to Isola Bella standard but it's edible, especially if I wash each mouthful down with champagne!'

We giggled like errant schoolgirls and raised our glasses to each other. Within forty-five minutes, we were on our second bottle and only a handful of other diners remained. By two, we'd had dessert [fresh fruit salad – no cream, no crème fraîche, not even plain yoghurt]; after draining the second bottle, we were laughing uproariously about the time Caroline and Bob were caught having it away in her mother's bathroom.

'Excuse me, ladies,' said Leone, 'but if you *have* finished, would you like to move through to the lounge for coffee?'

The tone was that of an imperative rather than an invitation.

'Smytainly,' I slurred. 'Lunsh was very, errr, shurprising.' 'Neish but shurprising,' I added, between hiccups.

'Let's go to our room for crisps and chocolate now – it'll only be a skinny latte on offer anyway.'

Propping each other up, we wove our way back to our room, and flopped down on the bed. Within twenty minutes, we were both fast asleep. When we woke an hour or so later, neither of us had a hangover [thus proving that practice makes perfect] but we were both really thirsty, our throats having the furry texture of corduroy.

'You'll never guess how many different kinds of water they've got in that coffee bar. This is just a small selection. Now, drink this; we'll toss for first shower, watch a bit of telly then repair to the dining room for another magnificent repast! I think we should go over the activity/treatment list over dinner and book what we want to do before going to bed.'

With palates stimulated by two glasses of wine and six Hobnobs, we arrived in the dining room promptly at 7.45.

Dinner was instantly forgettable – steamed vegetables with ponzu sauce, chicken, celery and radish salad;

Turkish chickpea burgers were among the highlights. By ten we were in bed watching Big Brother highlights, having already, with almost military precision, decided on our routine for Day 2:

8.30: Wake up and work out [30 mins]
9.15: Breakfast
10.00: Relax by the pool
11.00: Low impact spinning [45 mins]
11.45: Relax by pool
12.30: Sauna/steam room and shower
13.15: Lunch [restricted to one bottle of wine]
14.15: Relax by pool
16.00: Aquarobics [45 mins]
16.45: Relax by pool
17.30: Toning tables [30 mins]
18.00: Cocktails [i.e. wine] in room; shower etc.
20.00: Dinner

The reality of Day 2 was that the 'breakfast', 'lunch' and 'relax' components were scrupulously attended to but the only 'exercise' was the toning tables. You know, the ones where you lie down whilst different muscle groups are worked electronically by the table. The table can be set to vary the strength from one to ten. Caroline deliberately set hers at one. I would have liked about six or seven but the control would only work on three or nine, so guess which I selected?

On our way back to the room, we read the dinner menu … our distress mounted with each worthy offering.

'No way! Absolutely no way am I eating any of that. I'm hungry, and I want my mother,' Caroline whined.

I looked around anxiously to check on the proximity of any in-house spies …

'Cazi, sod this for a game of soldiers – why don't we go out to an Indian restaurant?'

'Love it! But …' she moved in closer to whisper, 'do you think it's allowed?'

'Allowed? What do you mean allowed? This isn't Holloway; I've told you that before. Of course it's allowed.'

I marched up to the reception desk but the fearsome sight of both Miranda and Helena manning the castle gates dented my confidence somewhat. But for their strikingly good looks, they could easily have passed for two of the more sadistic guards in *Tenko*.

'Hello, I wonder if you can help. Is there a small town or village within easy reach of here?'

'Well, yes, there are a couple of places. What exactly are you looking for?' Miranda responded snootily.

'Oh, you know, a pub, a shop, general store that sort of thing and oh … [as if by an afterthought]… an Indian restaurant if there is one.' Samantha arched an eyebrow.

Bugger this, I thought, I'm nearly forty years old – if I want an Indian I'm bloody well going to have one and I don't care what these china dolls think.

'Ah, I see,' smirked Miranda. 'There's an Indian restaurant in Wigston, which is about three miles from here. Turn left at the top of the drive and just follow the directions. You can't miss it … [and then, exchanging a knowing glance with Helena] the smell will guide you there.'

'Thank you *so* much, ladies.' I smiled sweetly. 'I'd bring you a bhaji back but I guess that's enough to get you the sack.'

Two hours later we lay on our beds, gazing up at the ceiling, having a deeply meaningful discussion on the relative merits of Indian starters [bhajis versus pakora], main courses [korma versus jalfrezi] and the amazing power of the body to ingest a Toblerone, Crunchie and wine gums even after an enormous Indian meal.

Day Three of our 'Tone up and Tune Out' break, saw us concentrating again on the 'Tune Out' part. More lazy hours by the pool relieved only by a Tropical Rainforest Mud Wrap for me and an Amazonica Floatation for my more adventurous friend. We left Cheverny Court after lunch, 4 lbs heavier and £350 lighter. God, life could be so good without a man in it!

Respite

Part 2 On a bender at Butlins

Easter was a welcome four-day break usually spent with Mum and Dad. This year though, they had gone off with friends on a coach tour of the Highlands and so I'd agreed to go with mad Janey [by now, totally forgiven for the Hugh incident] and two of her friends – Beth and Maureen – to Butlins in Minehead. Now, this would not be my first choice for a weekend away. In fact it was unlikely to be my 149th choice but Janey had persuaded me to go for the 'Tribute Band' weekend, promising a 'good laugh' and the chance of 'snogging a looki-likie' – far too good to miss.

Caroline thought it was 'wicked' – her son clearly wielded some sort of influence on her – reminding me that spending time with my girlfriends was absolutely the right thing to do at the moment, and that, you never know, 'Bruce Springsteen might be there.' I thought Bruce Forsyth was more likely but nevertheless agreed to go for the unbelievable price of £99 for three nights' dinner, bed and breakfast.

We arrived at Butlins at 7.15 pm, and headed straight for the restaurant. The man on the door looked like a bouncer; he was thickset and stubbly chinned – for a moment I thought we'd turned up at the wrong place; the room looked curiously empty.

'Good evening, Jeeves!' breezed Janey. 'No doubt you need our vouchers. There you are! We're ready to dine so do be kind enough to lead us on, there's a good chap!'

'Sorry girls,' he growled, 'dinner's finished. Last sitting's at six.'

'Six? What's he talking about?' whispered Beth to Janey. 'That's teatime not dinnertime.'

'But we're booked in for dinner, bed and breakfast,' said a confused Janey.

'And you can have your dinner between four and six and your breakfast between seven and eight-thirty,' retorted bouncer man firmly, crossing his arms now in a gesture of determination.

'Blimey! We'll have to get ready to go out *after* dinner and as for breakfast, forget it; I wasn't planning on getting back to our room before dawn!' Janey winked at the girls.

'OK, mate, maybe we'll see you at breakfast if the night doesn't live up to our, well, my, expectations!'

The weekend just went from bad to worse. Back home, I recounted the lowlights of the experience to Caroline.

There were gangs of men on stag weekends, wearing matching T-shirts with 'Fancy a Fcuk?' emblazoned across the chest and their name across the back. There was a high proportion of Lees and Deans – even a couple of Troys – but irrespective of name, they all had the same discomfiting look – TV *Neighbours from Hell* participants.

Janey, predictably, was in the thick of it – I've got clear memories of her kissing Noddy Holder whilst some mountain of lard on stage belted out 'Bat out of Hell' looking more like a Fruitloaf than Meatloaf. It was a cheap weekend, though, especially as the red wine was served in half-pint glasses. No, that was to be my one and only brush with *Hi De Hi* – I wouldn't be going back – ever.

Respite

Part 3   Lounging in Andalucia

Now, Marie – bless her – had something much more tasteful to offer. She'd told me that she needed a break from running The Fox, and mentioned her beautiful villa in the Spanish mountains – she'd bought this with the proceeds of her failed marriage to 'Richturd'; this was how she, somewhat unkindly, referred to her ex, Richard Patterson, one time successful stockbroker. Marie was a few years older than me and, at forty-five, personified the image of a glamorous divorcée, determined to enjoy the fruits of her hard labour, which is how she described her six-year marriage. She'd often suggested that I join her on one of her frequent 'escapes' to Andalucia, and , on this occasion – with time on my hands – I was happy to take her up on her kind offer.

The no-frills flight out there would have delighted Mike from Crewe. The hire car was ready and waiting at Malaga airport and in less than an hour we were in the centre of the nearest town, determined to stock up and enjoy every drop of the local produce. But, unbeknown to us, disappointment lurked beneath the bright Spanish flags that fluttered a warm welcome above the entrance to the local supermarket.

Juan-Carlos in the bodega section did his very best to explain.

'So veree sorree Seenyourass [was he winding us up?] but 'ere ina Spain we'ava speshal low – poleesmen say no halkohol een supermercado after ten ourz of night.'

Marie and I gaped like fish caught in a net.

'No alcohol? But, but, this is Spain: drink yourself senseless for ten euros you know, Juan-Carlos: Tempranillo, Rioja, Sangria. Por favour?' pleaded Marie.

'Iss no beeg problema beekoss the peepalz can buy much drink in barz but not een supermercado after ten ourz of night.'

'Damn it, sorry love,' she said, crestfallen. 'I know it's turned eleven and I've never arrived this late before but I certainly didn't know that the Spanish have the same stupid alcohol laws as us. Well, gracias anyway Juan-Carlos. Buenas noches! Never mind. We'll call at Pepe's on the way. He'll give me a couple of bottles to be going on with and we can sort it out tomorrow.'

We drove up the snaking mountain road to arrive at the villa just after midnight. It was too dark to see much of the surroundings but the villa itself was superbly appointed.

It comprised a lounge, dining room and kitchen downstairs with three en-suite bedrooms upstairs. All the rooms were furnished in contemporary style with the stark white walls boasting colourful prints and vivid Moorish carpets, hung like pictures. The crowning glory was the pool area, illuminated now by dim concealed lighting. I sat in a comfortably padded pool lounger, sipping a glass of chilled white wine courtesy of the obliging Pepe, and mused that either The Fox was doing much better than I ever imagined or Richturd had paid many times over for his short-lived marriage to Marie. But who cares? I was here and damn well determined to enjoy the next few days. Who needed a man to be happy – whether it was a dynamic electrician, a sophisticated antiques dealer, a price-conscious bank clerk or even an aspiring prime minister?

The next morning, stepping onto the terrace, I drew in my breath as I surveyed the vista. The villa was perched high up in the Sierra Nevada with a view that was truly sublime. 360 degrees of mountains, the distance dotted with clusters of dazzling white villages bathed in the warmth of Spanish spring sunshine. I guessed the nearest neighbours were about a quarter of a mile away and knew that a member of UB40 owned the largest villa in sight, unmissable owing to its pale pink rendering.

'Yes – sensational, isn't it?' Marie said, emerging from the house with a tray bearing orange juice, coffee and croissants. 'I love it you know; I often think about giving up The Fox – bit tired of serving Boddies every night to the Les Battersbys of this world – and moving out here lock, stock and barrel.'

'Well it's a nice thought Marie, but you know you'd miss everything from back home, unless of course Andalucia has a secret supply of tattooed smackheads and manic Man U supporters'

She laughed and added 'Well, I think I could live without them but I would need something to do with my time. Nothing too strenuous you understand and nothing that takes up more than a few hours a day...

The Midas Touch

'... and – promise you won't laugh – guess what I've been thinking about? Setting up an online dating agency for all the UK ex-pats out here. There must be thousands of them. Most of them are comfortably off but many don't have someone to share the good life with – tragically. It often happens you know – reasonably well-off people, in their mid/late fifties move out to Spain, and, two years or so later, the husband dies of a heart attack or something, leaving the wife stranded and lonely.'

'Marie. You're a born genius – I think that's a fantastic idea!' I said, gushing with enthusiasm. 'Can I let you in on a secret? I joined an Internet dating agency and I've already been on a few dates already. You won't think badly of me, will you love? Please …!' I begged, chewing on my knuckles in mock terror.

'Think badly of you? Of course not. I might be a bit surprised that a girl like you doesn't get plenty of offers without resorting to the net but think badly of you? Never!

In fact, if we *are* sharing secrets, I joined a dating agency last year – '

'You didn't but why – '

'No, not an Internet one,' she continued, laughing at my surprise, 'but one where you pay a hefty fee for someone to interview you personally then match you up with another member.'

This service – 'Midas Touch' – charged £1000 and for that, she was interviewed, photographed and profiled; then she was shown the profiles of three men supposedly 'discerningly selected' for their compatibility with her. The fee was so large because Midas Touch guaranteed that all their members were 'vetted to the highest possible degree' for their 'financial status, background and range of social skills.' In other words, Wayne and Waynetta updates need not apply. But as the Midas Touch company was only a dating agency and not a branch of the secret services such as MI5, Marie's stories of her dating disasters mirrored my own in so many ways.

There was 'Oliver' whose only claim to fame was that he had once opened the door for the Duke of Edinburgh who was on a visit to Manchester for the opening of the Commonwealth Games. He'd listed his job as 'Leisure Services'. Only later, after several flowing pints, did he confess to Marie that, rather than owning the hotel where he worked, he was actually a general dogsbody in the kitchen. He'd taken out a bank loan to pay the membership fee in the hope of wooing a 'posh bird' who could put him on the right end of room service for once. So it was a quick farewell to Oliver. Then there had been 'Colin'. She admitted that she didn't think they had that much in common but he'd stated his job as 'Reclamation' which Marie knew was a money-spinner these days. Luckily she'd gone to the agreed venue early and had spotted him as he backfired into the car park in his 1980s Sierra. She rapidly concluded that, for Colin, 'Reclamation' meant cars from a scrap yard rather than choice items from an unloved and dilapidated manor house.

'I can't say my dates ended up much different but I only paid thirty quid for my disappointments,' I began, as I recounted the lowlights of my recent dating history, pointing out that I supposed Hugh and James might be OK for the right women, but, as for Lenny, well he should really have been advertising himself in *Forum* rather than on Dateandsee.

'Do you think there might be someone for me?' Marie asked tentatively.

'Of course! Soon as we get back, we'll have a night in, surfing the net to see if there's a big fish for you.'

'Well, we don't have to wait that long' she grinned. 'Because guess what? I keep a laptop here.'

She set up the laptop [wireless naturally] in a shady spot by the pool and looked on with wide-eyed interest as I logged on to the dating site.

'Oh, look, Marie, I've got three new messages. I'll read those later after we've found an Adonis for you. Now, let's put in some search criteria.'

Age: 40 to 55
Location: North West and Midlands

In less than two seconds, Dateandsee.com returned twenty-five pages of possibilities. Marie's ex, 'Richturd' appeared halfway down the second page.

'The lousy, lying bastard!' Marie shouted, slapping her leg for emphasis. 'Only last week he was bemoaning the fact that he'd "lost" me and would do anything, buy me anything, take me anywhere, if I would only agree to see him again and, all the time, he's advertising himself on here. The lying scumbag!'

I kept a discreet silence. I'd never quite understood why Richard and Marie had broken up. To outsiders, they had everything going for them. Well liked by everyone, both were outgoing, positive people; they'd been really successful, with sufficient business acumen to assure a comfortable life. But the only time I'd ever broached the subject, Marie had brushed me off defensively, saying no one really knew him except her, and his demands had finally proved unacceptable. I wondered if these demands were 'Lennyesque' but that wasn't the impression Marie gave off. It appeared the problem was about control but not of the handcuffs and slap paddle variety.

'Marie, move the cursor on now. If you're no longer interested in Richard, does it really matter what he's up to?'

She continued to simmer but brightened up as more and more men popped up on-screen. In less than an hour, I had a list of a dozen possibles she intended to contact just as soon as she paid her £30 fee – paltry by comparison with the exorbitant amount charged by Midas Touch.

While she went off to shower and change before lunch, I went back to my three messages. Two from James – I was in no rush to read those, and one from a no-hoper called David in Wrexham [potholing had never been something I'd yearned to try]; standard reply issued. Getting into my stride, I did some more vigorous surfing, and then discovered 'Trevor' – or was it 'Twig?' … This was intriguing to say the least … a man with *two* names?

Chapter 13

AND NOW FOR SOMETHING COMPLETELY DIFFERENT

Yes, 'Trevor' did appear to have two names. The cold breath of menace blew down my neck. Did this hint at a man with a split personality perhaps, a schizophrenic even or possibly a latter-day Jekyl and Hyde? Well, he was certainly 'unusual'; yes that was it – 'unusual'; 'eccentric' might be a little too strong and 'strange' was a little too disconcerting.

It seemed that although his birth name was Trevor, his friends called him 'Twig'. He preferred the word 'encounter' to 'date'. Hmm … I found this rather precious. But never mind – what's the full picture?

THE MESSAGE: Hello Sally. I'm sure that you've never had a message from someone whose opening line is to say, 'We don't seem to have a lot in common'! You see, I don't know any of the film stars you refer to and the sort of food and drink you like is not to my taste – each to his own. But I think there's hope. We obviously agree that sport is a no-go area – great by me. Also, I think you're really funny and pretty as well. You do say that you're 'interested in different approaches to life' and this, perhaps, is where I may come in. Do read on if you've not mentally switched off by now. Twig

THE PROFILE:

Name: Trevor and Twig
Age: 43
Location: West Yorkshire
Status: Single
Children: Biologically, none
Job: University Lecturer [History of Art]
Height: 6'2"
Build: Medium
Appearance: Average
Eye Colour: Green
Hair: Brown
Religion: Buddhist
Star Sign: Aquarius
Smoker: Not tobacco
Drinker: Organic juices

INTERESTS: Art [especially painting and sculpture], New Age, nature, Druidism, eco issues

---

Bloody hell!

ABOUT ME: When I decided to subscribe to Dateandsee I had to ponder long and hard. As for 'Interests' should I put travel, cinema, sport etc. and risk attracting the sort of women who, if these things attracted them, would obviously not be my type at all. Well, here's the truth. I've never been out of England. The last film I saw was 'Carry on Cleopatra'

---

when I was still in short trousers. Sport has always left me cold; at school, when it came to P.E. or games, I was the only boy with a 100% absenteeism record thanks to my loving and understanding mother who wrote in saying I was asthmatic.

So, there you have it, I've been truthful. You might find me interesting if you too are drawn to crystals, gemstones and Ley lines. Also, I'm a vegetarian, and a Buddhist. Reiki is among my more recent enthusiasms. Above all, I worship at the High Altar of Nature in all of Her forms. It is this, which informs my love of Art.

I deliberately put 'Biologically none' to the Children field, because as a Buddhist, I firmly believe that we are all related – people, animals, reptiles, fish, plants, trees, flowers. If you're still reading this, then I have grounds for optimism. If you're even slightly drawn to someone who, by his own admission, is not one of life's followers, then do contact me.

P.S. I prefer to be called Twig as this name resonates more meaningfully within me.

> *MY PREFERRED REPLY: Dear Trevor/ Twig, when you read about me it might have struck you that we are not exactly compatible dating material. My life is essentially about the 'here and now' whereas yours I suspect, is about the 'everywhere and anytime'. But, on a lighter note, may I wish you success at your forthcoming Speed Dating session at Stonehenge. Do give my best wishes to your mates Freddy the Frog and Tommy the Toad next time you go off to the pub together for a swift half of nettle bitter. I sincerely hope that, before long, you will find a comfortable fig leaf to adorn your twig. Best wishes Sally*

My finger hovered over the send button. Then, my initial pause became a delay. And then the delay turned into a change of direction as I selected the delete button. My proposed reply was altogether too flippant, sardonic even. After all, he appeared honest – was this a characteristic to be scorned? He did have a job – university lecturer no less – was this to be underrated? He seemed to care about the natural world and people – were such sentiments to be derided? Oh yes, and there's one more thing – he was really good-looking! His handsome, if slightly gaunt, features, had a touch of the Ralph Fiennes about them; he needed some care and attention perhaps. There was an air of mystery about him too ... and weren't mysteries there to be unravelled?

> *MY ACTUAL REPLY: Dear Trevor, sorry this isn't 'Twig' but to use your special name so early seemed a little premature to an old-fashioned girl like me. All I know about your interests is what I pick up in Cosmopolitan and FeMail, not your regular reading material I suspect. Well, yes, why don't we meet up for an 'encounter' whoops, sorry, see I'm teasing you now, my dreadful sense of humour I'm afraid. Where would you like us to meet? Not in a Little Chef I'm sure. I look forward to hearing from you. Best wishes Sally*

Ping! Off it went. Now, how on earth would this one turn out? The slapping of Marie's espadrilles across the tiles disturbed my daydreaming.

'Oh, it's turned one already. Right Marie, give me ten minutes and we're off *El Toro Bravo* – tapas time!'

Holidays mean different things to different people but for me they meant getting up when I wanted to, rather than when I had to, eating what I wanted to, rather than what I should eat, drinking as much as I wanted to, rather than what was good for me and generally letting each day drift by as I sunned myself by the pool. Apart from gently raising a glass of refreshing Cava to my lips, and turning the pages of my latest Penny Vincenzi, the most energetic thing I did in five days was walk half a mile every day to claim my supply of fresh doughnuts before they were snapped up by fellow addicts.

Yes, it was true, Manchester *was* a long way away ... but the prospect of an 'encounter' with the enigmatic but alluring Trevor/Twig seemed very close. I really was intrigued by what he'd written and by his unorthodox but interesting outlook on the world ... and by his, well ... yes, his photo helped as well: I decided to make a priority of it as soon as I back home from sun-drenched Andalucia.

Preparing for the expedition

Even after just a couple of days, the glorious Spanish sun was just a pleasant memory, replaced now by a less uplifting northern grey. Although I'd returned relaxed and nicely tanned, I was almost suicidal about my weight gain. I had literally eaten and drunk my way along the Costa del Sol rather like one of those 'super size me' TV experiments.

Different positions on the scales [pirouetting to the right, craning to the left, the one-legged flamingo stance], removing everything including earrings, make-up, even nail varnish, were all – collectively, that is – just about capable of shaving off the odd ounce or two, but nothing short of a fortnight on birdseed was going to solve this problem.

But that preoccupation could be temporarily shelved. I was ready now to give serious thought to the Trevor/Twig challenge; after all, this was likely to be a rare combination of the spiritual, physical – and who knows? – the emotional. I pondered on the when and the where and the what to wear. Would the date be at dawn on the Yorkshire moors with the sun from the east bathing them in its early glow, or at dusk under the forbidding heights of Scafell Pike? And what to wear? What about those mock Amazonian bone earrings I'd won in the Knobbly Nipples competition at the Butlins weekend? Not as racy as Janey's but a little more stylish. What about borrowing from Cazi the famous faux fur thong – Twiglet [for thus was he now known] must surely approve of the artificial material and in the assumed Raquel Welch persona I might just turn him on … No, far too early for that. No, time to get serious.

Ping! A reply from him – perhaps.

Dear Sally, I'm sorry to be late getting back to you, it's just that I've been snowed under with the students' assessments recently and I've been chasing my tail. I'm flattered by your interest. Don't worry about my unusual pursuits. They are just part of who and what I am. But, occasionally, I feel I do need a reality check to stop me becoming out of touch with contemporary society – also, to prevent me from becoming too boring, too pompous or both. Now, could I suggest we meet at the Yorkshire Sculpture Park? It's no great distance away – just head for Barnsley and from there over to Wakefield. Yes, I know, I know, not exactly the Ritz but it's beautiful at this time of the year. I take my third-year students there because the exhibitions are always of interest. We could have an invigorating walk and then something to eat. There are lots of the pubs nearby offering vegetarian options – it's good for business these days. What do you think? Could you be persuaded? Regards
Twig

Barnsley … mmm. Perhaps I'd give satnav a rest and devise my own route. I really didn't want the slightest risk of any 'close encounter' with Jeff the tuba maestro over there! 'Vegetarian' … this was a little off-putting; I wasn't *that* paranoid about my weight.

> *Dear Twig, see, I'm getting there already; you must have some sort of hypnotic power that you can transmit over the Internet. As to the venue – fine, I'll find my way there without any trouble, my job has me driving all over the country. Shall we meet by the entrance about ten next Sunday? Best wishes Sally*

> *Dear Sally, I'm so pleased you've said yes. I'm looking forward to our date already – see you're influencing me as well now. This must be a good sign! Regards Twig*

Well, well. Fancy that, having a date with a Druid. Better not mention this to Caroline; she'd give me endless stick – or should that be twig? She'd conjure up all sorts of images of tree-huggers with dreadlocks, rainbow-coloured outfits and shoes made in the forest – Barks & Spencer perhaps?

Forewarned is forearmed

Before the appointed day I downloaded details of the sculpture park. My hunch had been correct, and I'd have no trouble in finding it. To prepare for conversation, I thought it might be a good idea to surf a few New Age sites. There was no shortage of these – several of them were distinctly top shelf material, rivalling the dating sites in terms of both their allure and astonishing variety.

ReikirulesOK.com *Don't trust quacks, subscribe to my unique tutorial course and within a week you'll be a fully accredited Reiki Master.*

Leylines&U.com I'd first heard about Ley lines from Janey who was convinced it was the latest and utterly mind-blowing sexual position – she was desperately disappointed on finding out the truth and demanded her money back.

Gemstones4all.com This site devoted page after page to a quasi-scientific analysis of the healing properties of different gemstones – '*all sorts of ailments, from Sciatica to Syphilis*' could apparently be cured effortlessly, simply by using the right one from the bewildering range on offer.

By now, it was getting late. I couldn't face the intellectual challenge of other sites such as:

BuddieswithBuddha.com and the other one, now what was it? Ah yes,

IfitsOKwithU-Zenitsfinebyme.com ...

Back in the office the rumour mill was achieving more spin than Shane Warne. There was some talk that, unknown to Lesley, Mike, her IT import, had shifted his interest to Leggy Bevvy. She was, it seems, flattered by his growing interest and responded accordingly. Her push-up bra produced peaks of Matterhorn proportions, her skirt could pass for a fashionable belt and her long flowing locks were as lustrous as any film star's. Well done, Mike – this would keep her out of Jonathan's sights ... Jonathan

291

for whom I retained a special affection … but apart from that furtive kiss, he'd shown no particular interest in me perhaps fearing a truly ego-shattering second rejection? *My* attention now switched to Brian, the Chief Twitcher; *I* needed *him.*

'Brian, something's come up. Could you possibly spare me a few moments, please?'

Scarcely were the words out of my mouth when Brian materialised by my side, not exactly perspiring but clearly in a heightened state of expectation.

'Yes, Sally, how can I help?'

'Oh, hello Brian – thanks ever so much for popping up. Look, it's like this. I've got to leave for an important meeting in five minutes but I need some details on the ten most common birds in Yorkshire. I'm in a pub quiz team you see and I've got some inside information that there'll be a section on birds. The Question Master's from Huddersfield, so he'll probably set questions about the local area.'

I softened, and gently placed a fragile hand on the back of his.

'Could you, would you, help me, please?' widening my eyes in a street beggar's appeal.

'Easy – got some paper and a biro there?'

In three minutes flat, I knew all I needed to know about rooks, woodpeckers, starlings, magpies and sparrow hawks. 'But you've not mentioned golden eagles, Brian.'

He looked at me with a mixture of pity and pain … clearly I'd said something ridiculous.

'Erm, no. For golden eagles you'd have to visit the west coast of Scotland to see them – honest you would. Actually

I wouldn't mind driving you up there for a weekend if you'd like to; it would be marvellous ...'

Sirens whining, warning bells clanging, red lights glaring, brakes screeching, paramedics' yellow jackets glowing! Danger!

'Very kind of you Brian but I'm allergic to Scotland. It's the midges, you know; I come out in red blotches all over. But thank you ever so much for your help with this – bye for now; see you soon!'

With that I scooped up my bag and was gone from the office before you could say 'Cloud-cuckoo-land' leaving a disheartened Brian behind me.

A walk in the woods

I found the venue easily and parked my VW Passat close to the entrance. It was a clear, bright day but as I was 'in the country' I made something of a drama out of donning my walking boots and cagoule.

The Visitor Centre resembled a 1950s youth hostel. However, there were obvious signs of an attempt to be modern and inclusive; as I walked up the ramp, I could see that the door was nearly obscured by an enormous 'Welcome' poster written in so many languages and different scripts that it could easily have passed for a restaurant in the United Nations building in New York. As I fished around in my purse for some money, my name rang out.

'Well done Sally, you found us then. Oh, don't worry about the entrance fee; I'm a patron here so I can bring guests at any time.'

I liked him immediately. He had a friendly twinkle in his eye and a Michael Douglas dimple in his chin. I noticed that his fleece was emblazoned with FOE – later, and not without a flush of embarrassment, I found out that it stood for Friends of The Earth. [I was sure, given the region we were in, it must have been Friends of Emmerdale but fortunately hadn't commented at the time.] I realised too that he was a regular here. Some of the female assistants greeted him warmly whilst giving me the once-over. Was I just one of many to have trodden this way, perhaps? 'Twig' – it still felt decidedly odd to greet a person as if they were a spare part on Bonfire Night.

'Oh, thank you and how are you? It's really nice to meet you. I'm sorry if I'm a bit late; I was passing some wetland and just had to stop to look at the woodpeckers swooping by. Don't they fly so low, in that sort of lurching movement?'

That should do it. I'm wearing walking boots, I've got my cagoule on after shaking out the spiders, I've mentioned 'wetland', and I've referred to a bird – if that lot doesn't establish my Green credentials with him then nothing will.

'Ah, yes, the woodpeckers,' he replied, raising a quizzical eyebrow.

Was his tone just a tiny bit supercilious? Oh no! Had I cocked up on the bird type? Perhaps he was the forgiving sort because he smiled softly, and took me gently by the arm outside.

Three hours and five miles later we found ourselves sitting in the crowded beer garden of a country pub close to the sculpture park. I felt totally reinvigorated – it was as if the combination of the fresh air and sound exercise had detoxified my system, a kind of colonic irrigation of the soul. More than this, the walk through the park had been really interesting, spectacular even. At first, I had inwardly dismissed the gigantic sculptures as cast-offs from an inner city children's playground but under his expert guidance I could see things differently. The material of each piece, its texture, its size, its design and, not least, its setting, all played a role. It was as if he was removing scales from my eyes. Finally a glum, overworked and overweight waiter arrived to take our order.

'Don't know about you, Twig, but after that marathon I'm starving. What about a drink first to get things going – my treat.'

As he opted for a jug of homemade dandelion and burdock, I felt obliged to settle for just a half bottle of the Pinot Grigio – no great problem; I was driving after all. It was much the same with our food; his tofu salad looked like emergency rations when compared with the gargantuan Mixed Grill that filled my plate, the sausages and pork chop still sizzling merrily in their fat. Did he look away in disgust, or was this merely my guilty imagination?

'So,' he began. 'I don't suppose a day like today is among your regular pursuits, is it – it's not been too tedious for you?'

'You're right there, Twig' I replied, feeling by now that this step of verbal intimacy was warranted. 'First time I've ever done anything like this. But it's been really interesting and refreshing. If you're cooped up like I am five days a week in air-conditioned offices or stuck in traffic jams on the motorways, you certainly need a fix of natural beauty every so often. It's been a real eye-opener for me. Now, tell me more about all that New Age stuff you're interested in, and what lots of people might call weirdo things.'

Twig grimaced. He said nothing. Immediately I wished I'd been more selective in my choice of words; he was obviously stung. He fixed his eyes on me.

'Well, Sally, if by "weirdo things" you mean an interest in life force, conservation, the health of our planet – and, not to put too fine a point on it, the future of our species, then yes, I grant you, from the outside it probably does look a bit odd. But just think about what's going on in the "real world" as you might put it. People, especially middle-aged men, dying prematurely from heart attacks due to smoking, bad diet, stress, whatever, and the problems in society caused by alcohol or drugs for example–'

'No, I didn't mean to–'

'*If* I may continue [God! I really had touched a raw nerve] – as for religion, yes, people may laugh at Buddhism but that's because they're not used to it; they don't understand it. But what if, one day, little green men *did* come down on a flying saucer and say to us, "Tell us more about these strange spiritual beliefs you have, where you say you drink the blood and eat the flesh of your god? And those other people – what do you call them – saints? Centuries ago, so you tell us, they went into convulsions or hallucinated or whatever and yet you pray to them." Do you see what I'm trying to say? There's a lot in our traditional culture that could also be classed as "weirdo", although personally I'd prefer the word "bizarre".'

He stopped and drew in his breath.

There. Lecture over. I shrivelled in my seat. I felt at bay – even worse, I was beginning to feel out of my depth. I wasn't used to dates that ended on some note of philosophical speculation. And yet, it was interesting; *he* was interesting. We chatted on into the late afternoon when I began to sense that he'd had enough – more than once I'd caught him glancing at his watch. Did he have something else on? A communal trance in the middle of the forest perhaps? Or a séance to attend in Shipley? I decided to take the initiative.

'Wow, is that the time? Gone five already. Twig it's been a marvellous day but I need to be heading home now. It'll take me at least a couple of hours – probably more with the weekend traffic clogging everything up.'

Pause. He didn't encourage me to stay even a bit longer. This was disappointing.

'Oh, fine, yes, I quite understand. I've got to be up at the crack of dawn myself; it's May 1st tomorrow; you know May Day, an important day in the Druidical calendar. [I just about managed to avoid coming out with some unwelcome wisecrack such as 'sorry Twig, was that "suicidal calendar" that you referred to?'] But before you go, hold on, I've got something in my car that may interest you.'

By sheer chance he'd parked his Morris Minor close to my shiny new VW, its Sahara red contrasting with the green and brown of the woodland around us. His car was just about big enough to accommodate three of the seven dwarves. It was plastered with stickers of every protest group imaginable; the inverted Y of the Ban the Bomb movement was still visible, though forlorn and faded now. 'Right to Roam', 'Foxes have rights too', 'No to nuclear fuel', 'Fight long-haul flights' had clearly ousted 'Greenpeace' and 'Cruise out!' – yesterday's preoccupations. He had everything covered except 'Save Gay Whales'.

Homeward bound

'Here, this is the park's latest brochure. You may find it useful if you decide to come back here ... with some friends.'

Hmm ... pregnant pause. 'With some friends' not 'with me.'

He stared at my car, frowning; his disapproval was all too obvious. 'Do you really think you need such a gas-guzzling vehicle?'

Whoa boy – challenge my choices, and you're challenging me.

'Twig, I drive hundreds of miles a week. I need a car that is comfortable, fast, reliable and safe.'

He turned to face me; there was a coldness in his eyes now. 'Sally you must know we all have a duty to restrict our carbon footprint.'

He mistook the look of utter bewilderment on my face for one of bored indifference, and grew even more vexed.

'I really can't see us meeting up again; it seems to me that our worlds are galaxies apart, but thanks for coming over today.' He virtually forced the brochure on me before shaking my hand, stiffly and formally. This was not 'au revoir' but most definitely 'goodbye'.

As I drove west over the Pennines, I felt my eyes stinging, my cheeks burning. The humiliation of it. Rejection – OK! But face to face rejection? Typical of a weirdo to behave like this, I decided glumly. Why couldn't he have been more devious, more hypocritical? Why couldn't he have followed the usual rules and dumped me by email like any normal bloke? And then, the simple truth hit me. This was exactly the point. Trevor/Twig wasn't 'normal' and so wasn't prepared to play by the rules. He was probably right. Our worlds, our outlook, our approaches to life were so very different, the one from the other. Perhaps I'd be better off sticking to ordinary men.

Safely back home, I decided that a remedial spot of surfing was called for but, after Mike, Hugh and James, would Dateandsee have any 'ordinary men' left? And yet, there was still Jonathan … but he was certainly out of bounds now, I concluded, probably regarding me as just another name in his extensive roll call of conquests. I did, though, fondly remember his 'sweet nothings' from just before the Christmas break … 'the old Jonathan will be back you know …'. Yes, perhaps there was still some mileage in the old saying: 'never say never'. For the moment, though, with a glass by my side and a contented Ringo on my lap, it was back to the drawing board or rather – back to the gallery of the Internet site … It was not empty of interest.

Tom enters the ring

THE PROFILE:

Name: Tom
Age: 42
Location: Shropshire
Status: Single
Children: None
Job: Quantity Surveyor
Height: 6'1"
Build: Average
Appearance: Attractive
Eye Colour: Blue
Hair: Dark Brown

Religion: None
Star Sign: Capricorn
Smoker: No
Drinker: Moderate

INTERESTS: Rugby, golf, football, cricket, architecture.

ABOUT ME: Hi I'm Tom. Blimey, it's hard doing this profile isn't it? Some questions were easy to answer but I wanted to add a postscript to others. For example:
Children = none that I know of
Religion= Yes, but only if you count worshipping at St Andrews, Twickenham and Old Trafford
Drinker = moderate except for any day that includes a sporting highlight [which is most of them thanks to satellite TV]
Now, ladies, don't be too dismissive of me. I'm only trying to show you that I have a sense of humour. Yes, I do love my sport but would never sacrifice a night out with you for a night in with Sky [unless of course it was the quarter final of the FA Cup or something equally important – another joke of course].
I like to think that I'm reasonably intelligent, good company, witty, and a good listener.
If you can see past this superficial description, please write to me – maybe you can make me walk on water much more often.

Now, I *really do* like the look and sound of him, I thought, drawing in my breath. After the date with Mr Twiglet I was certainly ready for a heavy dose of normality. I casually mentioned Tom to Marie during my next stint at The Fox.

'Careful! Don't you think he's just too much of a sportaholic? I mean some blokes with their sport – they can be very selfish you know.'

'Well, that's true – he could be I suppose, but I like someone who's clear about what's important to them. In his case it's obviously sport but, look, he mentioned other things as well – architecture for instance ... bit unusual don't you think? Perhaps it hints at hidden depths; anyway I've mailed him back, so let's wait and see.' I thought back to my reply and did wonder whether I'd been a tad too eager.

> *THE MESSAGE: Hi Tom. Guess what? I'm a devotee of Old Trafford as well – do you know that the shopping centre there was the first one outside London with a Selfridges? You see Tom, I am to sport what Desmond Lynam is to flower arranging but I don't necessarily think we are incompatible. Frankly I'm up for anyone who's intelligent, witty, good company and, oh yes, good-looking. [I love your photo – is that Tiger Woods in the background?] So if you like the look of my profile, why don't we get together and see if we can score a few points? Sally*

Chapter 14

A WINNING WINE BAR

Tom's entry on the dating site was of itself enough to put me in very good heart. There was also some good news at work – Lesley had been seconded to head office for a spell [God, they must be hard up] and so the prospect of returning to my duties was a little more palatable; the defining reason for my high spirits was, however, beyond any shadow of a doubt, the latest man in my life [... well nearly...] – Tom.

Since that first email, there had been a rapid exchange showing mutual attraction, and we agreed to get together soon. His dark, smouldering looks kept spinning around in my mind – unfortunately, Marie's warning did as well; a counterpoint to my growing interest in him. For the moment, I satisfied myself with the belief that he was just a true red-blooded male who liked his sport – fair enough … Little did I know …

He lived in Shropshire so where to meet was a little awkward. Then he had a brainwave. Alex, a close friend of his, lived in Rochdale where he worked as an accountant for a food processing company, and so Tom could easily stay over with him after seeing me in Manchester.

'Alex and I were great pals. Do you know we won the Hall of Residence drinking contest at university three, repeat, three years on the trot. [Oh dear God, please don't let him be a soak!] But those were the good old days; I'd be amazed if we could sink more than couple of pints now – must be getting old.'

On his friend's recommendation, we agreed to meet at 'WhyNose' the 'wine bar with a difference'; this didn't sound the most salubrious of establishments but I didn't feel I could be too choosy as it was Tom who was making the effort in driving a fair distance to see me.

The girls at work knew of 'WhyNose'; yes, it was a wine bar but also a comedy club. The girls claimed not to understand most of the jokes; apparently its current fame was due to its popularity with a certain kind of belligerent female – diesel dykes mainly, instantly recognisable from their outmoded navy blue boiler suits, cropped hair and the bottles of Guinness they swigged down in rapid succession as they indulged in some alarmingly frank repartee with the comedians on stage; they often got the better of these foul-mouthed entertainers: 'Oh yes love, and who invented you – Wallace and Gromit?' – much to the delight of the other punters. Imagining the setting, I didn't feel that the chic little cocktail dress I'd recently treated myself to would be entirety suitable so I decided on my beloved black jeans, sleeveless white polo neck and black suede jacket.

Tom had been careful enough to get to the bar really early. We spotted each other immediately. My first impression? Terrific! He was actually much younger looking than his photo and stated age of forty-two. His tousled hair and broad smile lent him an almost boyish air; he was wearing a light purple and black hooped rugby shirt with the sleeves pushed up just a little, dark cord trousers, fashionable tan shoes with a pale blue cashmere pullover draped around his shoulders to complete the casual effect. Very, very nice! Also, he wasn't wearing glasses; I knew I shouldn't be speckist but I couldn't get rid of my abiding impression that blokes with glasses look like dusty old professors.

He ambled up to me, gently took my arm and gave me a peck on the cheek. He smelt fresh and lemony, like he'd just jumped out of the shower.

'Hello Sally, it's really good to meet you in the flesh – as it were … Thanks ever so much for coming here – I was afraid you'd have second thoughts and make a diversion for the Take That concert at the GMEX instead. But honestly, this place isn't nearly as bad as you might think. And if it does get a bit rough we can always hide under the table.'

I liked the approach – open, warm, humorous; I felt good. The date went really well. He drank very little, sticking to pints of shandy and reminding me that his days of serious drinking were long gone now. 'All the articles you read these days about health and diet and lifestyle; makes you think doesn't it?'

'Oh, come on Tom, let me at least get you a glass of red wine – that won't damage the liver or expand the waistline will it?'

'Well, since you insist – yes, thank you – but just a small one though.'

Predictably, as the night wore on, the noise from the stage increased in volume and we retreated to the back area of the bar.

'So, aren't you going to tell me about you and your life? You mentioned university – Oxford? Cambridge? And what subject? No, let me guess … mmm, Physics perhaps? [He spluttered on his wine at this suggestion]. And your job – what exactly does a quantity surveyor do?'

'Right OK – the nearest I ever got to Oxford and Cambridge was watching the Boat Race on TV – now that's an epic encounter, one of the really great events in the sporting calendar. No, I just about scraped enough A-levels to get into Exeter to study History. At school, the old straightforward Maths was no problem but as for Physics, believe me, suicide was a tempting alternative. In fact, in the sixth form I'd had visions of becoming an architect but, frankly, I was to Physics what Dawn French is to celery. So, I thought, if I can't study buildings I'll study people and their history instead – and at Exeter, which in those days had a great reputation for sport. As for being a quantity surveyor – the thing was, like so many graduates with an Arts degree, I didn't have a clue about what to do. Then a friend of my dad's with a building business offered me a summer holiday job in the main office – you know, the "just till you find your feet" sort of thing.'

'Well, it obviously suited you because you're still there.'

'Yes, it did. I began to find it really interesting, working out how many bricks, how much sand and cement, how much timber, etc. would be needed for a development. I got a real kick from looking at a site plan and seeing a dozen or so impressive houses there only a year or so later. I got through the professional exams and when the senior guy retired, they gave me his job – quite lucky really: the old "right place and right time" syndrome I suppose. The building boom over the last ten years has been terrific for the company; mind you it's not always been plain sailing – we built a big detached place for this gentleman farmer type – loaded he was; turned out that the land inspection process was bit dodgy and we built it on a former slurry area. The building sank without trace a week or so before completion, I suppose you could call it "A room with a pooh"!'

'Oh Tom – spare me,' I said with a laugh.

Throughout the evening I found myself noticing more things about him. His hair curled ever so slightly at the nape of his neck and, below his shirtsleeves, his forearms were strong and sprinkled with dark hair. His hands were large but not podgy and his fingernails were short – definitely not manicured but clean and tidy.

' … Huge, black and that's why the girls call him The Horn of Africa!' Yes, the humour from the stage had predictably descended to cesspit levels but we were increasingly oblivious of it; we were so wrapped up in each other. I told him of my failed marriage and of how my schoolgirl ideas of loving husband, three children, and comfortable home had come to nothing. I even told him that children, or rather the lack of them, had sealed my fate. This was a first date, and yet I felt I could tell this man anything and everything. He listened patiently and, it seemed, sympathetically.

Sensing that the tone of the evening was drifting dangerously into the misery zone, I suddenly cheered up and exclaimed 'Well, come on Tom, what about you and marriage? Have you got any former wives buried beneath the patios on that Badger's Holt development you were telling me about?'

'Believe me, love – cross my heart and hope to die – not a single one. To be absolutely truthful I've been engaged twice but called things off. I suppose I wasn't ready for a permanent relationship at the time. But now, here I am, turned forty, solid job and a smashing house and I've got my sports and great mates ... but there's something missing and that's where Dateandsee came in – and you, I hope.'

He moved closer and kissed me warmly. Just then his mobile rang; I recognised the stirring *Match of the Day* ring tone.

'Bloody nuisance these things at times; sorry – impolite of me – I should have switched it off. What Frank? I told you we should have backed Tiger to win again – anyway, sorry mate, must go: visiting my maiden aunt in hospital – see you at the match next week – what, that shower to win? In your dreams mate! Cheers!'

He turned to me sheepishly. 'Very sorry about that: one of my golf mad friends – he thinks of nothing else. Now, where were we? Oh yes – relationships. Aren't things so different now to our parents' generation? For better or worse – who knows?'

We ordered something to eat and chatted on until way past midnight. As we parted in the chill of the early hours, he kissed me lightly on the lips as he ran his hand gently across my back, and we both felt that unmistakeable frisson of mutual attraction.

We agreed to meet again very soon ... and we did.

Chores galore

Towards lunchtime on the following day, I was busy in the kitchen. Why was it that emptying the dishwasher simply had to be the most boring job on the planet? Suddenly the tedium was shattered by the up-tempo *Relight my fire* ring tone on my mobile. This had gone off some months before at the cremation of one of my parents' old friends. Fortunately, the tune meant nothing to the small knot of distressed mourners but their eyes betrayed annoyance that the sepulchral calm of the Chapel of Rest had been so rudely shattered.

Mobile, mobile – where the bloody hell did I leave it? Bathroom, bedroom? Ah there, under that pile of old *Living* magazines. It has to be, let it be – Tom! No, sadly it wasn't Tom this time but Caroline. This was a real disappointment, and I felt a bit guilty about her reaction.

'Oh, hello Cazi, it's you.'

'Oh, thank you Miss Johnson – that's not quite the warmest reception I've ever received on the phone I have to say! Don't tell me, let me guess … yes, you had your legs firmly entwined around your latest bloke and just when he was about to–'

'Thank you Jordan; no actually I'm in the middle of my household duties which an ageing spouse like *you* should be doing anyway instead of accusing *me* of being in the middle of a midday orgy! No, sorry love, I suppose I'd hoped it was someone else – heard the phone go and I went for it quicker than you could say Calvin Klein!'

'Well I'll forgive you but only if you spill the beans … "Someone else" sounds to me like you're hiding something or someone … Now, who could it be? … '

'Since you ask, you clever thing you, I was with a rather nice new bloke last night but no! – I don't mean we ended up in bed together. Mind you, he's seriously good- looking and fun with it – I could have been sorely tempted.'

'Great news; I've been worried about you for weeks now. Giving up on men, you said, just because some control freak of a wannabe politician let you down. Then you go off on all those breaks – I thought you'd be buying a one-way ticket to the North Pole next. Anyway, you've landed a prize catch now and I'm glad your old instincts haven't totally deserted you.'

'Not at all, just the opposite – because this Tom's one hell of a bloke. So, there I was playing the old well-he-can-phone-me-first-see-if-I-care-game when you rang.'

'OK love, thanks for the update; I'll be keeping four fingers crossed for you – must go now to get the potatoes on; be in touch soon – bye!'

Right, back now to the grime of the kitchen and the magical properties of Flash! God, I'm sure I wasn't born for this. Oh Tom, please, please phone and one of these days soon I'll promise you the best bloody sh– The mobile again. There is a God!

'Hello Tom,' I whispered in my best come-and-get-me while-I'm-hot mode.

'Oh, sorry, I'm not Tom. My name is Jason,' said this unknown and particularly oily voice 'and I'm phoning to say "Hey congratulations" – you've won a trip for two to Las Vegas from that *Grazia* quiz you entered a month ago and all you have to do is to come along to a meeting – a very informal meeting – at the Midland Hotel next–'

'Jason, listen to me.'

'Err, yes.'

'You need to know that I am a trained lawyer, specialising in social harassment. You have just three seconds to get off my phone before I–' Click. Always works that one! 'But where's Tom?' I bleated.

To combat my growing sense of frustration and disappointment, I decided to check my notes for the imminent round of courses. The economy was picking up at last, and banks and mortgage providers were poised to profit from a new lease of life in the housing market. All of this had resulted in an exceptionally heavy demand for training, so much so that the board was even talking of appointing another trainer. Lesley had been fiercely opposed to this as an extravagance but – with her sidelined for the moment – it remained a real and welcome possibility. I ploughed on throughout the afternoon. It was only towards six that the phone interrupted my concentration. This time, surely, it had to be Tom!

Stylish dining at the Brummie Brasserie

Yes, it was Tom – but what threw me was the unmistakeable roar of baying multitudes as they shrieked their anthems of love and hate.

'Sorry, err, I'll just switch this thing off' [Bet you're just switching it down you cheeky bugger, I thought]. Just wanted to give you a bell to say how much I enjoyed it last night. Any chance of seeing you again soon … please?'

My mind raced through the probable order – and priorities – of his day. He would have reached his friend's place up in Rochdale very late, had a few cans as they chewed over old times, got up after midday, scoffed some meat pies in between the foaming pints at 'The Crown' before settling down to the Big Match at 4 pm precisely. And then, only then, nearly a full day since we'd shared a late-night embrace, had he bothered to call me – the sod! But … well, it was so good to hear his warm voice again and it wasn't really his fault that we'd had such a late night, and he'd driven all the way up from the Midlands just to see me … and …

'Oh, hello Tom – what a lovely surprise! Yes, it was great but that – what was it called? Wet nose – no, sorry,

WhyNose wasn't it – yes, funny place, but why don't we go for something a bit more intimate next time?' Damn, I've only gone and blown it again haven't I? Firstly I'm obviously gagging for another date and then I use a provocative word like 'intimate' – will I never learn?

'Top idea – count me in,' he enthused. Hmm ... the match must be over by now: I obviously had his full and undivided attention at last. 'Now, when would suit?' he continued, 'Boring old fart that I am, I've got absolutely zilch in my diary until ... well, until the London Olympics in 2012.'

'Oh yes? I don't believe that for a single minute. But, guess what, I'm training in Birmingham on Wednesday and Thursday next week – your neck of the woods – so what about Wednesday night in Birmingham – no shortage of good places to eat there, so what do you think? In fact, I'll be staying overnight at the Hilton, so we could meet there then decide where to go.'

His enthusiasm seemed momentarily curbed. His reply wasn't instantaneous; in fact, it must have been what? ... Oh, a full five seconds before he said, with noticeable deliberation, 'Ah now, Wednesday – could just be a little tricky, as I've got something on with my mates that night. But what about Tuesday, the night before?'

I suspected what was going on here. I knew from the lads at work that most big European matches were screened on Wednesday nights, and that's what he'd be up to then. As I pondered this likely scenario, he went on persuasively, 'I mean, presumably you could drive down to Birmingham early on the Tuesday evening to avoid a mad rush to get there before the training course on Wednesday morning – what do you think?'

I had to admire his resilience, quick thinking and coolness under pressure, as he succeeded in putting all the chess pieces in the right positions before inwardly shouting out 'Checkmate!' I'd trained in Birmingham on several occasions – the logistics posed no difficulty for me; getting there in good time for a ten o'clock start was no more a problem than heading the queue at a Debenhams sale. And yet, I desperately wanted to see him again and getting there early for once would mean I would be all bright and breezy for the training on the following day. Yes, OK, it all made excellent sense. I capitulated.

'Yes, that seems fine. Now, you know the Hilton don't you – yes, that's the one – in the Gas Street area – opposite is a place called the Brummie Brasserie – what are you laughing at? No, honestly it's not just mushy peas and faggots! Faggots? What do you …? Those are rissoles actually, you naughty boy!'

'Gas Street' – could there ever have been a setting with a more evocative name than this? He, however, sniffed victory.

'Your recommendation's good enough for me. I'll be there about eight if that's OK? Dying to see you again. Cheers!'

'Cheers' – what a blokeish term that was. Is that how he sees me – just another one of his pack of mates? … And yet I was falling for it – falling for him. I was cross with myself – well, just slightly cross really – for bending to his whims but, hey, this was a small price to pay.

The Brummie Brasserie certainly lived up to its name. It was a curious mixture of the traditional and the innovative, the indigenous and the foreign. The area nearby was criss-crossed by the intricate canal system of a bygone age. This accounted for the numerous 'waterways' artefacts that were dotted here and there around the lobby – enormous watering cans and buckets, gaily decorated with red roses and multi-coloured petunias. On the walls hung framed sepia prints of powerful horses straining on the towpath as they dragged the barges along, and also pictures of the bargees themselves, staring defiantly into the prying lens of the early cameras.

To my alarm, I spotted an overhead TV, easily within viewing range. Fearing the mind-numbing reiteration of the weekend's goals, tries and sixes, I promptly moved to a potentially less distracting section.

He arrived on time, and looked irresistible; I caught my breath. I couldn't have cared less where we were; I'd have been just as happy with him in a McDonald's. I loved his height and bulk, loved his dress sense and the fresh smell of him which I caught as he gave me a light kiss. Even better, his hair was still damp from the shower – a major turn-on; I fancied every inch of this man. Better go easy on the vino tonight or I'd be smuggling him into my room. I noticed too that the waitresses were eyeing him up, and I momentarily basked in the glory of my conquest … Hands off girls – he's all mine!

The design of the dining area was much more à la mode than the reception area and the contemporary feel was underlined by the nature of the menu. On offer were terrines, exotic salads with unpronounceable names, delicate fish and light cuts of meat. So much choice that submitting an order proved to be something of an ordeal; a customer felt subjected to a police interrogation. This even extended to the desserts.

'Blueberry frangipane tartlet? Certainly Madam – would you like cream with that?'

'Er. Yes please.'

'Would that be single cream, double cream, whipped cream, clotted cream, crème fraîche or pouring cream?'

He studied the wine list with interest. Birmingham had clearly moved on from Banks's bitter and Piat d'Or. New World vintages dominated and the special properties of each were described in predictably pretentious language. He said that he was looking forward to a few drinks as he'd decided to come by train. I was staying overnight in the hotel and so we could both indulge. It wasn't long before we were demolishing a second bottle of Chilean Merlot.

Skeletons in the cupboard

'So Tom, come on now – no secrets – how long have you been into the dating site? Have there been scores of conquests? Broken hearts perhaps?'

I bit my lip when I detected a slight irritation on his part. Why was it that women were always into this sort of thing and men couldn't be bothered with it at all?

'Oh, I'm sure you don't want me to bore you with all that sort of stuff — I mean we're here to–'

'No – relax – I'm not being nosey and I'm not an undercover features reporter for *Elle* magazine you know; it's just that I'm interested in people. And you.'

Momentary eye contact. Resulting warmth.

'Well, OK then,' he said, grasping my hand tightly and swivelling his head around the restaurant in mock dramatic fashion as if to satisfy himself that he could talk freely. 'I got into the dating site a couple of years ago. A mate of mine found out that his wife was having it off with their mortgage advisor. He'd had his suspicions from the minute she'd secured a 1% fixed rate for twenty years with guaranteed £500,000 cash back at the end of the term. Honest, that's true – more or less! Anyway they got divorced and that's when he got started on this Internet dating thing. He said it was terrific – he claimed it gave you more freedom, and was more exciting than the usual dating rituals and, believe it or not, he ended up marrying only the fourth girl he dated.'

He patted my hand in a 'what do you think of that?' gesture.

I felt a warm sensation churning away in the pit of my stomach.

'So,' he continued, now clearly warming to the task, 'I thought nothing ventured, nothing gained – why don't I give it a go? I found it a little odd to have to write about myself though – rather like submitting your CV for a job. When it said

"Attractive", I was sorely tempted to put 'Why not come and judge for yourself?' but chickened out and just said "Reasonably".

'So, no stunning femme fatale yet then?'

'Well, there was one who was particularly memorable for all the wrong reasons. Debbie, a youngish dietician from Leeds. She was mid-thirties I think, separated, dancing, sun beds, musicals, and eating out. Nothing too heavy there I thought. I normally steered well clear of the separated bit as my mate said it could get really messy but on this occasion the photo got the better of my caution. Coincidentally, our date was in Manchester to see that Abba musical–'

'Oh, I know that – everyone's saying how good it is,' I broke in excitedly …

'Yeah, and so I waited outside the Opera House for her – then spotted her – I didn't recognise her immediately though because she'd obviously been overdoing it a bit on the old sun bed – wondered whether I should chat her up in Urdu to be honest. But she was *ravishing*! I said, "Hello there, you must be the lovely Debbie from Leeds." She gave me a radiant smile. And then she opened her mouth … "Ee though – yoo are one fat lad are yoo – I bet your mum feeds you ten times a dare. I'll sort yoo out with some broccoli pasta lair-ta but reet now, I need t'loo." Obviously, not the most romantic start to a date I've ever had. But the show was terrific and I must take you to see it sometime–'

'Oh great, I'd love to see it – but go on: what happened next with the delicious Debbie?'

'Yeah, next it was something to eat and, over the meal, she gave me a calorie-by-calorie account of every diet known to man since the caveman had his first Bison burger and chips back in the Stone Age. She brought me right up to date with the Beverley Hills Diet, the Hays diet, the Atkins Diet and then moved on to the GI Diet just as I was about to plunge into my sticky toffee pudding. But she was actually great fun – bubbly, tremendous personality and before I could ask her out again, she stood up from her chair, right in the middle of the restaurant, and boomed out, "It would be nice to meet up again when you get rid of a few pounds!" Bloody cheek or what? I mean I wasn't exactly Mr Blobby. I'd been given the elbow more than once in my life but never because of my waistline and never via a kind of public address system – real blow to my self-esteem that was. So, what about you and the dating site?

No, no good looking at your watch – it's only half-eleven; fair's fair – it's your turn now. I bet you've been through the whole gamut, from landed gentry to city gent.'

I warmed to his wit and openness, and found myself increasingly attracted to him. I began my memoirs with Mike, the World Pizza Chomping Champion from Crewe; Tom was convinced that the daybook and supplementary bill were embellishments to the story but I swore blind they were true. I then moved on to Hugh 'so different, so urbane ...' [Tom probably detected a real sense of loss here] and then it was Endroo, the apartheid supporter and wine dealer extraordinaire.

'Mmm, he really must have been a turn-off for you to ditch him – a wine dealer no less.'

'Hang on a minute – yes, I do enjoy a drink but I'm not a total dipso you know.'

He spoke about his trip to South Africa following the England rugby team.

'We seemed to find trouble wherever we went. One night, honestly, we ended up in the local jail! I'm telling you those Afrikaner types could get really mean, and we were glad to get out of the country I can tell you.'

I thought I'd keep quiet about Mr Politician and Mr New Age, fearing endless teasing and, instead, amused him with earlier reminiscences; he suggested putting the famous tuba player from Barnsley in touch with the dietician from Leeds; 'Same region, same dialect – they'd probably get on like a house on fire but, believe me, Debbie would make sure that suet puddings would be off the menu.'

By now the waiters at the far end of the restaurant were clearing the tables.

'My God, is that the time?' he cried. 'I must be off, otherwise I'll miss my last train and be forced to sleep on one of those benches by the canal like some dosser. No you don't – put your card away; I'm picking up the bill – it's been great; do hope we can meet again really soon.'

Right, strike while the iron's hot – take him at his word and put him to the test.

'I've enjoyed myself so much as well – what about getting together next Saturday afternoon?'

Saturday afternoon. Yes, I was aiming a javelin at his vitals. I waited expectantly for his jaw to drop. Would he abandon his football, rugby, golf, whatever, just to dally with me as we strolled through the water meadows of south Manchester idly picking wild flowers?

'Saturday afternoon?' he replied. 'Umm yes, fine, we could take in the evening as well – great idea but ... but ... [he's weakening already, craven soul that he is!] promise you have no plans to force me on a route march along endless shopping malls ... please... [his hands clasped in fervent supplication] I beg of you, not that; I'd sit through three hours of *Eastenders* rather than that, honest I would.'

'Relax love, no; I promise shopping won't be on the agenda – my battered credit cards have about as much spending power as a Big Issue seller in Harrods. I could just about run to a pair of white knickers in M&S and that would be it.'

He licked his lips at this stirring mental picture, or was that just my vivid imagination working overtime again?

'What a relief! Right then, it's a date; I'll give it some thought and ring you soon with one or two ideas – really must be on my way now.'

He kissed me properly this time – a long slow kiss with just enough pressure to show his very real attraction. I responded in kind.

'Blimey,' he said, pretending to be coming up for air, 'I'd better go quickly or I'll be trying to convince your hotel receptionist I'm the pizza delivery boy.'

I fought down the urge to say he could deliver to me anytime, anywhere.

'OK then, off you go and make sure you do call soon.' One more quick kiss and we parted.

True to his word he phoned on the Thursday evening as I got home after two days' training.

'Did it go well Sally?' ... How nice of him even to remember, I thought, liking him more and more! ... 'Bet it did – I'm sure you had them all eating out of your hand! Now as regards Saturday – what about meeting up in London? You remember I said I've always been keen on architecture. Well, there's lots of interesting places to see, especially in the City and out towards Docklands – then we could take our time walking back and find somewhere to eat. What do you think?'

London. The fact was I had been there so often but had never found the time to do this sort of thing.

'Now there's an original idea – yes, love to, count me in.'

We agreed to meet at two in front of the National Gallery. Success! He's passed my test, I thought smugly; Saturday afternoon and he's spending it *with me*. What a victory. Roll on the weekend!

Seeing the sights

Tom was clearly in high spirits. He gave me a cuddle, saying 'You don't know how much I've been looking forward to this. I just knew this weekend was going to be the tops! It started yesterday afternoon on the golf course – me and Jack were in this four ball competition – semi-final would you believe – and we stuffed them 5 and 4!

He thrust a clenched fist into the air and passers-by could be forgiven for thinking he'd just been told that he'd won on the lottery.

'Oh well done Tom – great result. Let me give you a kiss – you're a hero!' [I didn't let on that, for me, understanding golf was even more of a challenge than breaking the Da Vinci code.]

He was still so high, so enveloped in this aura of success that he took my congratulations at face value and said, 'Oh, thanks sweetheart, I knew you'd be pleased for me – now, let's be off on our little expedition.' With a thrill I registered the 'sweetheart'.

Within half an hour we were buzzing along the Docklands Light Railway, heading east. He was as excited as a little boy watching the Changing of the Guard.

'Look, that's Canary Wharf in the distance, and can you see the Dome over there? What a fiasco that was! Hey, see those penthouses? Cool £2 million each they fetch now – unbelievable isn't it? Just think, thirty years ago, this place was a total dump. It'll be the same with the Olympics you know; we'll end up with another great piece of urban regeneration – fantastic but what a pity it didn't go to Birmingham or Newcastle instead. Oh look, there's the

Gherkin – what a stunning piece of modern architecture that is – see the art deco influence on it?'

I could scarcely keep track of everything, but was certainly infected by his boundless enthusiasm. We walked some of the way back and I pointed out the Tate Modern and Millennium Bridge nearby. I tingled when he grasped my hand as we gazed in awe at the majesty of St Paul's cathedral – all the more impressive now that Paternoster Square had been renovated. As we began to move along to Fleet Street, he showed me the Old Bailey and the Royal Courts of Justice. 'Can you believe it? Gary Lineker was on trial there a couple of years or so ago. No, I'm not joking – it was some sort of libel trial.'

'Gary Lineker, Mr Clean? In court?' I asked, genuinely surprised. 'Bet he won the case though.'

'He certainly did – and how!'

By now, my initial brisk pace had flagged into a more sedate dawdle, and I suggested stopping for a coffee. The frothing cappuccino revived me, and I was able to get my breath back, enjoying the sunshine and vigorously rubbing some semblance of life back into my aching calves and sore ankles. I hadn't worn the most suitable shoes for a jaunt of this nature and the combination of distance, sunshine and unyielding pavements had taken its toll.

'Tell you what, let's just press on to Trafalgar Square – there's always something going on there.'

I bravely – if reluctantly – agreed, and soon we were relaxing by one of the enormous lion fountains in the centre. He drew me to him, and I leant against his chest breathing in the fresh cotton smell of his shirt. God I loved this man. Loved? Loved?! What was I thinking? This was only my third date but it was true. I was besotted. Who would have thought it? Internet dating? Greatest invention since heated eyelash curlers. OK, so the others may have been pure dross – especially James – but I had found pure gold in Tom. I snuggled closer, just happy to be there with him.

Since the north side had been pedestrianised, Trafalgar Square was livelier than ever. Also, there was some sort of rally going on to celebrate London's success in the Olympics bid. Smiling clowns, perched high on stilts, tottered through the crowds, foreigners had their national flags stencilled onto their cheeks by eager face painters, and children milled around the ice cream vans and then begged their parents to buy food for the pigeons. Rock bands belted out their music against the weak competition from the buskers, and living statues peered blankly into the clicking cameras of the swarms of tourists. He slipped his arm around my waist, drawing me to him, kissing my hair and neck, enjoying my fragrance. We talked easily with no embarrassing silences to spoil the mood. This was wonderful; *he* was wonderful.

Buon appetito!

'Right,' he said, brightly, 'let's pop up to Soho; there's every kind of restaurant imaginable there – they've even got a Mongolian one now offering "All you can eat for a tenner" … [Hmm … must email Mike in Crewe with the address, I thought waspishly] yes, honestly, Mongolian – it's called "WOK you like".'

I giggled and said I was happy with almost anything, but not Thai – I'd never been particularly fond of Thai cuisine, regarding it as Chinese-with-attitude and it gave me indigestion.

We came across an Italian place, 'Il Contadino'; this would certainly fit the bill. As we strolled over to it, we passed by the many legendary offerings of Soho. Clearly, all sorts of appetites were catered for here – gay clubs, sex shops, peep shows, porno dens …

What was on public show was mind-boggling enough; God knows what sort of bizarre diversions they must have had on offer inside.

'One of my exes – girlfriends that is, not wives – used to work in the sex industry, you know.'

I was shocked – my eyes widened with surprise and just a little interest.

'Really? Would she have any useful tips to pass on to an innocent little girl like me do you think?' I said [fluttering my eyelashes provocatively]. 'You mean she was … erm ... she was a ...'

'Actually, she worked in factory that produced sex toys – you know: blindfolds, whips, masks, handcuffs … [beam me up Lenny] ... that sort of thing. Then, she applied for a promotion, as supervisor in the Penis Department, which had recently been extended – stop giggling; this is true, honest – but she made a mess of the interview by saying that she was always on top of the job and never made any cock-ups! Anyway, she left and got a job at an Ann Summers store, saying it was really classy compared with the other place, and the staff got a 25% discount and – '

'Are you sure you don't work for *The Sun* on the side Tom?' I broke in with a laugh. 'Hey, this place looks special.'

'Il Contadino' was really chic, stylishly furnished and with not too many tables. Subdued lighting, smart and attentive waiters – quite a contrast to the squalid replica up in Crewe, I thought, shuddering at the unpleasant memory of it all. Our delicious meal kicked off with a refreshing Pinot Grigio and ended with a delicate lemon liqueur, offered and served by the attentive padrone himself, who bowed to me, calling me 'Bella Donna'. It had been an absolutely perfect day but now, although it was still quite early – scarcely gone ten – I was beginning to think about getting back home. We took a cab to Euston. I'd been uncomfortable about travelling home late on a train ever since some drunken oaf had pestered me a year or so previously. It had taken the combined muscle of three Virgin staff to eject him at Harrow and Wealdstone, but the vivid memories were still unsettling.

'Thanks so much for a marvellous day?' I hugged him fiercely, grasping hold of the lapel of his jacket; I didn't know it – and in fact may well have scoffed at the very notion – but I was in rapture.

'I've loved every minute too sweetheart,' he said, gently pushing my hair away from my face and adding with mock severity, 'and I'll be in touch early next week and if you dare say no to another date, I'll get a friend of mine in the police to find out where you live and then I'll camp out on your doorstep until you say yes!'

He gave me another strong hug and kiss, and then waved a cheery goodbye. As he turned to make his way over to his platform, I clenched my hands together and chewed my bottom lip, as if suppressing my growing desire for him – sometime soon, it would have to happen; it couldn't come soon enough.

A sting in the tail

On the Monday morning, following some difficult business calls, I needed a shot of caffeine. Neil was in the staffroom. He was a nice lad, always in good humour; one of poor Roy's operatives, or 'opos' as he used to put it.

'No football for you lot on Saturday then,' I beamed. 'Must have been a dreary old weekend. What did you do instead – just reluctantly settle for all the lowlights of England's recent matches on that new DVD?'

'Oh, no,' he replied cheerfully. 'No problem at all – you see it was the last matches of the season, and all the Premiership games were played yesterday.'

Ha-ha … it was all becoming crystal clear now! Tom had unhesitatingly agreed to see me on Saturday afternoon because he knew for sure that the key games were to be on the Sunday. The cheeky so and so. We could still be together, and he could *still* watch his weekend football – what you call having your cake and eating it. I was decidedly miffed. But on reflection, I thought I was overreacting. After all he hadn't lied. *I'd* asked *him* about Saturday and he'd said yes – it was as simple as that. And Saturday had been really very special, he'd been so sweet, and soon, with any luck, we'd be locked in a tight embrace, our hot bodies almost fused together and … ooh, that lovely warm churning sensation was again spiralling down from my heart to the pit of my stomach … No! Enough of this daydreaming, I thought – there's lots of work to do. But it won't be long before we are together again – fabulous! Wait till I tell Caroline how well things are going.

Chapter 15

GIRLIE TALK

With a celebratory glass in my hand I phoned Cazi later that evening.

'Hi Cazi! Look, start saving up girl – I've got him; I've got my man! What? Yes, of course I mean Tom – I don't change my men as often as my tights you know! Oh, he really is such a wonderful bloke! He's so good-humoured, generous, full of fun and enthusiasm, so bloody sexy and so positive about everything! I'll be seeing him again soon as well. You know, I don't think I've ever been so genuinely close to a man for ages and–'

'*If* you'd just let me get a word in edgeways ... I'm delighted for you. Yes, I know I was a bit sceptical at first when you got into this Internet dating lark but, now, I'm quite prepared to eat an entire humble pie. You were right, I was wrong. Now, when do you see it all happening?'

'"It"? What do you mean by "it"?'

'God – wake up! What the hell do you think I mean? The preparations. Facelift plus boob job at Plastic Pierre's off Deansgate, and that's just for Bob! Yes, I'm talking wedding with a capital W, marriage, church bells pealing, pre-nups – not that you'll need them – house hunting, honeymoon in the Maldives, etc.'

'Wait a minute girl, give me a break! I've only been out with him a few times and now you've got me virtually hitched – I told you to start *saving* from now not *spending* from now.'

'Sally, listen – how long have we been friends? Thirty years or more isn't it? I know you better than I know myself. I know the signs and the fact is that you've fallen for him, hook, line and sinker. And if he doesn't ask you, you better be quick and ask him. We live in modern times now, don't we?'

'Not a bad idea that! No, it's just … well, we were just strolling through London yesterday and he touched my arm – I felt an electric shock all over. Yes, I know I'm sounding like a schoolgirl with an almighty crush but I really don't want to rush things. He's been honest enough to tell me he's been engaged twice before and broke it off at the eleventh hour, frightened of the "C" word. I'm scared to death that if I step on the commitment accelerator, he'll want to go straight into reverse. No, we're talking about going off to Rhodes or somewhere in the summer and that'll be a great step forward. And anyway, I want you and the girls to meet him sometime soon.'

'Say no more my dear, say no more – you're probably right. Now look, in May it'll be our silver wedding anniversary. Yes, twenty-five years would you believe – "Hard labour" according to Bob! But the good thing is that, given what we've been through in the last few months we're closer now than we have been for ages. We got to talking about our anniversary and we're going to celebrate in style with a really posh dinner – yes, with knives and forks would you believe. What, disco? No, relax, there'll be no disco, promise. I love mad Janey to bits but the prospect of her yelling out "Like a virgin" [what a joke] and flashing her purple thong from some tabletop for all to see would simply be too much to bear – *The X Factor* it ain't. So, it'll be black tie and cocktail dresses, the whole champagne and canapés bit and then a wonderful meal. What do you think? Right, the date for your diary my dear is Saturday, May 28th. Who knows? We might just be able to announce your engagement at he same time.'

'Ooh,' I shivered in delight. 'Now, that would be something – fingers crossed and all that! Right, must go; lots to do – ring you soon; bye.'

Things are developing nicely

No sooner had I put the phone down than it rang again. It had to be – it was – Tom.

'Hello sweetheart and how are your poor little tootsies? Sorry we did so much walking. Next time, I'll get in touch with Red Letter Days and hire a coach and four to whisk you off to wherever you want to go, except Harrods of course. It was great in London and I know it sounds like some soppy cliché but it really does feel as if I've known you for months rather than just weeks. Can we get together next week? Any chance – please?'

'I thought our London day was *fabulous* – and the walk probably did me a power of good – probably lost the odd stone or two! I've been down there so many times but what you showed me, well – it was like having blinkers removed from my eyes, so thanks ever so much. Now, remember the lovely Debbie and that Abba show you went to? Yes, it's on next week – back by public demand they say. Could you bear to see it again? Everyone I know who's seen it raves about it, and I'd really love to go.'

'Great stuff – count me in. I can doss down again at my friend's palatial mansion-cum-bedsit in Rochdale, no problem.'

I noticed he wasn't pressing the physical side: time for me to act.

'Look love, don't bother with that. After the show you can come back to my place and, as they say in films, I'll show you my etchings! I'll introduce you to the real love of my life as well – after you, of course [I thought I'd risk that] – Ringo, next door's tabby who saved me from the dangerous clutches of Mr Pervert; you know that Lenny bloke I told you about – that long-haired loser from Liverpool.'

'Oh yes, the big Brando fan and world authority on *Emmanuelle*. Fine, I'd be delighted to meet your great pal Ringo and stay over but only if it's really all right with you. I don't want to complicate things.'

'No, honestly, there's no complication at all. I'd like you to stay. Now, have you got your latest little silver gizmo with you? Good – are you free to join me on Saturday May 28th for a very, very special event?'

'Let's see. 26th, 27th…and, here we are, the 28th – ah! … the World Cup … [my heart plummeted] but no, I can record that so … yes, it's clear, no problem at all. It's in. So, come clean with me – you're not planning to wreak revenge and have me yomping over the Pennines in big hairy socks all weekend are you?'

'Of course not, darling – relax … [*darling* – the word had just slipped out – curiously, though, he didn't appear to have registered it or, if he had, then he didn't react to it] you know my close friend I've spoken to you about so often? Yes, that's her – Caroline – the one whose son is testing the Noise Abatement Act to its extremes with his manic drumming. Well, they're celebrating their silver wedding with a really special dinner and guess what? We're top of the invitees' list. I'm sure you've got a dinner suit tucked away somewhere in your wardrobe.'

'Sweetheart, this all sounds marvellous and yes, I do have a dinner suit. I'll have time to get it dry-cleaned; it certainly needs it after its last outing at the recent Gentlemen's Evening at the golf club. I'd really like to meet your friends; I've heard so much about them. Anyway, where were we? Yes, *Mamma Mia* – great idea but an entire week without you is simply too much … You're not training down in Birmingham are you? Later this week perhaps? We could do that Brasserie place again.'

I wriggled with delight. 'Tom, you're a genius. I'm due there this Thursday so why don't we meet in the bar at 7.30 and have a drink before the meal?'

'That's fantastic – see you then: must dash. Call you soon.'

I was just a tad disappointed. I'd have liked to keep on talking … hmm, I wondered, was there an important match on TV coming up?

Next day I had an email from Lesley to say not only had the bank decided to employ two additional trainers, but I would be arranging for their induction and training and, once underway, they would be reporting to me. In view of these extra responsibilities, I'd be given a substantial pay increase. Things were getting better by the minute. At the coffee break I phoned the Palace theatre to book tickets for *Mamma Mia*. To begin with I had to endure the seemingly endless and frustrating menu of options before making contact with a flesh and blood member of the human race. After all that, they only had the most expensive seats left but I felt he was worth every penny, and I was in line for a bumper rise! 'It's a rich man's world', as Abba would say.

About 6.30 in my hotel room on the Thursday evening I was just applying my make-up when my mobile rang.

'Hello love; yes it's me. Look I'm really sorry but I've just got to cry off tonight – I meant to phone you earlier on but had a few problems with my mobile … [I listened in silence, doubts as heavy as lead furrowing my brow] it's just that Slugger invited me months ago to this rugby club dinner in Gloucester and everything's booked and I can't let him down.'

I was really cross. 'Oh Tom, come on, it's really short notice and I've been looking forward to seeing you tonight and – '

'I know love, I know – I really am very sorry, honest, but I'll make it up to you, promise, and we'll have a great time at that Abba show at the weekend. Anyway, must dash now – bye love!'

Click. Suddenly, I'd lost my appetite. I settled for a sandwich from room service and then lay back on the bed, staring at the ceiling. Men, I thought – my God, they can be a real pain at times.

Take a chance on me

But, by the time Saturday came round, my irritation was long forgotten, and I was thrilled to see him outside the theatre at the agreed hour. He was in his usual high spirits. His favourite team, Arsenal, had just won some big match or other and he was most definitely 'Over the moon'. The fact that I looked absolutely DDG [or so he said – flatterer!] added to his delight. The show, as expected, was fantastic. Perhaps the storyline was a bit contrived, but so what? There was a string of hits and the finale with

'Waterloo' had the audience up on their feet, dancing in the aisles, roaring out the words and joining in the fun.

Back in my flat, Ringo took a real fancy to him. In turn, he was as soft as butter, speaking to him softly, stroking his fur gently and telling him what a clever little chap he was to have seen off a potential rival – Lenny – in such a resolute fashion. I looked on, catching my breath: that warm feeling again, butterflies in my stomach – my whole body felt alive … he was bloody fantastic.

This was the first time that we'd slept together. It proved to be everything I had naughtily daydreamed of amid the spreadsheets and bar charts that dominated my working life. We had a few drinks before going to bed and were so happy and relaxed in each other's company that I felt no embarrassment as we undressed and indulged in a lengthy bout of foreplay. I drank in his smell, and shuddered violently as he kissed my breast. His body was athletic. His chest and shoulders were broad, his legs were long with thick, well-muscled thighs and sleek calves. There was no sense of obligation, no hint of either seeking the upper hand, just a long satisfying night of shared pleasure and intimacy.

I'd never been happier and began to think that this man really was 'the one'. At breakfast, I hugged him close, and practically slobbered over him.

'Sallee!' he said with a laugh, untangling himself from me and pretending to be fighting for breath. 'No, another session like last night, and I'll be fit for nothing for the rest of the week.'

I pouted in feigned disappointment, my thoughts returning to our time in bed together as desire shot through me. He left at lunchtime to see his friend Alex in Rochdale. I noted how important his friends were to him; he was really close to them, and they were clearly an important part of his life. This mattered to me because I felt exactly the same about my friends. Here was a man who would genuinely want me to maintain existing friendships. He wouldn't feel left out or second best if I wanted a girlie night out. I remembered reading in a magazine article recently that, 'You can always tell genuine people because they always have friends of long-standing'; well this was as true of Tom as it was of me – surely we were made for each other?

The work/life balance

My two new recruits, though still a little wet behind the ears, were extremely well organised, eager to please and determined to do well. I felt as if I were taking an almost maternal interest in them. Jim had studied economics at university but had then changed tack by taking an IT conversion course. In contrast, Nicola was very much a 'home bird'. Although she'd done really well at A-level, she'd no interest going off to college but had plunged instead into computing. Given a new program, she would relish the challenge and invariably master it in a very short space of time. The bonus was that they both had outstanding interpersonal skills and proved popular with their colleagues. I knew for sure that I would soon be able to entrust them with the more straightforward training courses and thus reduce some of the pressure on myself.

Mum had phoned asking for advice, not about Dad's health this time, but about his obsession with flying out to Australia sometime to watch the cricket; this had been a lifetime wish. Given his age and uncertain health, she was more than a little doubtful.

'He's never right these days love and it's such a long way and you read about them big planes crashing and Mrs Rogers from the bingo well she lost her brother on one in Japan or somewhere far away and then there was this programme on the television talking about you getting a DVD or something like that if you didn't wear special socks and Dad said he didn't fancy the idea because they would get itchy and anyway you can't get up and walk around when you're six miles up in the sky and last night in bed I was getting really worried me chest started hammering just thinking about it and I thought I'd phone our Sally because you know all about these things ... and ...'

I sensed immediately that her mind was made up. They would not be indulging in any adventure down-under, however attractive such a trip might be.

'Well, you're probably right, Mum. A flight of nearly twenty hours wouldn't be too comfortable for either of you and anyway, it would be really scorching when you got out there. Why don't you explain this to Dad? You could also say that the ticket prices would be sure to hit the roof and, what with the flight and hotels and everything, it would all be simply too expensive, running into thousands of pounds. I'm sure he'd see the sense of it.'

'Oh thanks very much dear I don't feel so bad now and anyway with Dad's leg being a bit better so we can have a bit of a walk round the park with the weather being so nice as well and how's your new friend Tom did you say he was a quality supervisor or something like that is he all right?'

I felt it was much too early to divulge any more about him. If I did, the phone lines in the north-west would be buzzing with the world-shattering news that 'Our Sally's courting again.'

Preparing for the big day

The day of Caroline's wedding anniversary grew ever closer, and when we got together, we talked of little else. I discovered to my utter consternation that Anne would be bringing Mike from Crewe with her, he of the easyJet-pizzeria-daybook notoriety. How on earth was I going to play that one? I would waste no time on it. Early on in the evening, it would be a simple case of, 'Hello – isn't it a small world?' and that would be it. I could not NOT go to such a special evening simply because the Secretary of the Crewe branch of the EasyJet Supporters' Club was destined to make an appearance. I put this irritating detail to the back of my mind, confident it would be no more than a side issue.

The week that followed was one mad rush. The extra courses, demand being stimulated by an expanding economy, were proving really popular and the new, young lieutenants were proving exceptionally competent, constantly receiving positive feedback. Midweek, I had to drive over to Leeds but this time to undergo training ['Simulation Techniques in Training'] rather than deliver it. I really enjoyed the change. No responsibility for the day, no preparation, no pressure. Fellow trainers would be there too from the Midlands area and so there would be a good opportunity for socialising. Among these colleagues was Sunita.

Enter Sunita

Sunita was an elegant young woman of Asian background. She was also stunningly beautiful, her dark olive skin being set off by her gold earrings, necklace and bangles. Her lovely face was framed by an abundance of shining, jet-black hair. She was gregarious and very good with people, basking in that enviable confidence which natural good looks bestow on the fortunate few. Not surprisingly, therefore, she was the centre of attention.

We'd always got on really well and we were the first to volunteer for the customary role-play exercise. Later, in the coffee break, gossip replaced business matters. She confided that she had just avoided an arranged marriage. She'd stood her ground but, in rejecting her ethnic conventions, she'd soured family relationships, possibly for good. I told her I was dating 'a really nice bloke after one or two disasters earlier in the year.' We agreed to meet up soon for a longer chat – I was due in Birmingham in the not-too-distant future.

Counting your chickens

The day of the celebration had finally arrived. I'd been looking forward to it for weeks now, not only to share Caroline's and Bob's happiness, but also, if I was honest, to parade Tom to the assembled multitudes – well, to my gaggle of friends actually. I smiled to myself, not without a dash of self-satisfaction, that by eight o'clock he would have them all eating out of his hand, charmer that he was. My preparations began early. Caroline was going to wear an absolutely gorgeous midnight blue dress. Overlaid with dark sequins and velvet, it was exactly the type of 'posh frock' that Monsoon did so well. Mid-calf length and cut on the bias, which really flattered her curves. She would look fabulous and I didn't want to risk upstaging her in any way. So, I'd gone for a simple sleeveless, black crepe, knee length dress, which I planned to wear with just a couple of pieces of gold jewellery. I wore my hair down in casual waves. By early evening I was ready and waiting.

Tom was due to pick me up at a quarter to seven allowing plenty of time for the champagne and canapés. At 6.35 the phone rang. 'No, don't answer it!' was my immediate reaction. But I could see it was Mum. Duty called.

'Oh hello dear hope I'm not disturbing you or anything it's just that Dad's not too good again with his back what's been plaguing him all week and I don't know what to do.'

I was no medical practitioner and so could offer no clinical help but I listened patiently.

'Look Mum, don't get yourself so upset – we all know it flares up from time to time. Give it a week or so and he'll be back at the Line Dancing Club as fit as a flea.'

Mum was comforted by this but then ['Oh while I'm on'...] moved on to impart the latest news of family and friends; I inwardly groaned and glanced at my watch: five to seven.

'Now Mum, it's lovely to hear from you, but don't forget, it's Caroline's big do tonight and I mustn't be late – yes, of course I'll give them your love, and I'll phone tomorrow to see how Dad is, promise.'

Dead on seven. No Tom. I furrowed my brow, puzzled. Five past seven. Still no Tom. I was increasingly alarmed.

Where was he? What had gone wrong? Had he lost his way? He couldn't have – he'd been round lot of times. Ten past seven. The mobile rang. It was him. Relief flooded through me.

'Tom, where *on earth* are you? It's turned seven and we've got to be there pretty soon. I've been so worried.'

'Oh, hello I ... erm ...'

I knew in an instant that he wasn't coming; my stomach lurched.

'Actually, love ...' he continued lamely, 'I'm afraid I've got a bit of a problem with this party thing tonight and – '

'"Party thing"? "Party thing"? Tom, this just happens to be the most important occasion for my best friend! Now, what's this "bit of a problem" you've got?'

I was desperately trying to stay in control but tears were welling up in my eyes, my throat constricted, my heart pounded.

'Erm ... well, remember Alex? Well, his brother's managed to get some tickets for some big boxing match in Birmingham, and they were too good to turn down really and ... erm, I thought as I wouldn't know anyone at the do, you wouldn't mind if I ... well ... sort of ... didn't quite make it – is that all right?'

I fought for breath.

'I can't believe you're talking to me like this! What about me? And what about our hosts who've gone to all this trouble and expense – where are your manners? And another – '

'But Sally, they're – '

'No, don't interrupt; I know what you're going to say – that sport is very important to you: fact is, it's obviously more important to you than me! Now, get off this bloody phone – I never want to hear from you again you selfish, selfish bastard!'

Bursting into tears, I flung the phone across the room.

The show must go on

I lay on the bed, sobbing, pounding the pillow in disappointment and desperation. How could he do this to me? I felt sick to my stomach. The very last thing I wanted to do was go to the celebration alone … but how could I not go? This was Caroline's big day and I had to be there, *wanted* to be there – there was no way I could let her down. But the thought of all those other couples at the dinner and me on my own made me feel such a loser.

I regained a level of composure, restored my make-up to some degree of acceptability and phoned for a taxi. Most of the other guests were there by then but, fortunately, were too busy with the goodies on offer to notice me. I tried to make myself inconspicuous but naturally Caroline spotted me and quickly moved across the room, eyes wide with knowing suspicion – the radar of female intuition immediately sensing disaster; my hands went up in an attitude of self-defence.

'Don't ask – bloody men! Bastards, all of them as far as I'm concerned, Cazi. I'll give you the full story later but … ah, Bob, you lovely bloke, how are you?' giving him the biggest hug I could muster. He'd ambled over from the bar, happily quaffing a pint of foaming Boddington's – much more to his taste than the Maison Mercier on offer ['Champagne's for puffs'].

'100%, sweetheart, 100%! Now how's my favourite little banker, and can you rustle up a quick £25,000 loan for me and my long-suffering missus to squander on our celebratory holiday in Florida sometime?'

'Wish I could, Bob, honest I do. Cazi! Quick, cover Bob's eyes or he'll have another heart attack. Here's Janey. Janey, what *is* that you're wearing! Is it a dress or a knitted cuff? Well, I'm sure it'll look lovely when it's finished. Did they run out of material? I'm surprised you didn't get arrested in the street for public indecency.'

'No problem. Two coppers did come up to me but I just flashed my tits, gave 'em a kiss each and they let me off with a caution!'

I joined in the fun in a valiant attempt to stave off a possible torrent of prying questions about the 'dream man' I'd been describing to them for so long. Everywhere I looked there were couples clinking champagne glasses, touching each other in that familiar way couples do … little pats on the hand, slight leaning in to each other, and an arm casually but possessively placed on a shoulder. It made me sick to see it. I was utterly miserable. Over by the bar I spotted Anne; she looked glum as well. There was no one with her – this was pretty clear from the mini tower of canapés she'd deftly arranged on her plate.

'Oh, hello, Sally,' she began, licking wisps of puff pastry from her lips. 'Guess what! That tosser Mike from Crewe phoned me an hour ago to say he'd decided the train fare up here would be too much, considering he'd be with a lot of strangers, so he wasn't bothering to come. Tight bastard! Thank God you didn't have to meet him.'

Little do you know, my dear, little do you know, I thought before attempting to cheer her up. 'Oh, come on now Anne, buck up – lots more fish in the sea as we say. Now, pass me one of those pint jugs – time for a drop of champers I think.'

There was a short interval for photos. Obviously, the focus was on Caroline, Bob and their children. Richard, with his smart new suit and fashionable tie-less presentation, looked very much the modern teenager rather than the boy he still was, and as for Louise, she looked stunning. She'd let her hair down over her shoulders, and was wearing a full-length silver evening dress which emphasised her slim figure. I looked on in silent admiration and more than a little envy.

We moved to the long central table displaying name cards. I watched Anne snatch up **MIKE**. She tore it in two and furtively put the pieces in her handbag. I stared down at **TOM**, and my eyes filled up. Bloody, bloody bastard. The waitresses come along to serve the first course, and although I wasn't the slightest bit hungry, I did have something for appearances' sake. By sheer good fortune one of Cazi's relatives was sitting nearby; she was a born extrovert and a natural storyteller; she dominated the area where we were sitting, and this meant I could at least try to relax back, smile and join in the good humour as best I could.

The memories of the night before came flooding back. The animated conversation, the amusing speeches, the mountains of rich food, and the lakes of delicious drink … yes, the drink. And now, here I was, alone in my own bed. I had no idea of how I'd made it home. My mind was more preoccupied with my corrugated throat and searing headache. My hooded eyes drifted across the bedroom, and I could just about make out the bathroom door. In short, I was having the mother of all hangovers. Four bottles of Buxton water, three hours, two showers and one bath later, I felt in reasonable condition again.

Tom's smiling features were stuck to the fridge door. An A4 photo with 'Here's looking at you kid' scrawled across, a memory – or rather a relic, it seemed now – of happier times. The photo's shredded fragments soon littered the kitchen floor; I made myself a big mug of strong, steaming, black coffee. I saw my yellow Post-it note 'Phone Mum'. I was relieved to find they weren't in and left a cheery little message, warning Dad not to do too many press-ups at the gym. Then I felt guilty about being relieved and this only served to intensify the day's misery. Tom made several attempts by text, phone and email to contact me but all were met with a wall of silence. He didn't venture to my flat – probably fearing for his safety if he did so.

Three weeks had passed now since I'd dumped him. He'd phoned one last time in an attempt to win me back but even then I could hear frenzied football commentary in the background. Of *all* the men I'd met since my marriage broke up, he'd been the one I envisaged settling down with. I was devastated. I found it hard to believe that a mature person would sacrifice the possibility of a rewarding and long-lasting relationship just to watch some awful boxing match – a couple of overweight psychopaths pummelling hell out of each other. He'd let me down more than once before – then, it had been for football: ninety minutes watching twenty-two overpaid pampered ponces running around a football pitch that resembled a mud bath. And what had he said? He'd quoted some football 'legend' as saying, 'Some people think football is a matter of life and

death but it's far more important than that.' What a total
TOSSER!

After a month or so my deep disappointment was
gradually disappearing. And then, on one rather quiet
Sunday evening, the laptop on my dining table began to
work its magic … and yes, among several, there was one
rather promising hit. This might be the one to place Tom
firmly in the 'history' file.

Now, here was Jack. He was quite attractive in a
rugged/outward bound sort of way; I read his profile with
growing interest …

THE PROFILE:

Name: Jack
Age: 41
Location: Chester
Status: Divorced
Children: Two
Job: P.E. Instructor
Height: 6'1"
Build: Muscular
Appearance: Attractive
Eye Colour: Hazel
Hair: Brown
Religion: None
Star Sign: Taurus
Smoker: No
Drinker: Moderate

INTERESTS: *Adventure sports, horse riding, restaurants, cinema, reading [especially the history of warfare].*

ABOUT ME: *Hi, I'm Jack. I left the Army last year after 22 years' service, and as my marriage didn't survive the constant moving around, I'm back in 'civvie street' on my own and looking to make new friends and relationships. I like my job but I do miss the Service. I did some pretty exciting stuff in my time, the kind Andy McNab writes about ... well, almost ... and it's hard to feel that rush of adrenaline on the 7.38 from Whitchurch to Chester. So I look for it by doing adventure sports, rock climbing, white-water rafting, hang-gliding, abseiling, that sort of thing. So if you like my photo and are looking for a man who's light years away from a pipe and slippers, email me and let's see if we can create that rush together.*

THE MESSAGE: *Hi Sally. I think your profile is really entertaining, and you look gorgeous in your photo. In the event of a nuclear war, I'd stock up on clothing, carbohydrates and camping equipment. In other words the practical accompaniments to your Bollinger, Belgian chocs and Bulgari. You won't need Brad Pitt – I would more than make up for his absence! Now, I sense that sport is anathema to you but I'm cool with that. If we do get along and you don't want to be involved in that part of my life then fine. But I'm not talking about indulging in 'games' like football and rugby; I'm talking about THRILLS! Heart-pounding, gut-wrenching, head-spinning thrills! So how about meeting me for dinner and I'll tell you all about it? Jack*

MY ACTUAL REPLY: Dear Mr Adventure. Well, well, well! You are a turn up for the books, very different to the average Dateandsee subscriber. Yes, sport is anathema to me and I don't know anything about the 'adventure' sort either but it strikes me that white water rafting would involve expenditure on AquaDior, the best waterproof mascara on the market, and rock climbing would involve tucking my lipstick down my sock. Having said that, I like the look of you and I suppose I do need someone to handle practicalities in the event of world war so yes, I'd like to have dinner with you and as Chester is one of my favourite places, how about we meet there? Sally

P.S. You won't be in disguise will you? I mean, Andy McNab is a black silhouette on the cover of his books – bit sinister

So, Jack had come along. Although I didn't really think we had enough in common, he was really good-looking and I expected the date to be, at the very least, quite entertaining.

Chapter 16

AN EXTREME SPORT

A week later I arrived in Chester after lunch, planning to spend a few hours shopping and then freshen up and change before meeting Jack at seven o'clock in Café Rouge. Chester was special, with something for everyone. Roman history, top quality shops, stylish restaurants and even a racecourse for those interested in the Sport of Kings. I went every year to Ladies' Evening at Chester races. It was a bit like Ladies' Day at Ascot but without Tara Palmer-Tomkinson and other celebrity skeletons.

I immediately spotted Jack at the bar. My, oh my, he really was handsome in a Ramboesque kind of way. He was casually dressed in light Chinos and a blue polo shirt, and his smile indicated that he was as pleased with my appearance as I was with his. We ordered drinks and fell easily into conversation.' … No, it's not all that dangerous. *You* are securely strapped to the instructor and *he* has a parachute *and* an emergency chute.'

I shivered, 'Brrrr, well, I've no desire to fling myself out of a plane. I mean, what's the point?'

'The point is the thrill of it all and the sense of achievement you get from doing it. The satisfaction of being able to say, "I conquered my fear." That must be a good feeling, don't you think?'

'Well, I don't want to devalue your experience, but frankly, I get all the thrill and fulfilment I need from beating someone else to the till with the Reiss bargain of the century.'

'Yes, very good but it wouldn't do for us all to be alike so you're not going to put me off that easily.'

The evening passed pleasantly enough. He was certainly good company but I knew I would quickly tire of stories packed with references to crampons and stabbing fish with a home-made spear. Having said that, when he invited me to attend an adventure charity event, I readily agreed to go.

Between a rock and a hard place

The event *sounded* perfect. I thought of my many futile attempts to convince Lesley that the bank ought to get involved in local charity events. I'd pointed out that it needn't be expensive – only a few hundred pounds' worth of prizes, but it would raise the profile of Barclays, demonstrating that we were interested in small businesses/customers as well as the multinationals. The adventure sports on offer would be totally different to the usual run-of-the-mill tombola stalls and coconut shies and would undoubtedly attract young people. This was another selling point to Lesley because head office had identified the under twenty-fives as *the* key consumer target group for the year ahead.

The venue was Weston Park, Staffordshire – ancestral home of the Earl of Bradford but more famous in recent years for the annual 'V' concert, the Midlands equivalent of Glastonbury. The aim was to raise funds for a national charity to provide adventure holidays for underprivileged kids. I arrived promptly at noon. My 'wardrobe' had been a problem but I did at least have my walking boots, scuffed reminders of my ill-fated venture to the sculpture park;

also, from my first ever visit to Millets I'd secured a pair of faux combat trousers and a sort of bum bag thingy big enough for my lipstick, mirror, Kleenex, Polo mints and, on this occasion, rosary beads. It was a promising start as the weather was fine – sunny and with relatively little wind. Jack absolutely looked the part. Resplendent in khaki, he was the epitome of macho strength and courage. I half-expected him to deliver a speech worthy of Lord Nelson ['England expects every man to do his duty!'] to the huddle of youngsters kitted out and eager to try climbing the fifty-foot 'rock face' before them.

He patiently explained the safety ropes and then gently encouraged the kids as they scaled the wall. They couldn't get enough of it – quite literally rising to the challenge. One exclaimed loudly that it was miles better than climbing onto the roof of their maisonette to get in when his mum was too drunk to hear him banging on the front door, while another said his brother had been caught housebreaking when he fell off the drainpipe he was attempting to climb. I shook my head, wondering how these youngsters intended to put their newly found skills to use but for now, at least, they had no motive other than to have fun.

Suddenly he turned … I froze as his commanding gaze settled on me. 'OK, Sally – your turn,' he boomed out.

'Meeee?' I squeaked incredulously, my eyes immediately sweeping over the area in a vain search for a place of refuge.

'Yes, you! Private Benjamin over there. Come on, let me attach your safety ropes and show us all what you're made of.'

'But, but, but, I don't like heights. I get dizzy on a step stool. Honest, I'll fall off and ruin everyone's day when you have to call an ambulance. We're a long way from *Holby City!*'

'Come on love, you've just witnessed a group of nine to twelve-year-olds climb this. Don't tell me that you can't do it. You're not going to let this beat you, are you?'

'Yeah, go on Miss,' one of the kids shouted. 'It's dead easy. Even my mum could do it and she smokes forty fags a day, and she's even fatter than you!'

By now, the rest of the pack had encircled me rather like predatory wolves rounding on their hapless prey. Then they started on a disturbing chant 'Eezee …eezee…eezee' to the deafening accompaniment of rhythmic, tribal handclapping.

I looked venomously at the self-appointed leader of the pack. He had the grey pallor of deprived inner-city living and his facial expression was sly and cunning, challenging me to prove him wrong.

OK, you little brat, I thought. I'll show you what twenty years of Weight Watchers meals have done for me. I'm a lean, mean, climbing machine … and then, just ten seconds later …

'Jack! I'm losing my grip! Get me down!'

I was dangling about fifteen feet above the ground, oblivious of the laughter of the kids who had been joined now by a gaggle of adults, curious to know what all the noise was about.

'*Sally*, listen carefully to me,' shouted Jack, Action Man incarnate. 'You will NOT fall because your safety rope is secure. You *might*, however, strangle yourself with it if you don't stop swinging from side to side – stay calm: with your right hand feel for the grip; it's only about six inches above your head now.'

'I'll bloody strangle *you* if you don't get me down off here right now this minute,' I yelled. 'I told you I couldn't do it, you tosser!'

'Right,' he said, in a tone of resignation, realising this was one pupil destined for abject failure. 'Calm down. Stay exactly where you are and I'll come up to get you.'

He reached me in about four easy steps.

'OK, I'm here sweetheart – now relax and let me attach this rope to yours. There you are. See? You can't possibly fall.'

'Don't you "sweetheart" me. I knew this was a mistake. Get me down. RIGHT NOW!'

He expertly placed my feet in each of the footholds, and slowly we descended. The crowd, which had swelled considerably, roared their approval, chanting 'JACKO, JACKO, JACKO' in admiration of his 'heroism'.

Several of the mean-spirited onlookers were equipped with camcorders [nicked, I thought savagely, my erstwhile liberal outlook on life now hastily swinging to the extreme right] anxious to record my sorry plight for the amusement of future generations. The minute I was detached from Jack, I pushed him aside and shakily pulled myself upright. Tears of fear, embarrassment and relief coursed down my face as I surveyed the grinning faces of my audience. My mouth opened and closed like a landed fish as I struggled for words … then a quiet voice in my ear said, 'Nice arse.'

Peeping Tom

I wheeled round to deliver a stinging reply and very nearly fainted when I saw that the arse fancier was none other than … Tom!

'You, you, you MORON,' I screamed at him. 'What are you doing here, you bastard?'

'Hey, steady on girl. I could ask you the same question – never had you down as the Lara Croft type! But, you know, it's strange – I thought I recognised that rear end. It's good to see you again, especially from that angle,' he chuckled.

'Humph. You are a total idiot. Get away from me. I'm leaving.'

I stomped off towards the car park, slowing down only when I'd put enough distance between me and the rock face to muffle the sound of the kid asking his mother, 'Why has that lady got black streaks down her face?'

I had intended driving straight home but realised I was too upset for that and needed a strong black coffee first. Half an hour later, comforted by caffeine and a huge slice of fruitcake, I made for the car park. Passing the lake, I caught sight of Tom again. He was demonstrating the way to strap on a lifejacket before placing kids into two-man kayaks. I remained out of sight, watching him as he worked patiently with them. Well, well. What do you know; the Neanderthal has a charitable streak after all. What's he doing here giving up his precious sporting Saturday?

I drove home contemplating the email I'd have to send to Jack but my overriding thoughts were about Tom. I simply could not square his cavalier attitude to me with the Tom I'd just witnessed giving up his precious social time to help underprivileged children. The curiosity was eating me up, and I resolved to email him as well.

Hello, Jack – yes, it's me, little Miss Timid here. Thought I'd better email to apologise for my behaviour earlier today. Yes, I was terrified and really embarrassed by my fear, but that's no excuse for the way I treated you. I'm truly sorry and hope it didn't spoil your day, because I could see how very much you were enjoying it. It was really good to meet you, but I suppose what today has taught me is that we're too different to make a go of things. So, I'll just apologise once again and wish you all the best for the future. I'm sure Dateandsee has any number of ladies willing and eager to share the wilder side of life. Best wishes, Sally X

Right, that should sort Rambo out. Next up, it's my dearly beloved Tom!

Dear Des Lynam. I won't say it was good to see you again but on reflection it is pleasing to know that my derrière managed to look OK in combat trousers, the hour spent in that draughty Millets changing room was obviously worth it. I confess to being absolutely gobsmacked to see you there. I never had you down for a 'do-gooder', much less on a Saturday. So what's the connection between the Sportsman of the Year and that sorry bunch of apprentice muggers? Rear of the Year.

Jack replied within twenty-four hours accepting my apology and also accepting the truth in what I'd said – that we were probably incompatible and the episode was best put down to experience. On the other hand, Tom made me wait a whole four days before replying. Was he twisting the knife?

Darling derrière. How are you? Dignity fully restored by now? You know, you really ought to lighten up. What happened was funny! People were not laughing at you, we were laughing with you except that … you weren't laughing. Too bad, if you could have only seen yourself … anyway, enough of that I won't tease you anymore. It's a shame that we didn't spend more time together because if we had, you'd have learnt that every year I give up a few weekends to 'YES' the Youth Encouragement Scheme run by a sports charity to help wean inner city kids off stealing cars and into playing sport. I'm one of the Midlands helpers so the Weston Park event was in my backyard so to speak. Yes, sport is the foundation of my social life but I've witnessed firsthand how it can encourage children to make something of themselves. I enjoy doing it so it's no hardship. So Sally, has this made you think differently about me or am I still, what was it now? Ah yes, your fragrant words drift back to me … 'A moronic sports addict bastard with the intellect of Wayne Rooney and the emotional capacity of a cricket bat?' If, in the extremely unlikely event that I've gone up just a notch or two in your estimation, then please let me know because the fact is, I miss you and I'm more than willing to give it another go. Love, Tom xx

… 'Give it another go'… Despite myself, even from seeing his familiar face a few days ago and now from reading his explanatory email, I could feel myself being drawn back to him; it was as if a comforting warmth was gradually enveloping me. He hadn't mentioned the silver wedding celebration; perhaps he accepted that he'd been, at the very least, guilty of rank bad manners on that occasion. But had it really been a hanging offence? After all he wasn't my husband, fiancé, or partner, even though that's really what I would have wanted. Yes, his behaviour had been unworthy, but had my own reaction been, well, out of proportion? ... In less than a week, I was seeing him again. And, one month on, it was as if our relationship hadn't suffered the rupture, which, at the time, had seemed terminal ...

Chapter 17

Lovely Tom's cabin

Tom was, by now, a frequent lodger at my flat. It struck me that I'd never actually been to his home … and curiosity got the better of me.

'You know love I've never seen your place in Shrewsbury – and you did tell me it was a "smashing house" didn't you?'

Silence … a hint of resistance here perhaps? Was I invading his space, his private domain? But why should it be private – we were an item now, weren't we?

'Well, I don't know about "smashing" … It's not that bad a place but it's not exactly a palace either.'

'I'd be surprised if it was, but I'd still like to see it and perhaps I could help with a few feminine touches …'

His continuing lack of enthusiasm made me even more determined.

'By sheer chance, *sweetheart* [the emphasis wasn't lost on him], I'm due in Birmingham again next week and instead of that Brasserie place I could easily scoot over to Shrewsbury and cook you a nice dinner.' Without even being aware of it, over the last few weeks I had slipped into 'homemaker' mode.

'Well love, arm … that sounds fine but–'

'No buts this time, and don't you dare let me down again …' I tweaked his ear jokingly although my intentions were deadly serious '… so I'll reach you about seven, OK?'

For once his stock of pretexts, excuses, evasions appeared to have deserted him.

'Yes, fine love – let's do it,' he conceded; there was though a certain distance in his eyes – he was clearly not enthusiastic about the plan.

He lived on the outskirts of Shrewsbury. I found his house easily enough, it was just a case of punching in the postcode and letting the magic carpet of satnav do the rest. This was just as well because the estate was one of those modern, sterile developments. The house itself was featureless with nothing individual about it to mark it out from the countless other 'units'. There was a postage-stamp lawn at the front; his gleaming Saab stood in the drive. From inside he spotted me, and summoned up enough eagerness to give me a cheery wave.

'Hello love, come on in – I've been slaving away for hours to make the place presentable for you.'

The interior matched the exterior. It was all tidy and functional. The L shaped sitting room/dinette was predictable in the way that bachelors' homes tend to be. He'd made minimum effort to turn this house into a home. A set of dark wood carriage-style lamps hung low from the centre of the ceiling; the carpet was straight from the early 70s, an unimaginative expanse of dark green patterned with enormous orange diamonds. The broad arms of the black leather sofa and easy chairs were ringed with traces of beer and wine glasses. A large, austere cupboard almost filled one of the walls with nothing – no photographs or glass – to relieve its plainness. A huge plasma TV filled the corner recess, surrounded by almost industrial-scale speakers and an untidy, coiling jumble of wires and cables. The walls were bare for the most part – just one was decorated with a colourful poster from Mijas or somewhere advertising a bullfight. There was a plain table and two

357

chairs in the dining area, which looked out onto a small, barren garden. The patio boasted two earthenware tubs; both were empty. Mmm, definitely room for a woman's touch here, I thought, a little wistfully.

He looked uneasy. 'I'll give you the full guided tour later love, but look, I thought we'd go over to that Indian place I mentioned – save you cooking.'

The disquieting image of his grease-smeared cooker was the only encouragement I needed to agree.

'Yes, OK – I'll just pop to the loo and I'll be straight with you.'

I'd spotted the pale avocado suite through the cloakroom door. Inside it was clean, but there was a strange dampness about it and the potent smell of excess disinfectant; I cringed. On the way to the restaurant, Tom was in top form: warm, loving, teasing but sadly this didn't last …

When we got back to his house, I brought in my overnight bag together with a Threshers carrier.

'I thought a drop of sparkling wine would be good to celebrate my first time here,' I said cheerily.

'Great idea love – I'll get a couple of glasses.'

As he went off the kitchen, I retrieved from my bag a number of travel brochures.

'Look, darling, remember we were speaking about Rhodes? Well, I picked these up in town the other day – I thought we could read them through and then book for ourselves over the Web – much cheaper that way. I can easily take a week off mid September but it's a bit difficult after that.'

His smile froze; the brochures lay unopened on the table.

'What's up? Don't tell me you can't take time off?'

'Look love, any other year it'd be fine, but not this year – the Ryder Cup – remember? I can't miss it and there's even a chance of flying over to Dublin for a day or so to see some of it; Slugger was saying that a mate of his – '

'Tom, not damn sport AGAIN! For Christ's sake …! The Riders' Cup? You've never shown any bloody interest in horse racing before!' I was livid. 'Whenever we think of doing something, some bloody sports event always seems to come in the way – it's not fair!' I felt close to tears.

'But you know what I'm like, love – it's part of me – and, just for the record you silly thing, the Ryder Cup is *golf's* major international event and after all, it only comes round every four years in Europe – come on, give me a kiss, we can think about Rhodes a bit later in the year, come on now.'

He pulled me closer to him, clearly hoping that a kiss and cuddle would win me over.

He was right, and I was weak. The tournament did only come round every four years, and perhaps mid September in Rhodes would still be a little uncomfortable with its hordes of holidaymakers and torrid heat...

'OK,' I conceded reluctantly, 'I suppose I could shift my holiday week to sometime in October instead but when this golf thing's over, you've got to promise to think about our holiday properly or – '

'Of course, promise. Now come on, have another drop – we could take the rest of the bottle upstairs if you like ...'

Chapter 18

Goin' courting

What really thrilled me in these months was the way in which Mum and Dad had really taken to him – even more so, the fact that Dad seemed to have recovered some of his former vitality with 'my young man' being around. It was as if he was the son they'd never been fortunate enough to have, the son Dad would have been proud of.

A weekend in early September had been typical. I'd seen a lot of Mum but as for Dad and Tom, well they'd spent most of it down at the social club watching England play against Pakistan. Sport was the strong glue holding them together. There was even talk, again, of a family visit to Australia in the year ahead; Dad had always been a man of modest horizons but the one ambition he'd cherished for years was to go to Australia to watch an Ashes series. By way of reinforcing his case, he pointed out to Mum that they could even visit their cousins – they'd emigrated to Perth in the late 1950s. She was still less than eager, retaining fears about his health but she was warming to the idea now that I would be with them. As far as Tom was concerned, there could be no stronger incentive than cricket Down Under.

Since our reconciliation, I'd learnt to accommodate his sporting mania whilst he had kept his promise to maintain some balance and, when it mattered, to put me and our relationship first ... first – well most of the time. We'd had a blazing row when he'd let me down – again – and once more it involved Caroline and Bob. We'd

made arrangements to go out for a Chinese meal together
– everything was organised, including the taxis so that
everyone could enjoy a few drinks. I was out shopping with
Caroline in the Trafford Centre on the Saturday morning
and the place was heaving; suddenly, my mobile rang.

'Hello love, it's me. Yes, fine. But look, something's
just come up. I've had a phone call from the golf club
and they've brought forward the date of that big match
I mentioned to you ... [I had no recollection of this but
it wasn't the time or place to argue] and now I've got to
go down to Shrewsbury this afternoon for this regional
tournament – semi-finals you know, so wish me luck. Say
sorry to Cazi and Bob for me won't you? But don't bother
waiting up – it's bound to be a late one.'

I was bristling with rage, and shamefacedly explained
everything to Caroline.

'Oh, don't worry love. We all know what these blokes
are like with sport. Just like schoolboys. And Bob won't
mind for a minute – he always says my cooking's better
than that "Chinese crap which is only fit for pandas" – so,
no, don't give it a second thought; we can easily rearrange.' I
thought I'd got off lightly, and I resolved to have it out with
Tom the next day. What on earth could I do to prise him
away from his wretched sports?! I was still full of anger
as I steamed down the motorway to Shropshire. Barely
had I sat down on his paper-littered sofa when I went into
action, all guns blazing.

'Tom, you really upset me again last night – we were
all set to go to that Chinese and you casually phone up
about your bloody golf match and – '

'Love, let me explain – '

'No, *you* bloody listen for a change will you! I thought we'd got over all that sort of thing months ago and were more like an ordinary couple now and –' I couldn't continue; I felt my bottom lip quivering and I began to cry.

He came over and put his arms round me. Against myself, I leaned into him, and the sobbing ebbed away.

'Look, sweetheart, I'm so sorry – you're right: I was bloody selfish about it; I should have just scratched from the competition – bugger my trophy ...'

I raised my head hopefully – perhaps my tears had succeeded with him where my words had failed.

'... I know I've got to make it up to you, and to Caroline and Bob as well. Tell you what – we've got that Simply Red concert next Saturday but let's see if they're free on Friday and we can all go to that Indian place you said Bob liked; I'll pick up the tab – least I can do. Honestly, I'm so sorry to be upsetting you like this.'

He gently stroked my shoulder, kissed my neck, my salty eyes and mouth ... and I responded, reluctantly at first, but then with increasing intensity.

Friends

We'd arranged to meet Caroline and Bob inside the restaurant at about eight o'clock. We were just about to leave my flat when I spotted a group of hoodies looming up from the dusk outside. They stopped on my drive, looking at Tom's smart Saab.

'Tom, you'd better have a look at this lot.'

'Yeah, OK – I'll have a quick word; it'll be fine.'

I peered anxiously round the curtain as he ambled rather than marched up to them. They all seemed to be chatting away easily enough as he appeared to be explaining some of the car's specification. Then, with a cheery wave, they went on their way; what a relief! I recalled how well he'd dealt with the youngsters at the Weston Park festival some months earlier – no doubt he'd put his people skills to good use yet again on this occasion.

'OK love – all sorted; no probs,' he shouted cheerfully. 'Let's be on our way; I could eat a horse.'

'Straight with you!'

I skipped over to the dining table for my handbag, and noticed that he'd left his laptop on. Bending down to switch it off, I saw the screensaver. It was a photo of him – with Alex, I thought – and two attractive women in their thirties. They were in someone's living room and seemed to be having a good time. There were lots of wine and beer bottles around, and they were all smiling. The camera had caught Tom gazing with admiration down the blonde's cleavage, and she appeared to be enjoying his attention. This was worrying – not least when I realised that it must have been quite recent as he was wearing the red Nike T-shirt I'd bought him in the August sales. I swallowed hard, a flood of unwelcome images filling my mind.

I heard a horn beeping.

'Sorry.' I said, I put on my safety belt, 'I had to find my handbag and then I noticed you'd left your laptop switched on …'

'God, I'll be leaving my head behind next,' he joked, turning the ignition. 'Did you see that screensaver by any chance? Alex mailed it to me last week – took the photo when I was up in Rochdale watching the cricket on TV with him. His sister and another friend came round too; now they really could drink us under the table: that's modern women for you! Long live girl power! Now, what's the best way to that Indian?'

I could see he was using humour as a smokescreen, but his beaming smile could not conceal the furtive look in his eyes. I had to think quickly. If I challenged him further about the screensaver, this would definitely put the damper on the evening ahead – one I'd been working at for months. I couldn't – wouldn't – risk it. Perhaps he was right to pay so little attention to it – just a friend of his ... but, in retrospect, I realised that the incident did little to bolster my belief in his fidelity.

I was glad I hadn't made a fuss about it because the four of us got on like a house on fire. All women liked Tom and Caroline was no exception. He was so good-looking and a real charmer – quick-witted too and easily exchanged sporting stories and jokes with Bob.

'You know, mate, I was utterly gutted when we got knocked out of the last World Cup – that wanker Sven! He should have spent his time stuffing his various birds instead of stuffing our chances out there in Germany!'

'Dead right mate and bloody Rooney didn't help either, getting sent off like that – and then we had that human beanstalk Crouch; he should be playing basketball instead – bloody tosser!'

By the time they'd drained their fourth pint of lager, it was if they were old friends. I looked on, almost with pride. Caroline squeezed my hand under the table and this, together with a slight nod of her head, was all I needed to know that Tom, not unexpectedly, had proved to be a great hit. There wasn't the slightest suggestion of any continuing rancour about the spoiled evenings in the past, and we ended up at Caroline's house for more drinks.

Tom caught sight of young Richard who had sloped down to the fridge to help himself to more ice cream.

'Aah, you must be Richard, the famous drummer,' said Tom genially shaking the boy's hand. 'You know, I've got all the old Phil Collins stuff from his Genesis days and if you like I'll burn it on a CD for you.'

'Fantastic, cool – that'd be great.'

So, I thought, as I slipped into bed later, wrapping myself up in a cocoon of satisfaction, he's even passed the Richard test! The bedside clock ticked steadily in the silence of the night. I stretched out my hand, stroking Tom's face and chest, pulling him towards me. His boyish features were caught in the moonlight that filtered into the room. I had a huge lump in my throat. I loved him. Plain and simple. I loved him more than words could say.

Room to breathe

Several changes at the bank in recent weeks had made my professional life more exciting and therefore more fulfilling. The remote upper echelons of the business clearly rated Lesley highly; the whys and wherefores of this esteem remained a total mystery to the entire workforce. One outcome was that she had been invested with a new and more responsible brief. Whilst retaining overall management responsibility for the Manchester branch, she was now termed 'Regional Mentor'. Her job was to travel across the north-west, acting as a guide and mentor to branch managers in the early months of their tenure. Her 'extensive experience' would, it was believed, play a significant role in their professional development. For me, however, this meant that Lesley, even the reborn, slightly human Lesley, would be out of my hair for at least fifty per cent of the time. In addition to this, a further team of trainers had been appointed, and it would be my task to attend to their needs. I thrived in this sort of role and was really looking forward to getting started with them.

So, with Mum and Dad more settled, the job more rewarding, and Tom both literally and figuratively at my side, my circle of happiness was complete. And then, straight out of the blue, an email came … from Jonathan.

Billet doux

Sally, good morning to you. How are you? I've not seen so much of you in recent months. And no, it's not that I've been away on golf tours all the time it's probably that you've been away training a lot. And when you are in the office, you seem to scuttle off promptly at the end of the day to your … love nest perhaps? Do I know the lucky fellow? Anyway, I'm mailing you to say that the annual ball at the Midland isn't too far off now – it's a month or so later this year – and if in the wholly unlikely circumstance that you might be 'available' I'd love you to come with me. Now, if I don't hear from you in the next day or so, I'll need to assume that you're 'otherwise engaged' as they say. That would be really nice and I'd be genuinely happy for you. Love, J xx

Jonathan, it was really nice to hear from you. There was I thinking that I'd blotted my copybook with you for ever since I had to let you down at the eleventh hour last year – my God, doesn't time fly! Well, yes, there is a man in my life at the moment and I love him lots even though he is something of a cross between Quasimodo and Trigger out of Only Fools and Horses. So I do hope you have a really great time at the ball and as to your likely escort ... I've noticed one or two new young women up in FX recently, not that you'd give them a second look ... same boring old model, it's as if they're clones – lovely, blue-eyed beauties, long blonde hair, figures to die for [scratch, scratch] legs that disappear up a microskirt – not your type at all in fact! Love S xx

Going Greek

'So, where exactly is this place called Rhodes? It's not that I'm totally thick but remember at university I did history not geography.'

This was a welcome surprise as I'd been afraid that I'd have another battle on my hands because of all the sporting events dominating TV.

'Right, OK, let's see.'

I took two long cheese straws out of the tin on the coffee table and made a rough 'X' out of them. I was as excited as a child with a new jigsaw.

'Right, that 'X' is Italy and my coaster on the right is Greece – roughly of course. Now this blue napkin – this is the sea and the TV remote you've got there is Turkey. Down there to the south, where I put your coaster – that's the island of Rhodes.'

'God sweetheart, that's brilliant. You should phone up to go on that *Millionaire* quiz programme. OK, let's check dates and then onto the Web to make the booking; you know, I'm really looking forward to it – it'll be great fun.'

Beware the Greeks bearing gifts

Our hotel was next to a tiny chapel, topped by a bell-tower in Lindos. Dazzling white, its reflection shimmered in the clear, blue water. It was quite modest but had the key advantage of air conditioning; an absolute must even at this time of year. We went sightseeing early and late in the day and then relaxed in between at one of the countless tavernas. The local culture was obstinately Greek with all the signs written in Cyrillic and the translations in English underneath. There were so many monks and priests around too; with their unusual dark square hats and heavy black robes they stood out like flies on a white tablecloth. I loved the little donkeys too but felt sorry for them; their matted coats were encrusted with dirt and the burdens they were carrying seemed impossibly heavy. Perhaps the best part of the holiday was the evenings, as the setting sun streaked long tapering fingers of red, scarlet and vermilion across the gathering sky.

Over a candlelit dinner on our final evening, Tom reached out for my hand. He raised it to his lips and kissed it, smiling at me fondly.

'Well darling, it's high time I spoke to you about something really important – important for both of us.'

The candles flickered in the light evening breeze. I caught my breath and felt my heart pounding as he dipped into his pocket. This was it, it had to be – the old-fashioned proposal to be confirmed by a sparkling ring nestling in a purple box. I almost squirmed on my chair with pleasure.

'Yes, Tom,' I said hoarsely, barely able to speak such was my rising anticipation.

From his pocket he produced a brown envelope, folded several times so that, at a glance, it appeared to have the square compactness of a small container. From it he retrieved a creased letter. Dramatically he smoothed it out on the tabletop and began to read, affecting a posh accent of authority.

' ... *And so we are pleased to confirm your appointment as Chief Surveyor, North West region. Your base will be in Stockport and your new responsibilities will begin on Monday, October 16th.*'

'There we are, sweetheart,' he added with a flourish, clinking his glass against mine. 'Here's to Stockport, here's to us, and here's to a new beginning.' He leant forward and embraced me.

I was rigid with shock and disappointment. I felt my heart faltering. Perhaps it was the drink, or perhaps it was just the sort of man he was, but he failed to notice my reaction. I swallowed, determined to be positive.

'Oh darling, I'm so pleased for you; you work so hard and you deserve it, and as for living up there – '

'Oh, no problem sweetheart – I've already got it worked out; remember my mate Alex who lives in Rochdale? Well I can easily doss down with him – it's only half an hour's drive from Stockport and I can clear £500 a month by renting out my place in Shrewsbury – great isn't it?'

'Tom,' I replied, with perhaps a little more emphasis than I had intended. 'No, not Alex's place – don't you see? You could simply move in with me – it's so much more logical and then,' I paused, 'then we'd be a proper couple, we really would.'

My eyes looked at him appealingly. Silence. I thought he flinched at the suggestion initially as he drummed his fingers on the tabletop; but, then, somehow, just a moment or so later, he appeared to see the sense of it all.

'Oh yes, sweetheart, of course; yes, I see what you mean. Why not? Time I settled down a bit I suppose. Great, now if that doesn't merit a bottle of champagne, nothing does. Waiter!'

Love's young dream

Who said only women were hoarders? It was moving-in day and I couldn't believe the amount of rubbish that he wanted to bring with him. Tin trophies dating back over twenty-five years, souvenirs of countless victories on the rugby/cricket/football pitches of his youth and tattered programmes from long-forgotten matches; and, to cap it all, surely every single copy of *Today's Golfer* that had ever been published littered my spare room. He was struggling into the hall with yet another packing case. That did it – I launched my attack.

'Tom, just how much *more* of this junk do you plan on shipping in?'

'Junk? JUNK?! I'll have you know I've got some of the finest sporting memorabilia in existence. None of it is *junk*! People pay good money for this sort of thing on eBay – not that I'd even consider parting with a single item. Pass me that rugby ball please.'

I couldn't see a rugby ball but did spot a dirty squashed lump of once white leather. I screwed up my nose, and then held it out at a fair distance in front of me, lightly grasping it between two fingers like a festering sock.

'Do you mean *this?*'

'Yes, that's it. Now look at it carefully. See the names written on it? That's every member of the Barbarians' winning team. Well, all except Jonny Wilkinson that is – he'd already been carted off, vigorously protesting, to A & E minus a chunk of his right ear.' Tom was lost in reverie. 'What a great day that was – breakfast in The Cricketers, crate of Stella on the coach, blinding performance from the lads then an invite back to the players' dressing room. I'll never forget it and if I ever do ...' he waved the deflated ball menacingly at me '... this will remind me. So find a safe place for it – there's a good girl'.

I hesitatingly took the cherished memento from him. I wanted to fling it out of the window there and then but thought better of it. Placing it gently on the precarious pile of magazines, I said, 'Well all right then, but if you want to keep all this cra – err, all these precious things, then we'll have to make a trip to IKEA for more storage.'

He rolled his eyes heavenwards in irritation. I knew what was going through his mind ... 'Bloody hell – IKEA ... endless displays of cupboards and shelving, interminable discussions about which size was most appropriate, mind-numbing decisions on the relative merits of dark beech versus light beech veneers. And at the end of it all? A bloody Swedish open sandwich – just big enough to fill a hamster. God!'

Was this pique about the IKEA expedition though just the tip of the iceberg? Floating below might have been a deeper dissatisfaction with the recent massive change in his relationship with me; perhaps he was thinking ... 'I only wanted a place to kip near my new office and what have I got instead? An opportunity to take part in one of those bloody makeover programmes ...'

But hang on a minute. He was getting much more than that. He'd said I was a terrific girl – best girlfriend he'd ever had. I *knew* he was truly fond of me and my family and friends but perhaps it was all a bit ... well, quick for him? One minute he's tucking into the dolmades in Rhodes and the next minute I've talked him into moving in with me instead of Alex who, by the way, was 'well gutted' as, apparently, he'd thought Tom would bring his plasma TV with him. Ah well, it's done now and I bet he's thinking that if the worst happens [which it *won't*] Alex would always be available as a safety net because Tom says no woman in her right mind would have *him*. No, I think he's really going to try and make this work.

He bit his tongue and said 'OK love, no problem – we can go over to IKEA next weekend. There's not much more stuff to come anyway.'

As the weeks went by, we both made adjustments. He tried to remember to lower the toilet seat and squeeze the toothpaste from the bottom of the tube. On the other hand, I accepted that he didn't like his socks colour co-ordinated and his boxer shorts folded into neat squares. The major accommodation though, was on my part. I finally understood that he needed sport in his life the way I needed make-up and perfume – something to be savoured every day. So, we bought the *TV Times* every week, and he highlighted what he absolutely 'could not live' without seeing. I then fitted my life with him and my friends around these key sports fixtures. He promised things would get even better with Sky+ and that then we'd have '... even more flexibility ...' – mmm, yes, I thought to myself grimly, and his sports viewing would probably treble.

I'd recently given up my job at The Fox, which, after all, I'd only taken for the lack of anything else to do at the weekends. Whilst Marie was sorry to lose me, she did approve of Tom and was genuinely happy for me. When I'd finished my last shift, she hugged me warmly and said, 'I'm so pleased for you love. He seems a great guy and he's absolutely gorgeous. I really hope it works out for you. By the way, do you remember Emma who used to work here? She's sure her mate Julie had a couple of dates with Tom a few months back. Met him on the Internet but I don't think it was the site you used. Anyway, obviously it all fizzled out and now he's all yours, you lucky girl.'

I pretended not to pay much attention to this piece of news. He hadn't mentioned any 'Julie' to me but then perhaps neither of us had really shared our full dating history, although I felt pretty sure that I'd been the more open on the subject. Nor could it have been 'a few months back' because he was seeing *me* then. Marie must be mistaken. Interesting to note though that he was – or rather had been – on more than one dating site; he really had cast his net wide. Still, he belonged to me now and I'd never been so happy. I loved the whole domestic scene. I loved doing his washing and ironing, loved curling up next to him on the sofa and loved sleeping with him. Our sex life got better and better and I was overjoyed that I'd never have to go on a 'first date' again. Even shopping for two was much more pleasurable than shopping for one. I'd swapped single portion ready meals for fresh meat and vegetables and, of course, I'd snapped up a variety of cookbooks in Waterstones. In fact, on one particular night I remember all too clearly, I was cooking something special; this was a chicken dish from Jamie's Italian cookery book.

Tom patted his stomach in appreciation. 'That – was – bloody – superb. Come here you goddess – have you been taking lessons from Jerry Hall?'

I sat on his lap. 'I know what you're thinking about. A maid in the house, a cook in the kitchen and a whore in the bedroom. Tom, you are the ultimate caveman but I wouldn't have you any other way.'

I sprawled over him, kissing him deeply on the lips.

'Get up, get up, you Jezebel. It's only eight o'clock. Save yourself for later. Now, before I make mad passionate love to you, I've just got to pop out to my car – there's something wrong with the rear mirror, and I've got to adjust it before the drive to Lancaster tomorrow.'

He slapped my bottom lightly as he went outside to the drive.

I carried the dirty dishes through into the kitchen; his mobile, lying on the hall table, rang. I scooped it up, and called out to him from the front door. 'It's your mobile love.'

He was engrossed inside the car, fixing the mirror. 'Oh, could you take it sweetheart and say I'll get back to them in a tick – nearly finished this.'

I stepped back into the hallway, and pressed the button. But before I could even say 'hello' a man's voice, full of excitement and against a rowdy pub background, blurted out 'Tom, sorted mate – it's on for next week and I'm telling you, that bird Sarah's gagging for it and – '

'Who's speaking please?' I said, steadily.

'Oh, sorry, you must be Sally – sorry about that; erm, is Tom around please? It's Alex.'

'Yes, he is but he's just working on the car at the moment; he'll phone you back in ten minutes or so.'

'Oh, thanks; that's fine – cheers!' He seemed glad the call was over.

I gazed at the mobile, utterly bewildered, turning over his words once again in my mind: ' … it's on for next week mate and I'm telling you, that bird Sarah's gagging for it …' – *gagging for it* – no prizes for guessing what that was about but with whom? Alex? Surely not Tom. I raised a hand anxiously to my forehead. Just then, he came back in. I was quiet, and simply stared at him, the mobile glued to my hand. Quick as a flash, he was able to put two and two together; it was almost intuitive.

'Bet that was Alex wasn't it, love? He's been banging on about some birthday do his sister's having; I'll give him a ring now – he can't seem to get the message that my party days are over.'

He took the phone from me, and called Alex, joshing and joking with him. He went through the theatrics of speaking more slowly and louder than usual to make sure that I took in every word, maintaining steady eye contact with me as he did so.

'No, I don't care if Angelina Jolie's going mate – I'm not interested. Well, yes, but the tickets for that match will cost a fortune – anyway, must go; cheers mate!'

'Bloody Alex – time he grew up if you ask me,' he continued, avoiding my unwavering gaze for a moment.

'So, you don't know anyone called Sarah then?'

'Sarah, mmm, let me think,' he replied in a puzzled tone. 'Well, no, not really, but she's probably the one Alex fancies from his work's accounts section … but come here you lovely Sally Johnson you, and let me give you a big kiss – that dinner was fantastic.'

I thought about pressing him more sternly on this but remembered how far back he and Alex went … and I didn't want to ruin a marvellous day by dwelling on something that was probably just trivial … and, after all, Alex's words were ambiguous – at least as far as my Tom was concerned. Instead, I let myself be hugged, kissed and petted as he led me to the bedroom.

Into November now, and I could hardly remember a time without him. We had an enviable lifestyle, with the rent from his house more than covering the monthly outgoings. Both of us earned good money and had nothing to spend it on but ourselves. Evenings out with Caroline and Bob were a regular feature; if their son Richard respected Tom for his all-round musical knowledge, then Louise simply worshipped him.

By now I was really looking forward to Christmas, expecting it to be so different at Mum and Dad's with Tom by my side. His new job was going well although he often worked really long hours and had to spend a few nights away from home. Following his last trip away, I'd found a Visa slip for the Brummie Brasserie in his trouser pocket – £82.35: a bit steep for a single dinner so I assumed he must have been schmoozing a client. I paused for a moment, lost in the memory of our date at the Brasserie, a time when I'd hoped Tom would be everything I was looking for and so he had proved to be. I didn't mention the restaurant; simply laid the receipt on his bedside cabinet with a note saying 'Found in navy blue trousers – in case you need it for expenses claim – by the way, the night we were there, I wanted to drag you back to my hotel room!'

I was finding it difficult to quell Caroline's excitement at the prospect of a spring wedding. Prospect was the right word. We had never actually discussed marriage but I knew he was the man for me and supposed it would only be a matter of time before we tied the knot.

Truth to tell, marrying him was never far from my mind. Louise, for example, Caroline's daughter, had developed a warm friendship with Lucy who was now flourishing in her new career in customer services at Manchester Airport. After one of our recent joint trips to the cinema, the scheming pair had enthusiastically offered their services as bridesmaids.

'Ah,' I said wagging my finger in mock reproof. 'I get it now – that's why you both treated me to that double vodka in The Fox on the way home. Well girls, we'll see how things go but I promise, if and when the big day comes, I fully expect to have you both by my side, provided you don't make eyes at my Tom.'

The girls whooped in delight with Louise begging her mother to do some serious shopping at Pronuptia when they got back from Florida; their family holiday was now imminent.

The discovery channel

I had an easy start to the day. It was simply a case of calling in at the office, responding to some emails and picking up one or two items before leaving for one of the periodic 'training the trainer' sessions in the Midlands. By two o'clock I was at the venue and delighted to see a friendly face – Sunita.

'Hiya Sally' she said cheerfully 'How's it going – good weekend?'

'Great, thanks. We went round to my friend Caroline's for a takeaway. The blokes watched some boxing on TV – leaves me cold but they enjoyed it and had far too much to drink! Mind you, Cazi and me – we didn't exactly stint ourselves either. Now, what did you get up to?'

'Oh you know, another Saturday night with a DVD and a box of chocolates, but I'm hoping things will change pretty soon.'

'Oh yes – why's that?'

'Well, I'm bursting to tell someone but you must promise to keep this to yourself.'

'OK,' I said with a laugh. 'I promise – mum's the word. Now, what's the mystery – not running off with a rabbi are you?'

'Sall-ee! No, nothing as madcap as that – no, it's just that I started subscribing to one of those Internet dating sites and had my first date last week. It was great! And this hunk of a man said he'd email again this week. He was away on some rugby tour or other at the weekend so couldn't see me, but I'm sure he'll contact me again!'

'Fantastic! I'm really pleased for you and, you know, there's no shame in dating by Internet. That's how I met my Tom although I did have to kiss a lot of frogs before I met the handsome prince. Come on then, let's have it then: name, age, occupation, location, etc.'

'His name's Simon, he's forty, lives somewhere in the Midlands, near Wolverhampton, I think, though I'm not sure about that and he works in an architect's office. Sort of draughtsman.'

'Sounds good. So what's he got in the looks department?'

'Oh he's absolutely gorgeous! Or at least I think so. Tell you what though, why not judge for yourself? Come over to my desk when we have a tea break later, and I'll log on to the site and show you his profile.'

I thought back eighteen months to the start of my Internet adventures. I mentally reviewed the highs and lows of Meany Mike through to Mr Adventure aka Jack. The thing that struck me was that, with the possible exception of pervy Lenny, all my dates were actually quite normal. They may have had interests and personality traits completely alien to me but, nevertheless, they were ordinary people just like me and all looking for the same thing. I was so lucky to have found Tom and inwardly thanked Jack every day for the invitation to that charity event over at Weston Park. Just thinking about Tom made me feel good, and I instinctively dipped into my bag for my mobile.

'Hello, darling. I was just talking to one of the girls about Internet dating and thought I'd just ring to remind you how very lucky you were to meet me on Dateandsee.'

'Something I tell myself every day, sweetheart,' he replied.

'Well, I'll be counting the hours until I'm home on Wednesday and I promise to nuke something special for you.'

'No, love, let's make it a takeaway – you'll be a bit fragile after two hours' driving along the M6 during rush hour.'

What a truly thoughtful and caring bloke he was. 'OK, whatever you say. Give you a ring later, darling.'

The tea break was announced to thunderous applause; the latest software had been more complex than usual, and an entire afternoon in front of a screen had left everyone reeling.

Sunita winked at me. 'Right let's go over to my desk. Boss man isn't around – he always clears off early on Mondays for his weekly thrashing on the squash court.'

I was certainly intrigued and eagerly crossed over to her desk.

'Taadaaaa,' she trumpeted, as she stood to one side in a movement of mock drama, allowing me the best possible view of the screen that now revealed a smiling face, a face I knew only too well ...

'That's Simon. Isn't he just the best?'

I stared at Tom's familiar features. Though it was only seconds, it seemed like hours. I was poleaxed. I staggered to an empty chair. I was immobile with shock. I simply sat there, not uttering a single word. I felt the colour draining from my face ... my stomach churned ... I began to retch.

'Oh, come on Sally,' joked Sunita, 'I only said he was gorgeous, not drop dead gorgeous! What's up? You've gone white. You look as if you've just seen a ghost!'

I looked – was – shattered. A hefty blow to the solar plexus would have had less effect than that of the appealing, all too recognisable image on screen. I faltered for a moment. I choked and just stumbled out a reply.

'Oh yes, sorry – I just feel a bit light-headed; it must be the heat in the training room.'

'Don't worry love, I'll just pop round to the rest room and get you a glass of water – only be a tick!'

Tom's warm voice kept ringing in my ears, snippets of conversation splintering my mind. Then it all began to make sense ...

'Must shoot down to Birmingham midweek to see the Villa game. I'll be a bit late getting back – all right love?'

'OK if I go down to Shrewsbury this afternoon for this regional tournament – semi-finals you know, so wish me luck but don't bother waiting up for me – it's bound to be a late one.'

'Slugger had invited me months ago to this rugby club dinner in Gloucester and everything's booked and I can't let him down.'

'One-day international at Bristol – sort those Kiwis out! Should be back early hours Sunday ...'

And then there'd been that screensaver business, the unusually expensive bill receipt from the Brasserie, that 'gagging for it' remark from Alex, the overnight 'business' trips ... the time-worn expression darted into my mind 'love is blind and marriage is the eye-opener'; well, we were 'a couple', admittedly not married, and it was obvious to me now that we never would be. The central truth of that cliché was devastating. I had ensnared Tom, but never actually tamed him. There had been a dream, a wonderful vision of domestic bliss, true love and solid partnership and I had turned it, or so I'd thought, into reality ... but, here, in the office with Sunita ... this turn of events had shattered my dream as surely as a power cut brings with it a strange silence, a sudden chill and an ominous darkness.

The long and winding road

Just as Sunita reappeared with the water, her boss phoned. He'd forgotten to ask her to complete and send off an urgent report to an important client before the end of the day, and it was obvious from her dutiful responses that she would attend to the task without fail. She turned to me, clearly uncomfortable.

'I'm really sorry about this but boss man insists I get a report off. I feel terrible about letting you down – you're obviously off-colour and we were going to have that drink we'd promised ourselves. I feel awful about it.'

'Oh, don't worry,' I replied bravely, drinking the water gratefully. 'We're due to meet towards the end of the month again aren't we and we can have that glass of wine then, perhaps even more, to make up for tonight,' I said, forcing a smile.

The drive home was totally wretched. I couldn't concentrate, my eyes kept misting over, and flashbacks confused my thoughts. I finally did put my key in the door, stared into the hall mirror and burst into tears. I hurled myself down onto the sofa, weeping uncontrollably. Predictably [fortunately?], Tom, again, wasn't there. He was away. It was, I remembered, another 'boys' night out' … or was it, in reality, another '*boy's* night in' – with some other gullible and available female from one of the many dating sites. Still sobbing, I made myself a strong cup of coffee and decided to act.

I beavered away for almost two hours with dogged determination, pausing only to dry the tears streaming down my cheeks; it was a heartbreaking job but the end result was worth it. The hallway was now full of his clothes, packed away into three suitcases, his CDs and DVDs neatly stacked, his treasured sports equipment propped up against the wall – the classic backcloth to a final parting but without the normal accompaniments of tears, shouting and insults. I picked up my mobile. Fighting back the tears and gritting my teeth, I texted him.

I'm going away for a couple of days. Your things are in the hall, ready for you to collect. There's no need to contact me. Sunita sends her love.

'Going away' in fact meant nothing more than driving round to Caroline's house as they were still in Florida. Little had I suspected, when I cheerily waved them off at the airport, that their house was to be a temporary place of refuge.

Overnight, my resolution didn't weaken – if anything it strengthened. I phoned work to say I'd gone down with a virus but hoped to be back in soon.

Morning has broken

Monday morning. Back in the office, back to work. Yes, back to work. I suppose I could have chosen to dig in for several months, hibernating in a burrow of despair and misery, but, after all, other people were dependent on me – also I was drawing my salary, and felt I had to earn it. Work would keep my mind occupied as well and help fill the void that currently seemed bottomless. I scrolled through my emails, deleting several from Tom just as I'd done with his texts and phone calls. I'd reached home on the previous night to find the flat dark and eerily silent. A note had been sellotaped to the fridge door: 'Darling, can we talk about this?' This time though, there would be no happy reunion; that was a certainty. I groaned too, realising that I'd need to let Mum and Dad know about all of this as the plan had been for us to see them over the Christmas period. They would be really disappointed; I was heartbroken.

'Hello, Mum. How are you and how's Dad?'

'Oh hello love Dad's doing a spot of tidying in the garden believe it or not oh yes, we're fine and we can't wait to have you and Tom up here for Christmas [my heart sank] and it'll all be lovely because that nice Mr Neal's done up the spare bedroom and it's looking really contemporary and–'

'Mum, I don't know how to tell you this,' I broke in, fighting back the tears, 'but we won't be seeing you–'

'Oh love don't say that honestly there's no problem we've got more than enough room–'

'No Mum, no. It's just that Tom and me, well it's not really worked out … Anyway, I've got to go now – early start tomorrow but I will phone you again soon.'

I hoped she hadn't been aware of my sobbing.

Lack of appetite and a series of sleepless and tearful nights very swiftly left their mark. I winced whenever I looked into a mirror. A dull pallor had replaced the natural freshness of my complexion, and layers of cosmetics somehow failed to remove the permanent smudge from around my eyes. I lost weight so that my clothes seemed to hang on me. I felt too that I'd lost my sense of humour, and, most noticeably, my positive attitude. I was never abrupt or impolite, but I'm sure that I no longer initiated conversation and, when asked a question, replied simply, with a monosyllable. In a way I thought my personality had been ironed out of me. Colleagues guessed something was badly wrong but were too polite to pry. I kept my friends in the dark and, thank heavens, Caroline was still away because, at present, I wouldn't be up to discussing this catastrophe – even with her, my dearest friend.

Trying hard to concentrate on my work one Tuesday afternoon, an email popped up on screen.

Hi Sally, the rumour mill tells me that you're not your old self at present and I'm really sorry to hear that. You know, it's the office party in a fortnight's time and all the FX dolly birds have spurned my once irresistible advances, so I could be on my ownsome. I'm not even going to try and persuade you to come with me because I can guess what you're going through right now. Been there, done it … it's not only women who sometimes have broken hearts you know. Anyway, this is really just a note to say I'm here for you, whenever. Lots of love, J xx

This bloke Jonathan – why on earth couldn't he have shown up on the dating site instead of that sorry stream of losers I fetched up with. Then I corrected myself, realising I was wrong and losing a sense of balance here. Virtually all of the dates had been enjoyable, and certainly all had been memorable though for very different and sometimes entertaining reasons. I read through his email again. I was deeply touched by it.

Jonathan, what a lovely bloke you are. Thank you so much for your kind thoughts, they mean a lot to me. I hope you have a very happy break. Love, Sally xx

Work kept me busy. Lesley was back and relentlessly piling on the pressure. She'd lost her IT Mike to Bevvy and had immediately reverted to type. And then there was Caroline – she would be back from her Orlando experience soon and then I'd be able to share the heavy burden of my disappointment with her.

Shortly before Christmas, I phoned Mum and Dad to say I'd gone down with a heavy dose of flu and unfortunately wouldn't be able to see them at all over the festive period. I did promise faithfully to ring them on Christmas Day and see them as soon as I felt better. Mum's heavy disappointment cut through me like a knife but I kept my resolve, reconciling myself to a lonely and forgettable Christmas.

Dinner time?

It was the afternoon of the first Friday in the New Year. That time of the week when the phone calls peter out and the atmosphere in an office palpably relaxes. Among the flurry of emails – in the main from fellow trainers/ financial institutions/demanding clients – one stood out; it was from Jonathan.

Hello Sally. Happy New Year! I've been thinking, it seems a lifetime since we had that great lunch together ... and I thought you might be tempted again ... please? You need thoroughly spoiling and dear old Jonathan is just the man to do it. Dinner, sometime soon, next Saturday perhaps? Love, Jonathan xx

I smiled and yes, maybe I could squeeze into that little black Ghost number now. Taking a deep breath, I mustered enough confidence to pick up the phone.

'Hello Jonathan, yes it's me ... oh, I'm fine, honestly – fine. Now, about next Saturday: thanks ever so much – it's really kind of you. What time do you think we should meet ...?'

Author's note

It's true that Sally's experiences of Dateandsee have not – like life – been entirely successful but that doesn't mean that Internet dating in general fails to meets its objective. In the modern world, meeting people over the Web is just another tool in the global business of relationships.

If you are over, say, thirty-five, you know how difficult it is to meet single people of your own age. You also know how dispiriting it can be to trawl endless bars and, worse still, nightclubs, looking for that small number of mature single people, hoping against hope that at least one of them will have something in common with you.

Yes, the Internet *is* certainly an effective way of meeting people but it has not changed human nature. Some people are a little dubious, objecting that, on these sites, you can claim to be 'anything you like' – yes, this is true – but you can in 'real life' as well. All the technology does is to enable you to connect with large numbers of others on the same quest. That's all these sites do. Once that connection has been made, all the normal 'rules' of getting to know someone apply.

With just a little common sense, Internet dating is perfectly safe and even if it ultimately fails to find you that one special person, you can certainly have a lot of fun looking! So, what are you waiting for?

Printed in the United Kingdom
by Lightning Source UK Ltd.
135241UK00001B/55-93/P